Web-Based Instruction

A Guide for Libraries

second edition

Susan Sharpless Smith

AMERICAN LIBRARY ASSOCIATION
Chicago 2006

Design and composition by ALA Editions in Minion and Legacy Sans Book using QuarkXPress 5.0 on a PC platform.

Printed on 50-pound white offset, a pH-neutral stock, and bound in 10-point cover stock by McNaughton & Gunn.

The paper used in this publication meets the minimum requirements of American National Standard for Information Sciences—Permanence of Paper for Printed Library Materials, ANSI Z39.48-1992. ∞

Library of Congress Cataloging-in-Publication Data

Smith, Susan Sharpless.
    Web-based instruction : a guide for libraries / Susan Sharpless Smith.— 2nd ed.
      p. cm.
    Includes bibliographical references and index.
    ISBN 0-8389-0908-6 (alk. paper)
    1. Library orientation—Computer-assisted instruction. 2. Web sites—Design.
  3. Library Web sites—Design. 4. Web-based instruction. 5. Libraries and the Internet.
  I. Title.
    Z711.2.S59 2005
    025.5'6'0785—dc22   2005015011

Printed in the United States of America

10 09 08 07 06   5 4 3 2 1

Contents

3 Design and Development Cycle   *39*

4 Selecting Project Development Tools   *54*

5 Designing the User Interface   *86*

6 Multimedia: Using Graphics, Sound, Animation, and Video   *134*

7 Interactivity   *174*

Figures

Acronyms

ADC	analog-to-digital converter
AIFF	Audio Interchange File Format
API	application program interface
ASP	Active Server Page
AU	Audio File Format
AVI	Audio-Video Interleave
BMP	bitmap
CBI	computer-based instruction
CCD	charge-coupled device
CDR	CorelDRAW
CD-ROM	compact disc–read-only memory
CD-RW	compact disc–rewritable
CGI	Common Gateway Interface
CIS	contact image sensor
CMS	course management system
CMS	content management software (or system)
codec	compressor/decompressor
COM	Component Object Model
CPU	central processing unit
CRT	cathode ray tube
CSS	cascading style sheets
DAC	digital-to-analog converter
dHTML	Dynamic HTML
DOM	Document Object Model
dpi	dots per inch
DSL	digital subscriber line
DV	digital video
DVD	digital video disc
FTP	File Transfer Protocol
GB	gigabyte
GHz	gigahertz
GIF	Graphics Interchange Format

HCI	human-computer interaction
HTML	Hypertext Markup Language
IE	Internet Explorer
IIS	Internet Information Server
IM	instant messaging
ISP	Internet service provider
IT	information technology
JPEG, JPG	Joint Photographic Experts Group
JSP	JavaServer Page
LAMP	Linux, Apache, MySQL, PHP (or Perl, or Python)
LCD	liquid crystal display
LED	light emitting diode
LiOn	lithium ion
LMS	learning management system
MB	megabyte
MHz	megahertz
MIDI	Musical Instrument Digital Interface
MNG	Multiple-Image Network Graphics
MOO	Multiuser Domain, Object Oriented
MPEG	Moving Pictures Expert Group
MP3	MPEG-1 Audio Layer-3
NIC	network interface card
NiCad	nickel cadmium
NiMH	nickel metal hydride
OCR	optical character recognition
OPL	Open Publication License
OS	operating system
PC	personal computer (IBM compatible)
PCI	Peripheral Component Interconnect
PCMCIA	Personal Computer Memory Card International Association
PDA	personal digital assistant
PDF	Portable Document Format
Perl	Practical Extraction and Report Language
PFR	Portable Font Resource
PHP	[Personal Home Page] PHP Hypertext Processor
PNG	Portable Network Graphics
ppi	pixels per inch
RAM	random access memory
SCORM	Shareable Content Object Reference Model
SCSI	Small Computer System Interface
SGML	Standard Generalized Markup Language
SMIL	Synchronized Multimedia Integration Language
SVG	Scalable Vector Graphics
SVGA	Super Video Graphics Array
SXGA	Super Extended Graphics Array
Tcl	Tool Command Language

TIFF	Tagged Image File Format
Tk	Tool Kit
3-D	three dimensional
UID	user interface design
URL	uniform resource locator
USB	Universal Serial Bus
UXGA	Ultra Extended Graphics Array
VGA	Video Graphics Array
VHS	Video Home System
VHS-C	Compact VHS
VoIP	Voice over Internet Protocol
VRML	Virtual Reality Modeling Language
W3C	World Wide Web Consortium
WAV	Waveform Audio File Format
WBI	Web-based instruction
WMA	Windows Media Audio
WYSIWYG	what you see is what you get
WWW	World Wide Web
X3D	Extensible 3-D Graphics
XGA	Extended Graphics Array
XHTML	Extensible Hypertext Markup Language
XML	Extensible Markup Language
XSL	Extensible Stylesheet Language
XSL-FO	Extensible Stylesheet Language-Formatting Objects
XSLT	Extensible Stylesheet Language Transformation

Acknowledgments

A book containing a great deal of information about technology and the Internet is guaranteed to need a revision or it will become quickly outdated. It's been four years since the first edition of this book was published, so an update is long overdue. However, embarking on this sort of project can be daunting and would not have taken place without help and encouragement from colleagues and family.

Laura Pelehach, my editor at ALA Editions, deserves credit for guiding me into agreeing to attempt a second edition. She was supportive throughout the process in the most positive way, even when I missed a deadline or two. Helen Court did a fine job with copyediting the manuscript; her subject expertise in Web development was appreciated as much as her grammar skills.

Colleagues at Z. Smith Reynolds Library repeated their role of providing moral support and solid technology input during the months of writing. Thanks to Erik Mitchell, Giz Womack, Rosalind Tedford, and Tim Mitchell.

As always, my family provided constant support without which this project would never have been completed. Ron, Sarah, Josh, and Nancy, I appreciate everything you do for me!

Introduction

Welcome to the second edition of *Web-Based Instruction: A Guide for Libraries*. In the four years since the first edition was published, the Web has continued to grow as an avenue for the delivery of services by all types of libraries. This introduction to the second edition will review the reasons why Web-based instruction has shown such great potential and why it continues to do so—and what makes a revision of this book in order.

THE PROBLEM WITH TRADITIONAL BIBLIOGRAPHIC INSTRUCTION

There are common themes that appear in discussions about traditional bibliographic instruction, also called library instruction. This instruction is designed to teach library users how to use the library and its resources effectively. Increasingly, library instruction goals are expanding to encompass a more comprehensive concept—information literacy, in which library users gain "the set of skills needed to find, retrieve, analyze, and use information."[1] Instruction has traditionally been delivered face-to-face, lecture-style, by a librarian with subject knowledge of the course being taken by students, but research has shown that using some sort of practice to reinforce the instruction is more effective than straight lecture. The information environment has become more complex with the growth of online resources. In addition to teaching students about traditional print library resources, including electronic databases and journals, as well as World Wide Web resources, is now imperative. This requires even more instruction on search and evaluation methods. Because the availability of information on the Web has exploded, there is also a critical need to teach learners the ethical and legal issues involved in using the Internet for research purposes.

Other issues come into play also. As demographics change libraries are finding that their constituencies have transformed. Students who are not native English speakers may find it especially difficult to retain all that is taught in a face-to-face class. Many libraries now support distance education programs and must find a way to reach out to those students. The students may be dispersed globally and culturally.

These situations present challenges to providing effective library instruction. It means (and this comes as no surprise) that instruction librarians have to do more—and with limited staff, resources, and time. Planning subject-specific, interactive classes is time consuming and labor intensive. Hiring more instruction librarians is usually not an option. Classroom space is finite and access to a classroom that is configured for interactive hands-on learning is even more difficult to find.

WHY USE THE WEB FOR LIBRARY INSTRUCTION?

In light of all these difficulties that stand in the way of providing effective library instruction, there is recognition of the need to develop alternative solutions. Because we have turned to the World Wide Web for so many of our day-to-day activities, it is an obvious place to turn to find a possible answer to the library instruction problem. Some characteristics of the Web are very attractive: It is a way that library skills can be taught to large numbers of students. It is interactive and can be programmed to give immediate feedback to students as they proceed through the material. There is no limitation of time or space; students can access the instruction twenty-four hours a day from wherever they can connect to the Internet. One of the most appealing attractions is that it presents the same information to all students, removing the unavoidable variations in human delivery.

WHEN IS WEB-BASED INSTRUCTION INAPPROPRIATE?

Web-based library instruction may not be the answer for everyone. It's important to understand your institution's mission and decide whether Web-based instruction supports that mission. For example, if your institution places a high value on classroom instruction, not only in the library but also throughout the campus, then Web-based instruction may be determined to be inappropriate for that environment. There is also the risk of losing the personal touch that face-to-face instruction provides. Many students are hesitant to come ask for help with their research problems, but when they have become acquainted with a librarian through instruction, they feel more comfortable in seeking assistance. Finally, such basic roadblocks as inadequate infrastructure may be a legitimate reason to reconsider the desire to turn to Web-based instruction. If your institution is limited in its hardware, software, and networking capabilities, you may be doing your students a disservice if you attempt to channel instruction through an online environment.

THE EFFECTIVENESS OF WEB-BASED INSTRUCTION

Before embarking on a major undertaking to produce an interactive Web-based tutorial, you may well ask about the effectiveness of such instruction. Developing effective Web-based instruction is a time-consuming task and it would be foolish to devote limited resources to a project that will not be a worthwhile tool.

However, a review of the literature written on the effectiveness of computer-based instruction (CBI) in general, and its value in delivering library instruction specifically, is reassuring. In almost every study reviewed, neither instruction delivery method (face-to-face or computer-based) was found to be significantly different from the other.

An interesting resource to consult is Thomas Russell's *The No Significant Difference Phenomenon: As Reported in 355 Research Reports, Summaries and Papers: A Comparative Research Annotated Bibliography on Technology for Distance Education.*[2] Russell decided over a decade ago to document the fact that technology improved instruction. Instead, he found that, in the majority of studies, no significant difference could be claimed to support that technology improved or caused a decline in effective instruction. In this compilation of research results from studies on whether technology improves instruction, Russell cites 355 studies that support this finding. His conclusion is that "no significant difference" provides evidence that technology doesn't denigrate instruction, which, in essence, opens up our choices for selecting the type of instruction that works best for our institutions and missions. A Web site has subsequently been made available to present citations of studies done after the publication of the book (http://www.nosignificantdifference.org/nosignificantdifference/).

You may want to carry out your own local research to see if it is right for you. In 2000, we conducted a study at Wake Forest using six sections of a survey course, Business 100. Half of the sections received face-to-face instruction and the other half were administered the same content in a Web-based tutorial. We compared effectiveness by analyzing the differences in pretest and posttest scores. Our findings were consistent with what others have determined. In our study, neither face-to-face instruction nor Web-based instruction was found to be more effective. However, students increased their pretest to posttest scores in both methods of delivery. These results helped us confirm that our approach to Web-based instruction is the right course for our university, where we have chosen to supplement traditional instruction with Web-based.

WHAT'S NEW AND DIFFERENT SINCE THE FIRST EDITION?

The first edition of *Web-Based Instruction: A Guide for Libraries* was published in 2001. In Web years, this is an eternity. New technologies, approaches to online learning, library instruction subject content and resources have emerged over the last four years. The use of the Web for instructional purposes continues to increase and its scope continues to expand. After the publication of the first edition, much valuable feedback was delivered via reviews and other venues. In this edition an attempt is made to address most of the suggestions received, including adding an overview on concepts related to learning theory, pedagogy, and distance learning. Discussion is included on some trends that have appeared in recent years, including the move toward reusable learning objects and modular instruction, and the increase in sophistication of library Web instruction through authoring with interactive technologies such as Macromedia Flash. Some newer Web trends and issues are introduced, such as Internet safety, file sharing, and spam; all are fodder for instruction opportunities. A glossary has been added to make it easier to define the sometimes technical, library, and educational jargon, and the resource section at the end has been expanded to cover more subjects and include more print resources. Because the Web is so fluid (not to mention that Web companies buy, sell, and merge products), many of the URLs included in the first edition have changed or gone away. All have been updated or revised. Screen shot examples have all been updated to give a peek into instruction that has been created by a variety of institutions since the first edition.

An effort has been made to be more inclusive toward nonacademic libraries. Although library instruction remains a larger focus for academic libraries, due to the nature of their mission, it has a solid place in other types of libraries. They, too, are turning to the Web to address their patrons' instruction needs. Screen shot examples still favor academic sites simply because they are more plentiful and seem to have more resources to develop the technical expertise required to incorporate the more complex technologies that are discussed. No slight is meant to other libraries; the technologies discussed can be used by any library!

A note of explanation and clarification is offered to all concerning examples of software and technologies pictured and discussed. If you are in a Macintosh environment, as many school libraries may be, you may find that Mac references are not as plentiful as you wish. In addition, you may wonder why certain specific software applications are highly represented, while your favorite gets a mere mention. The practical side of doing a project such as this is that one uses the hardware and software owned and licensed by the author. This is not an indication of particular preference or recommendation over another product. It is instead the cost- and time-effective method of writing on a budget!

WHAT CAN YOU EXPECT FROM THIS BOOK?

This second edition of *Web-Based Instruction: A Guide for Libraries* will help you decide if you would like to implement Web-based instruction and, if so, will lead you through the process. It is aimed toward the library instruction practitioner who has some basic knowledge of and experience with Web authoring procedures but who has no previous experience in creating interactive educational Web sites. If you are completely unfamiliar with Web authoring and its terminology, you will want to read one of the many books available on authoring Web pages. Although Web-based instruction is concentrated in academic environments, public, school, and special libraries are also finding it a valuable way to instruct their patrons about the Internet and about research in an online setting.

This book is organized in the order that planning and executing a Web project takes place; therefore, you may encounter an early mention of some technical terms that are fully explained in later chapters, where the sequence of dealing with those topics would normally take place during a project. Chapter 1, which was written for this second edition, is an overview of concepts relating to Web-based learning and pedagogy. Chapter 2 presents best practices and explores the different types of Web-based instruction being created by institutions. Chapter 3 is geared to help you organize a project from start to finish. Chapter 4 presents considerations for selecting development tools for a Web project and identifies and assesses potential hardware and software authoring tools. The importance of user interface design guidelines and principles is explained in chapter 5. Use of multimedia and the importance of interactivity are looked at in detail in chapters 6 and 7, where tools that will help accomplish their use are also discussed. Chapter 8 focuses on an overview of evaluation, testing, and assessment methods for your project and to measure student progress. Each chapter includes practical information to ensure that a library Web project is a manageable, enriching experience.

Notes

1. Institute for Information Literacy Executive Board, "Introduction to Information Literacy." ACRL Information Literacy Web site. http://www.ala.org/ala/acrl/acrlissues/acrlinfolit/infolitoverview/introtoinfolit/introinfolit.htm.
2. Thomas L. Russell, *The No Significant Difference Phenomenon: As Reported in 355 Research Reports, Summaries and Papers* (Raleigh: North Carolina State University, 1999).

1
Setting the Stage

Conversations about the use of educational technology in the classroom and instructive environment take place with regularity. It would be easy to take for granted that this audience is already well acquainted with the terms and meanings associated with Web-based learning, or why read this book? Rather than making this assumption, this chapter will introduce and discuss some of the basic concepts that are involved in discussions of the topic. This chapter is not meant to be a comprehensive coverage of the various topics, but a brief introduction. The resources section at the end of the book points readers to more in-depth coverage of the topics.

HISTORY OF WEB-BASED INSTRUCTION

In the years since the introduction of the World Wide Web in 1993, the use of the Web to deliver instruction has grown immensely. It may seem apparent to most what is included when discussing Web-based instruction (WBI). It was defined in 1997 by Khan as "a hypermedia-based instructional program which utilizes the attributes and resources of the World Wide Web to create a meaningful learning environment where learning is fostered and supported."[1] However, it may be useful to review where it came from in relation to other concepts that preceded it.

Distance Education/Learning

When many people first think about Web-based instruction, they immediately picture instruction that takes place in spite of a separation of time and place. They visualize materials made available by an instructor so that students can access them from anywhere, at any time. This model has its beginning in what is traditionally thought of as distance education. Distance education, in some form, has been around for a long time, although it has become known by this term only recently. As it has evolved, so have the factors that define it. Zvacek specifies the components:

physical distance that separates teachers and learners

use of mechanical or electronic means to deliver content

interaction between teachers and learners

the influence of a formal educational organization that outlines the roles of the participants, the expectations and the expected outcomes[2]

Using these criteria, it is easy to see the variety of instructional methods included in the definition of distance education: correspondence courses, videotaped classes, and audio classes where the students and instructors communicate by telephone are just a few examples. As technology has advanced and come into use to deliver distance instruction, improvements in interaction and delivery have followed. Interaction between an instructor and students via a print-based correspondence course is much harder to maintain than it is via Internet technologies. Zvacek also identifies three guiding principles that frame the purpose of distance education:

to provide educational opportunities for unserved or underserved populations

to save money (particularly in corporate training)

to offer a wider variety of courses to students than would be possible in one physical location

Distributed Learning

Distance learning is actually a subset of a broader concept: distributed learning. Distance learning has its focus on students who are separated in time and space from their instructor and peers. Distributed learning can take place on- or off-site (campus, school, work) but provides a student with flexibility as to time and location. Both do have a commonality: technology is integral to the process.[3]

Distributed learning is a method of instructional delivery that includes a mix of Web-based instruction, streaming video conferencing, face-to-face classroom time, distance learning through television or video, or other combinations of electronic and traditional educational models. The term *distributed* has its roots in the networking community, which used it to indicate distributed intelligence on the network as opposed to central intelligence in a mainframe computer.[4] Although distributed learning can be implemented in a combination of ways, it always accommodates a separation of geographical locations for part (or all) of the instruction, and focuses on learner-to-learner as well as instructor-to-learner interaction.[5] It also is referred to as mixed-mode, hybrid, and blended learning.

Distance learning seems to be more closely associated with adult learning because, increasingly, adult students find that it often fits into their busy lives better than traditional models of education. They find savings in commuting time, comfort with the independent structure of distance education, and have the self-motivation it requires.[6] Distributed learning expands the potential student base because it can be molded to different age groups and learning styles. It can be effective in the K–12 arena as well as postsecondary and corporate environments. Consider that today's young people have grown up *digitally*. They don't remember a time without computers. They are comfortable with cell phones and MP3 players. Not only that, but they are able to multitask and use these numerous systems simultaneously! A distributed system that uses multimedia approaches in combination with traditional classroom may be a model that engages today's student in a more multisensory educational experience.

The Internet and the Web

The popularity of the Internet is a new opportunity to expand the capabilities of conducting instruction outside the classroom. According to Nua Internet Surveys, as of late 2002 there were 605.60 million Internet users worldwide.[7] A 2001 analysis of Internet use by children ages five to seventeen concluded that 59 percent use the Internet and that for high school students only that figure is 75 percent.[8] A study by Pew Internet and American Life found that 86 percent of U.S. college students use the Internet and believe that the Internet is essential to their academic lives.[9]

These types of statistics illustrate why delivering instruction over the Web is an attractive option. Today's learners are adept at using the Web to discover and learn. According to a 2001 report from the American Council on Education, the Web holds a number of implications for learning environments and students:

Exploration. Today's students use the Web as an exploratory tool to find information and resources.

Experience. The Web offers wide-ranging learning experiences, from synchronous learning to threaded discussions to self-paced study.

Engagement. The Web captivates learners by enabling creative approaches to learning that foster collaboration and sense of community.

Ease of use. It is easy to use for both learners and learning providers. Content is platform independent.

Empowerment. Tools can be provided for personalization of content and that allow learners to choose the way they learn best.

Effectiveness. A growing body of evidence shows that distributed learning can be more effective than the classroom lecture.[10]

WHAT IS INCLUDED IN WEB-BASED INSTRUCTION?

Web-based instruction "encompasses the integrated design and delivery of instructional resources via the World Wide Web and promotes student engagement with text-based, hypermedia, multimedia, and collaborative resources for the purposes of teaching and learning."[11] As the technologies have evolved, the possibilities for multiple approaches to the design and delivery have expanded considerably. WBI can be used to perform basic support functions such as providing a repository of student resources such as a course syllabus, assignments, and instructor notes. But it can be much more with the incorporation of multimedia, which offers the capability to engage students with streaming video, audio, and simulations and animations. Khan identified key and additional features that can be conducive to learning in a well-designed WBI program:[12]

Key features: interactive, multimedial, open system, online search, device-distance-time independent, globally accessible, electronic publishing, uniformity world-wide, online resources, distributed, cross-cultural interaction, multiple expertise, industry supported, learner-controlled, etc.

Additional features: convenient, self-contained, ease of use, online support, authentic, course security, environmentally friendly, non-discriminatory, cost effective, ease of coursework development and maintenance, collaborative learning, formal and informal environments, online evaluation, virtual cultures, etc.

MEDIA

There are a variety of media that can be used in the delivery of educational content: text (printed, including graphics), (analog) audio, (analog) video, and digital multimedia.[13] Each of these can be delivered in a variety of ways. In this book, we will be limiting discussion to the fourth listed, digital multimedia. However, within this category, there are a variety of technologies that can be utilized to transmit the media. For instance, digital media can be transmitted over the Internet, stored on a CD-ROM or DVD, or transmitted via satellite. Bates identifies major distinctions that are made in the technologies that are used to transmit digital multimedia, and you will come across these in more detail throughout this book:

Broadcast versus communication technologies. A broadcast is a one-way technology that moves information from the producer to the receiver, but doesn't include a mechanism for two-way interaction. In contrast, communication technologies facilitate equal communication back and forth among all participants.

Synchronous versus asynchronous technologies. Synchronous technologies operate in real time; all parties must participate simultaneously. Asynchronous technologies allow participants to choose a time and place convenient to them.

Figure 1.1 shows how different digital multimedia technologies fall into these two structures.

FIGURE 1.1
Multimedia Technologies Adapted

	TECHNOLOGIES			
	Broadcast (one-way) applications		Communication (two-way) applications	
	Synchronous	*Asynchronous*	*Synchronous*	*Asynchronous*
Digital multimedia	webcasting audio streaming video streaming	Web sites CD-ROMS DVDs learning objects multimedia clips blogs	chat MUDs Web conferencing Voice over IP (VoIP)	e-mail discussion forums

From Bates and Poole, *Effective Teaching*, 55.

PEDAGOGY

The basic definition of pedagogy is the art of teaching. The important point to under-stand is that effective Web-based instruction starts with instructional strategies based on theories of learning and transforms them to work in the Web environment. In Khan's book, Thomas and Patricia Reeves present a model that represents ten peda-gogical dimensions of interactive learning that illustrate important values to be ana-lyzed in creating instruction. Each element reflects a range from one end of the spec-trum to the other:[14]

> *Pedagogical Philosophy—Instructivist ↔ Constructivist.* The instructivist approach assigns the learner to the role of passive recipient of instruction. At the other end, the constructivist approach focuses on the learner who constructs knowledge based on previous knowledge and experience.

> *Learning Theory—Behavioral ↔ Cognitive.* Behavioral psychology is the learning theory where behavior is shaped through the use of stimuli, feedback, and reinforcement. There are many examples of this approach to be found in today's WBI. A tutorial contains instructional material offered in a presenta-tion, followed by a short quiz with feedback provided depending on the responses given by the student. The cognitive end of the spectrum places emphasis on internal mental states and incorporates a variety of learning strategies, including memorization, direct instruction, deduction, drill and practices, and induction, depending on the type of knowledge being con-structed by the learner.

> *Goal Orientation—Sharply Focused ↔ General.* The goals for any given educa-tional experience can vary from a highly focused one such as learning a spe-cific medical procedure to broader, higher ordered ones such as motivation of employees. Different goals call for different tactics.

> *Task Orientation—Academic ↔ Authentic.* Traditionally, instruction occurred via academic exercises that did not necessarily offer any context or relevance for learners. A basic tenet of adult learning theory is that context is highly impor-tant to them. An example of an academic exercise would be to diagram sen-tences to learn proper sentence structure. In an authentic learning experience, students would learn by doing more practical activities such as writing a résumé.

> *Source of Motivation—Extrinsic ↔ Intrinsic.* Motivation plays a role in all learning theories. Extrinsic motivation draws from external sources to motivate—such as working to receive a passing grade. It is easier to offer extrinsic than intrin-sic motivation. Intrinsic motivation depends heavily on individual learners and what they value about taking from the educational experience. Presenting a way for the learner to determine his or her own outcomes from the instruc-tion is one way to try to intrinsically motivate the learner.

> *Teacher Role—Didactic ↔ Facilitative.* The traditional didactic teacher role is that of *sage on the stage* where the instructor is the possessor of the knowledge to be imparted to the student. The facilitative role is one of being the *guide on*

the side. This approach puts the responsibility for learning with the student; the teacher functions more as a mentor.

Metacognitive Support—Unsupported ↔ Integrated. Metacognition refers to the learner's awareness of objectives, ability to plan and evaluate learning strategies, and capacity to monitor progress and adjust his/her behaviors according to need. An integrated system would provide a means for students to reflect on their progress, assess their needs, and adjust their learning processes.

Collaborative Learning Strategies—Unsupported ↔ Integral. WBI instruction can be constructed to disregard or promote collaborative learning opportunities. Using synchronous or asynchronous technologies to allow students to work collaboratively in small groups is one example of integrating this dimension into a learning experience.

Cultural Insensitivity—Insensitive ↔ Respectful. Because the Web is far-reaching, it is important to consider cultural implications in designing Web-based instruction. Accommodating diverse cultural and ethnic backgrounds should be a WBI goal.

Structural Flexibility—Fixed ↔ Open. A fixed system is fixed in time and place, for instance, the traditional class held in a specific room at a specific time. An open system accommodates asynchronous learning, thus permitting greater flexibility for the learning experience.

LEARNING STYLES

People have different preferences for acquiring and processing new information. Some are visual learners, and learn best through seeing the material. Some are auditory learners, and prefer to gain knowledge through hearing information first. Still others are kinesthetic, and do best through experience. There are numerous learning style classification systems. For instance, Kolb's Learning Style Inventory focuses on concrete experience versus abstract conceptualization, reflective observation, and active experimentation.[15] In another example, Gardner takes a different path and puts forth a theory of multiple intelligences. He proposes that each person has a different biological composition made up of the following intelligences: linguistic (sensitivity to spoken and written language), mathematical-logical (capacity to analyze problems logically, calculate mathematics, investigate scientifically), musical (skill in the performance, composition, and appreciation of musical patterns), spatial (potential to recognize and manipulate patterns of wide space), bodily-kinesthetic (potential to use one's body to solve problems or fashion products), interpersonal (capacity to understand the intentions, motivations, and desires of other people), intrapersonal (capacity to understand oneself), and naturalist (capacity to recognize and classify species).[16]

But no matter what learning style system is subscribed to, the Web is capable of accommodating the various types within it. Figure 1.2 shows the example of Gardner's multiple intelligences and potential online teaching strategies to address each type.

FIGURE 1.2
Online Technologies and Multiple Intelligences

INTELLIGENCE	DESCRIPTION	ONLINE TEACHING STRATEGY
Verbal-linguistic	Preference for reading, writing, and speaking	Web-based research, computer-mediated communication
Mathematical-logical	Aptitude for numbers, reasoning skills	Problem solving, data analysis
Musical	Ability to produce and appreciate pitch, rhythms, learns well through song	Music and composition software, multimedia
Visual-spatial	Visual and spatial stimulation; learners enjoy charts, maps, and puzzles	Web-based presentations, object and document analysis, 3-D modeling
Bodily-kinesthetic	Good sense of balance and hand-eye coordination; handles objects skillfully	Virtual reality, interactive simulations, whiteboard
Interpersonal	Ability to detect and respond to moods and motivations of others tries to see things from another's point of view	Collaborative learning, WebQuests
Intrapersonal	Uses self-reflection to remain aware of one's inner feelings	Online journaling, reflective assessment
Naturalist	Enjoyment of outdoors; ability to detect subtle differences in meaning	WebQuests, case studies, virtual field trips
Existential	Capacity to handle profound questions about existence	Computer-mediated communication, online journaling, authentic learning

From Jennifer Gramling, "Learning Styles," in *Education and Technology: An Encyclopedia,* ed. Ann Kovalchick and Kara Dawson (Santa Barbara, CA: ABC-CLIO, 2004), 420.

LEARNING OBJECTS

Developing materials for Web-based instruction for a variety of learning styles may be well worth the effort, but there is no doubt that it can be a time-consuming and expensive proposition. Additionally, most course development is undertaken on a local level with similar subject matter being developed simultaneously at different institutions of learning. The concept of learning objects was originated to address these types of issues. A learning object is any digital resource that can be reused to support learning. Synonyms for the term include digital learning materials, content objects, chunks, modular building blocks, and Lego. The idea behind the concept is that instructional designers can break down instructional materials into small reusable components that can be used in different contexts. They are generally understood to be deliverable over the Internet on demand so they can be accessed by any number of people at any time. Learning objects can include small objects such as digital images or photos, live data feeds, live or prerecorded video or audio snippets, small bits of text, animations, and smaller Web-delivered applications like a Java calculator. Larger objects could include entire Web pages that incorporate text, images, and other media.[17] The University of Wisconsin–Milwaukee's Center for International Education expands on the characterization of what comprises a learning object.[18] Learning objects

> are a *new way of thinking* about learning content. Traditionally, content comes in a several-hour chunk. Learning objects are much *smaller units of learning*, typically ranging from two minutes to fifteen minutes.
>
> are *self-contained*—each learning object can be taken independently.
>
> are *reusable*—a single learning object may be used in multiple contexts for multiple purposes.
>
> *can be aggregated*—learning objects can be grouped into larger collections of content, including traditional course structures.
>
> are *tagged with metadata*—every learning object has descriptive information allowing it to be easily found by a search.

To leverage the use of learning objects, repositories have been created and maintained. One of the best known is MERLOT (http://www.merlot.org). A cooperative effort, MERLOT is the acronym for Multimedia Educational Resource for Learning and Online Teaching and is an open resource primarily geared toward higher education. Learning materials are peer reviewed, catalogued by discipline, and categorized as simulation, animation, tutorial, drill and practice, quiz/test, lecture/presentation, case study, collection, or reference material. All materials are freely available to anyone to use. An example of a repository aimed at K–16 can be found at Wisconsin's IDEAS (Interactive Dialogue with Educators from Across the State, http://ideas.wisconsin.edu). This site is searchable by grade level, subject, and keyword.

Figure 1.3 illustrates a library-specific example of a learning object repository. CLIP (Cooperative Library Instruction Project) was created "to assist integration into the curriculum of comprehensive and systematic instruction in the use of information resources."[19] The purpose of the site is outlined.

Modules have three parts—a Flash tutorial, an exercise, and a multiple-choice test. Each tutorial is scripted in PowerPoint and then converted to a presentation using Macromedia Flash or Camtasia. The modules can be made available through course management software like Blackboard. Presentations run on the Internet, will download over dial-up lines, and can be done as homework so they don't take up class time. The test can automatically be graded and posted though course management software.

The modules are meant to address three levels of instruction—basic, program, and course levels. Basic level modules address the needs of incoming students and cover topics like the use of EBSCO, NetLibrary, JSTOR, Project Muse, OPAC, ILL,

FIGURE 1.3
CLIP: Cooperative Library Instruction Project

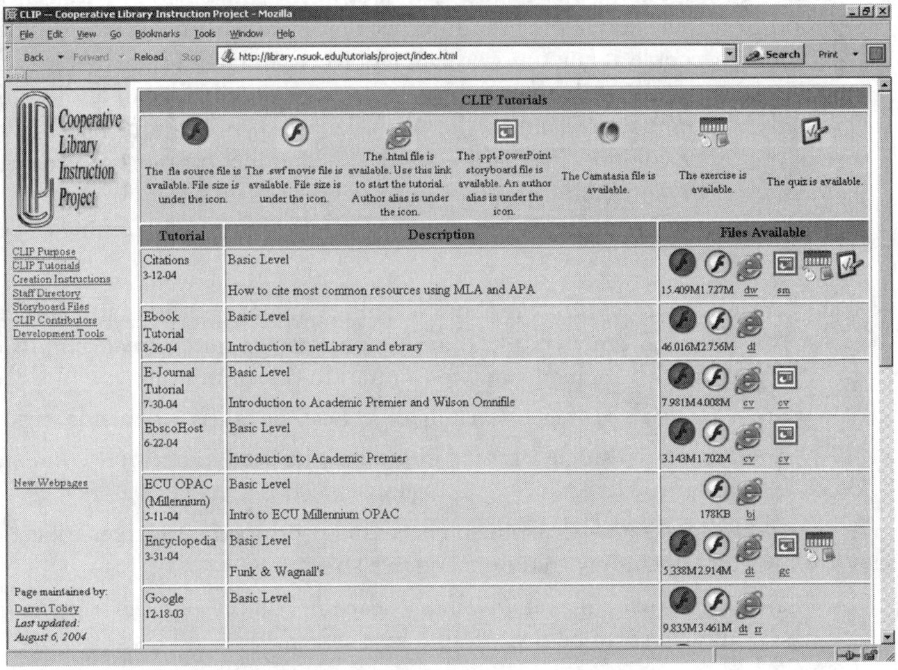

From John Vaughan Library, Northeastern State University, Tahlequah, Oklahoma.
Available: http://library.nsuok.edu/tutorials/project/index.html.

Google, evaluation of Web sites, and citing sources. The modules can be associated with a completely Internet-based class dedicated to the library's information resources, be part of a mandatory freshman orientation class, or be integrated into freshman classes like the composition classes.[20]

The use of the modules is varied. During the fall semester of 2004 at NSU's John Vaughan Library, four CLIP routines were included in a mandatory College Strategies course for all incoming students (thirty-nine sections with more than 1,250 students). Currently they are also being used to train library work study students. Future plans include integrations into all the university degree programs.[21]

Notes

1. Badrul Huda Khan, ed., *Web-Based Instruction* (Englewood Cliffs, NJ: Educational Technology Publications, 1997), 6.
2. Susan M. Zvacek, "Distance Education," in *Education and Technology: An Encyclopedia*, ed. Ann Kovalchick and Kara Dawson (Santa Barbara, CA: ABC-CLIO, 2004).
3. Diana Oblinger et al., *Distributed Education and Its Challenges: An Overview, Distributed Education: Challenges, Choices, and a New Environment* (Washington, DC: American Council on Education, 2001), 1.

4. Tony Bates and Gary Poole, *Effective Teaching with Technology in Higher Education: Foundations for Success* (Hoboken, NJ: Jossey-Bass, 2003), 116.
5. Whatis.com. http://whatis.techtarget.com/definition/0,,sid9_gci550900,00.html.
6. Judith L. Johnson, *Distance Education: The Complete Guide to Design, Delivery, and Improvement* (New York: Teachers College Press, 2003), 1.
7. Nua Internet Surveys. "How Many Online?" 8 Aug. 2004. http://www.nua.ie/surveys/how_many_online/.
8. Matthew DeBell and Chris Chapman, *Computer and Internet Use by Children and Adolescents in 2001, Statistical Analysis Report* (Washington, DC: U.S. Department of Education, National Center for Education Statistics, 2003).
9. Steve Jones, "The Internet Goes to College: How Students Are Living in the Future with Today's Technology" (Washington, DC: Pew Internet and American Life Project, 2002).
10. Oblinger et al., 6.
11. Brenda Bannan-Ritland, "Web-Based Instruction," in *Education and Technology: An Encyclopedia*, ed. Ann Kovalchick and Kara Dawson (Santa Barbara, CA: ABC-CLIO, 2004), 638.
12. Khan, ed., 8.
13. Bates and Poole, 53.
14. Tom Reeves and Patricia Reeves, "Effective Dimensions on Interactive Learning on the World Wide Web," in *Web-Based Instruction*, ed. Badrul Huda Khan (Englewood Cliffs, NJ: Educational Technology Publications, 1997), 59–66.
15. David A. Kolb, *Experiential Learning: Experience as the Source of Learning and Development* (Englewood Cliffs, NJ: Prentice-Hall, 1984), 68–69.
16. Howard Gardner, *Intelligence Reframed: Multiple Intelligences for the 21st Century* (New York: Basic Books, 1999), 41–52.
17. David A. Wiley, "Connecting Learning Objects to Instructional Design Theory: A Definition, a Metaphor, and a Taxonomy," in *Instructional Use of Learning Objects: Online Version* (2000), 7.
18. Center for International Education. "Learning Objects: What?" 13 Dec. 2002 (Milwaukee: University of Wisconsin), http://www.uwm.edu/Dept/CIE/AOP/LO_what.html.
19. CLIP Contributors Northeastern State University. "CLIP: Cooperative Library Instruction Program." http://library.nsuok.edu/tutorials/project/index.html.
20. Ibid.
21. Allen W. McKiel, 10 Sept. 2004.

2

Library Instruction on the Web

CHARACTERISTICS OF GOOD LIBRARY INSTRUCTION

One of your primary goals as you start to think about how to develop a Web-based library instruction project will be to incorporate the characteristics of good library instruction. What constitutes the best practices? Much research has been done over the years to identify these characteristics. This list, gathered by Nancy Dewald, is a compilation of best practices:[1]

Library instruction is best received when it is course related and, more specifically, assignment related. Anyone who has worked with students has found that retention is much higher when it relates to a specific subject being taught or when an assignment is attached. In these situations, students are more highly motivated to learn. When instruction is delivered for some unknown future use, students tend to dismiss what is being covered.

Incorporating active learning into instruction is more effective than instruction by lecture style alone. Providing exercises or other activities helps reinforce the lessons being taught and helps determine whether the students are grasping the material. With straight lecture, a one-way dissemination of information, it is difficult to assess the students' mental engagement.

Collaborative learning can be beneficial. Having students interact in small groups to help each other learn is a powerful way to encourage critical thinking and problem-solving skills. Although this technique may not lend itself to a one-shot instruction class, it can be used in a longer information literacy course.

Information provided in more than one medium is helpful. Students have different learning styles. Some learn primarily through visual means; others prefer auditory means. Combining a lecture delivery with a visual demonstration can reinforce the message through two mediums.

Establishing clear objectives is important. Students are much more likely to grasp what is being taught if they know the direction the instruction is heading.

Teaching concepts is preferable to simply teaching mechanics. When students understand the concepts being taught, they can transfer that knowledge to other learning situations. For example, information literacy concepts include Boolean logic, keyword versus controlled-vocabulary searching, evaluating resources, and methods for focusing a search.

Good library instruction does not end with the class session but includes the option of asking the librarian for help in the future. Often, library instruction is just the beginning of the research process. Students usually have a need for follow-up help and should be assured that it is available and is an anticipated part of the process.

Is it possible to incorporate these criteria into Web-based instruction? Does it make a difference if the instruction is totally online rather than a supplement to face-to-face instruction? As you start to consider how to transfer these characteristics over to a new medium, you will find, as Dewald did in her analysis of twenty online tutorials, that there are comparable techniques in Web tutorials that demonstrate the use of best practices. In this and subsequent chapters, these techniques will be identified and examples from different tutorials will illustrate the incorporation of good instruction criteria including active learning, collaborative learning, and the use of multiple mediums. A main goal of this book is to teach you how to integrate active learning and collaboration into your Web-based instruction through using interactive technologies and to use graphics, sound, and/or animation to deliver information through more than one medium.

Dewald's list of good library instruction characteristics also covers items that are not necessarily solved by simply using a certain Web technique. Delivering course-related content, establishing objectives, teaching concepts, and providing ongoing assistance are pedagogical issues that you and your team must build into the instructional design of your tutorial. No matter what format your instruction takes, these are issues that every good instructor addresses when developing a class or course.

DEVELOPING EFFECTIVE WEB-BASED LIBRARY INSTRUCTION

Drawing from Dewald and others, the ACRL (Association of College and Research Libraries) Instruction Section has assembled several tips on the pedagogy of Web tutorials:[2]

Outline the objectives and outcomes clearly to establish purpose and expectations.

Provide a clearly defined structure that reflects the objectives and provides for both linear and nonlinear learning.

Include interactive exercises.

Give attention to concepts.

Incorporate contemporary language and topics, be succinct, and don't be afraid to entertain.

Provide a way to contact a librarian.

When a tutorial is used, try to make it course-related.

IDEAL LIBRARY INSTRUCTION TUTORIAL FEATURES

In a presentation at the 2003 ACRL conference, Kornelia Tancheva discussed her examination and assessment of over forty library tutorials. She assembled a list of features that she considers essential to an ideal Web-based library instruction product:[3]

Preliminary assessment. Use of a pretest will ensure at which level a user is at the outset and thus the relevance of the system to meet his/her needs.

Branching capabilities. A structure that progresses through material in a path that depends on the learner's response or needs can be achieved through a modular approach with increasing levels of complexity.

Problem-based. The tutorial should be discipline- and/or assignment-based to ground it in a realistic need for the student.

Concept-based. The goal of a problem-based approach is to enable the user to transfer what is learned to concepts that can be transferred for future use elsewhere.

Interactive. To encourage concept-based learning, users should be active participants in the process. Interactivity via simulations of live links to databases and catalogs provide a controlled, positive experience while engrossing the learner in a real environment experience.

WHAT TYPES OF LIBRARIES ENGAGE IN WEB-BASED INSTRUCTION?

Academic libraries come to mind most often when the subject of library instruction is discussed simply because the concept originated in academia more than a century ago. It was in the academic environment that it developed and matured. Undoubtedly, most of the literature available on the subject focuses on the academic library's research into and experiences with the subject. However, in today's complex information-overload world, it is not practical (or prudent) to expect students to wait until their college years to learn information literacy skills. Nor should non–post secondary schooled adults have to struggle to understand how to find, evaluate, and use information in the most effective manner possible. So, unsurprisingly, other types of libraries are turning to the Web to meet the needs of their constituents.

As is true with the academic library, the school library media center has become a central player to "ensure that students and staff are effective users of ideas and information."[4] Library media specialists and teachers collaborate to integrate information literacy skills into the school curriculum. An examination of the Web site *Resources for School Librarians* (http://www.sldirectory.com/index.html) in figure 2.1 shows the involvement that school librarians have in the education of their students.

Public libraries have become the place people expect to be able to find online access. As of 2000, 95 percent of public libraries provided this service.[5] As might be expected, patrons also turn to public library staff to provide instruction on how to use

FIGURE 2.1
Resources for School Librarians

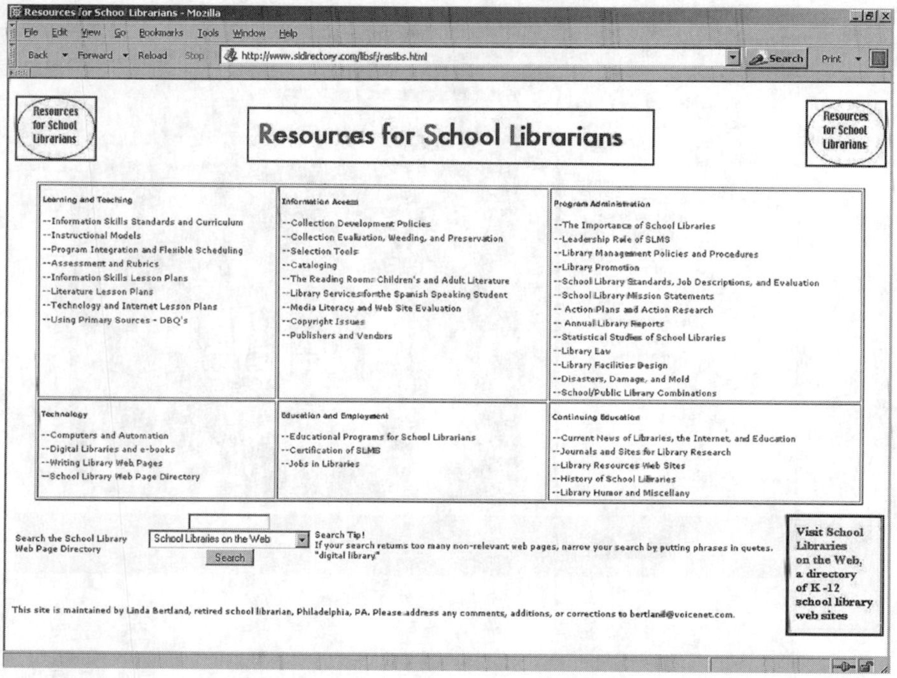

From Linda Bertland, Philadelphia, Pennsylvania. Available: http://www.sldirectory.com/index.html.

technology and the Internet.[6] The NCLIS study also showed that 62 percent of public libraries provide Internet training services, 55 percent to adults and 44 percent to children or youth.

You will find that there are many examples of uses of the Web by school and public libraries to assist their patrons in learning a wide range of topics. Topics covered include those that are typical of academic library instruction plus different approaches to engage students and life-long learners by zeroing in on specific target audiences such as children, teens, and seniors. The list of online self-paced tutorials offered from the King County (Washington) Library System Web site (http://www.kcls.org/comptutorials/) provides a glimpse at the range of topics that interest learners today: Computers 101, Computer Safety, Selecting a Computer, E-Mail on the Web, Selecting an Internet Service Provider, Word, Publisher, and Excel are among their offerings. Another example can be seen in figure 2.2. It shows a tutorial, TeenLinks, from Hennepin County Library, which is designed to teach teen patrons how to use library resources.

Special libraries cover a wide variety of potential students and educational needs. The designation *special library* encompasses many types. Examples include special academic (that is, business, law, medical), art, museum, corporate, government agencies, newspapers, and film, to name just a few. Because these are so varied and diverse, the educational needs of the users of these libraries are wide ranging also. But the

FIGURE 2.2
TeenLinks

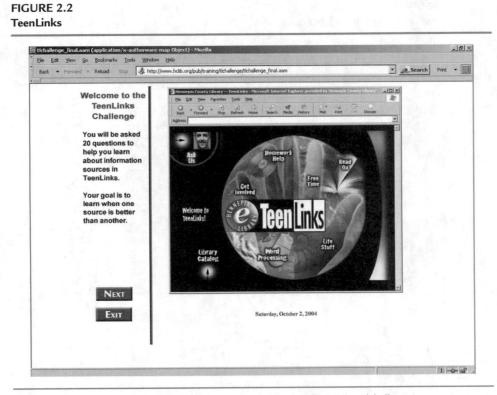

From Hennepin County Library. Available: http://www.hclib.org/pub/training/tlchallenge/
tlchallenge_final.aam.

importance of offering library instruction spans all types of special libraries. In an era when money is limited, many special libraries are forced to justify their budget and their existence. A good library education program can keep a special library visible and valuable.[7] Many special libraries have patrons who are geographically dispersed and are busy adults who need to become proficient with computer technologies and the Internet to perform their jobs in today's global economy. Web-based instruction can be one cost-effective avenue to reach each targeted audience. Driscoll cites economic advantages for using Web-based training:

> Information and job skills are changing so quickly that it is not practical to ask employees, business partners, and customers to attend traditional instructor-led classes.

> Training at the desktop reduces travel and the lost productivity that occurs while a learner is in class.

> The need to install special computers or develop multiple versions of training software for different platforms is eliminated.

The costs of duplicating, packaging, and mailing materials are eliminated.

Updating courses and making revisions from a central point ensures that changes are uniform and that learners have access to the most current training materials.[8]

Figure 2.3 shows an example of how one special library uses Web-based instruction. The Illinois Fire Service Institute Library has developed Web-based video modules to educate staff, students, Illinois fire departments and firefighters, and other fire/emergency-related users on a variety of topics relating to services and locating library materials.

FIGURE 2.3
Training Module #2: FireTalk

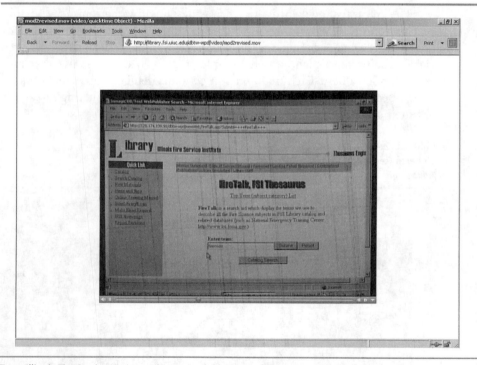

From Illinois Fire Service Institute Library. Available: http://library.fsi.uiuc.edu/dbtw-wpd/video/mod2revised.mov.

TYPES AND EXAMPLES OF WEB-BASED LIBRARY INSTRUCTION

What kind of library instruction can be delivered via the Web? An examination of existing tutorials shows that you are limited only by your imagination. Still, there are several major categories of tutorials. The following sections deal with each of these and provide examples.

General Research or Reference Skills

One common type of Web-based library tutorial deals with how to undertake research in general. Although at first it might appear that this type of instruction will not meet the criteria of a course-based focus, this type of tutorial can be integrated into many different disciplines as a supplement (or learning object) because the research process follows a similar path in many subject areas. Furthermore, as mentioned, Web-based tutorials can also be the primary method of instruction for distance education students who will not have an opportunity to receive face-to-face course instruction. Typical topics covered in this type of tutorial include planning research, identifying/refining a topic, using available research tools (online catalog, periodical indexes), evaluating information, citing resources, and differentiating between various resource types.

The tutorial shown in figure 2.4 was designed by the Kentucky Virtual Library Teachers and Kids Workgroup to teach K–5 children how to do research. Designed to be interactive and engaging, the tutorial guides a student through the research process via six main steps: plan, search for information, take notes, use the information, report, and evaluate. Each main section contains detailed subsections that introduce basic research concepts that will form a framework for conducting research throughout their school years.

FIGURE 2.4
General Research Skills for Children
All the Information in the Known Universe: How to Do Research

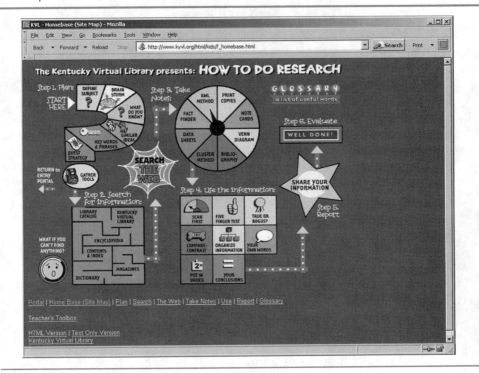

From the Kentucky Virtual Library. Available: http://www.kyvl.org/html/kids/f_homebase.html.

Another example of a general research skills tutorial from the College of DuPage Library can be seen in figure 2.5. In this academic tutorial, students are introduced to identifying types of information, determining the right type of information for their needs, and the available search tools to use.

Online Catalog Skills

A library's online catalog is its main tool for finding materials in its collection. A tutorial that instructs library users on how to search that specific system can be helpful to all concerned. Most online systems today are sophisticated enough to permit complex search strategies. If the tutorial is developed to teach the concept of searching in one system, the strategies learned can be transferred to other online systems. Concepts that can be conveyed in an online catalog tutorial include keyword versus subject searching, the meaning of call numbers and how they are structured, when to try different access points to find materials (author, title, subject, keyword), and how to search different fields simultaneously using Boolean logic. Students can be taught about different types of information available in the library and how to interpret and refine the

FIGURE 2.5
General Research Skills
Doing Research: Finding the Information You Need

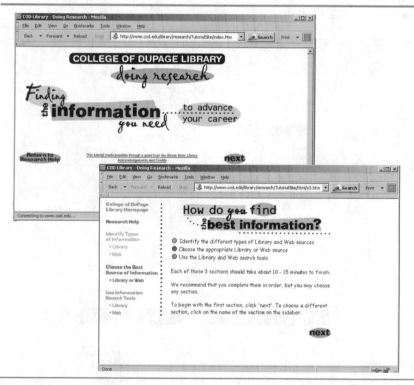

From College of DuPage Library. Available: http://www.cod.edu/library/research/
TutorialSite/index.htm.

results they retrieve from the catalog. Figure 2.6 illustrates a section in the interactive Information Literacy tutorial from Western Michigan University Libraries that introduces their online catalog WestCat. In this section students learn to

recognize that WestCat contains more than books

find books on a topic using a guided keyword search

find books by title, author, or subject heading

find journals by using a journal title search

identify the location of books or journals

read a call number and use it to find items in the library

find an item placed on reserve using a course reserve search

Database- or Software-Specific Search Skills

This category of tutorials covers those developed to teach users to use specific databases or to master particular search-software interfaces. Because there are so many database interfaces, it is necessary to help users learn how to navigate them. Some search software, such as Ovid or ProQuest, provides one interface to search multiple databases. Tutorials designed to teach how to search specific interfaces can be inte-

FIGURE 2.6
Online Catalog Research Skills

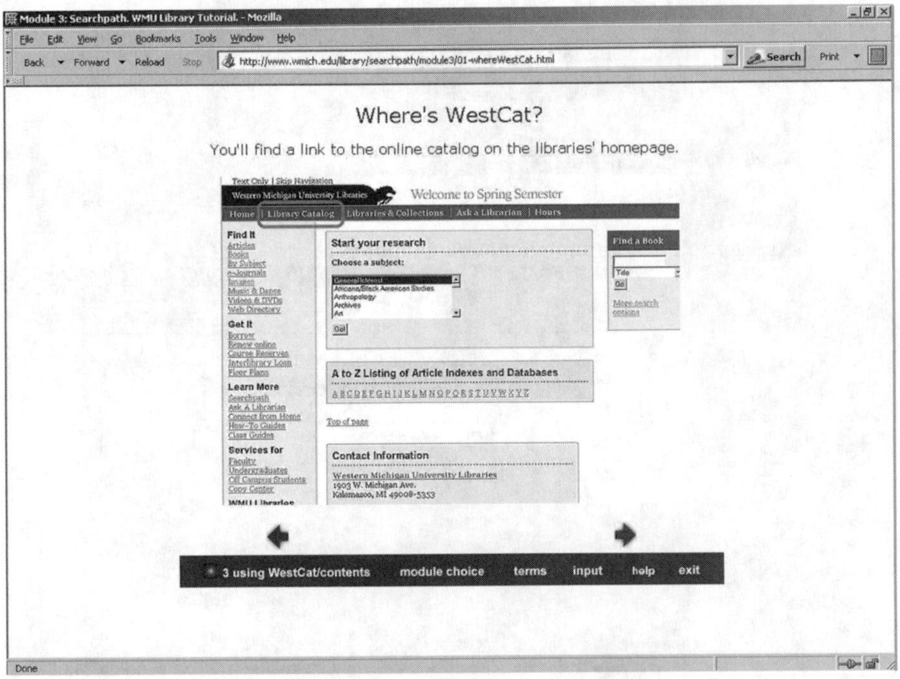

From Searchpath, Western Michigan University Libraries, Kalamazoo. Available: http://www.wmich.edu/library/searchpath/module3/index.html.

grated into subject-specific and course-related instruction by focusing on an appropriate database for that field. Mastery of the search software can be translated into knowledge of how to use the program in another discipline.

The University of Wisconsin System Women's Studies Librarian's Office has created a tutorial that teaches students how to search Contemporary Women's Issues in Lexis-Nexis. In this tutorial, shown in figure 2.7, the student is taught search strategies,

FIGURE 2.7
Database- and Software-Specific Search Skills Tutorial

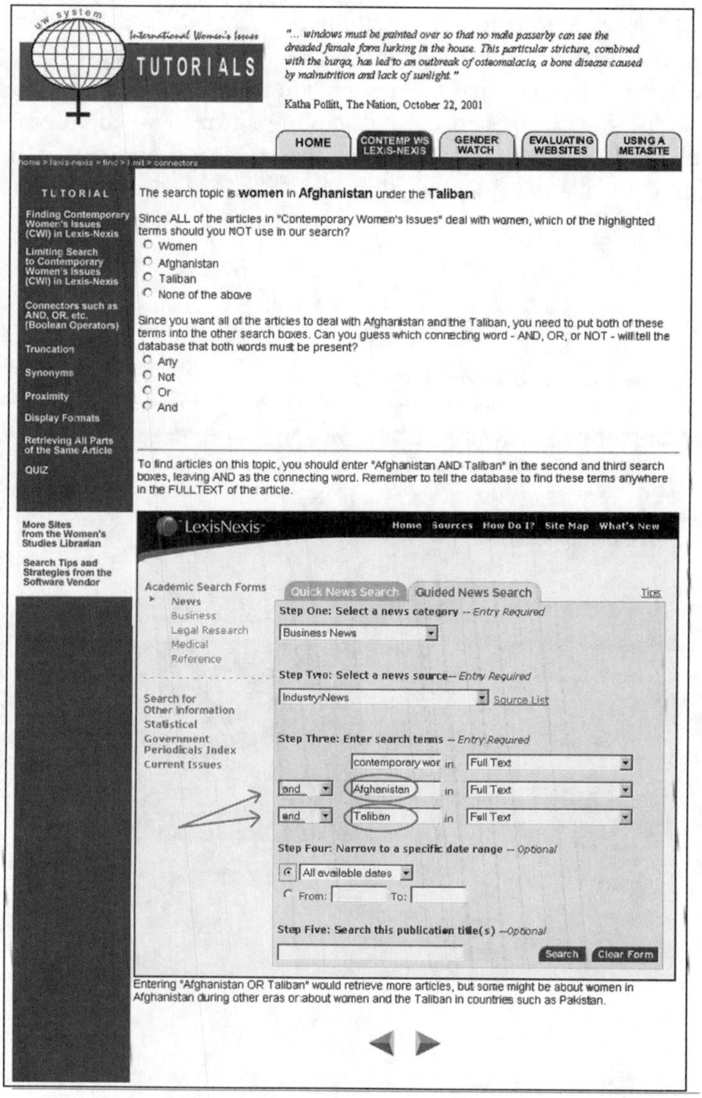

From University of Wisconsin System Women's Studies Librarian's Office. Available: http://www.library.wisc.edu/projects/ggfws/iwitutorials/lexisnexis/ iwslexisnexisfind.htm.

display formats, and retrieval strategies. Because Lexis-Nexis is an aggregator of many databases, skills learned in this tutorial can be transferred to other disciplines.

Discipline- or Course-Specific Research Skills

Tutorials in this category zero in on teaching a student to conduct research in a certain discipline. A humanities student approaches a research project in a much different manner than a physics student does. Usually a discipline-specific tutorial supports a particular course, often a survey course with multiple sections. This type of tutorial will be quite focused and provides the student with in-depth instruction on how to do research in a particular field. It will include information about appropriate sources and research processes unique to that discipline.

Richard W. McKinney Engineering Library, part of the University of Texas Libraries, has developed several tutorials that are designed to teach engineering students how to do research in specific courses in their discipline (http://www.lib.utexas.edu/engin /tutorials.html). Figure 2.8 shows a tutorial that teaches how to find information about vibration control and cable stayed bridges.

FIGURE 2.8
Discipline- or Course-Specific Research Skills Tutorial

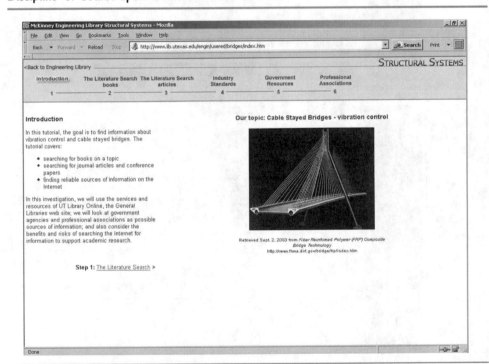

From Richard W. McKinney Engineering Library, University of Texas Libraries at Austin. Available: http://www.lib.utexas.edu/engin/usered/bridges/index.htm.

Assignment-Specific Tutorials

A tutorial can also be developed to guide a student through a specific assignment for a course. This is a perfect opportunity for a librarian to collaborate with a professor to create an interactive Web research project.

In an art history course at Wake Forest University, the professor had a set assignment that she used to teach students how to conduct research. The art history librarian and I started with the written assignment and developed a tutorial designed to make the assignment an interactive lesson that was much more engaging to the student than a text handout (see figure 2.9).

Internet Instruction

In many libraries, teaching topics about Internet has become a standard part of the instruction mission. This type of instruction can range from teaching the mechanics of navigating the Internet to using the Web for research. Different libraries have included a vast assortment of instruction topics about the Internet in their lessons. The following list of potential Internet topics will give you an idea of the possibilities.

FIGURE 2.9
Assignment Specific Research Skills Tutorial

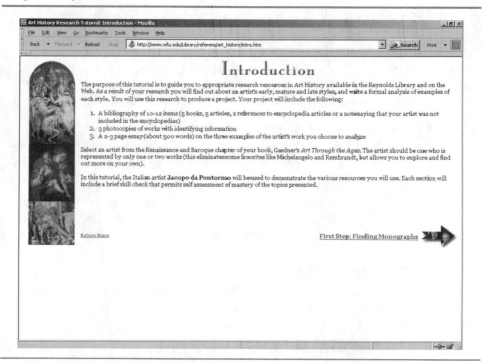

From Z. Smith Reynolds Library, Wake Forest University, Winston-Salem, North Carolina. Available: http://www.wfu.edu/Library/referenc/art_history/.

Introduction to the Internet

Even though the Internet may seem to ubiquitous to us, there are still many people who seek instruction on how to access and use it. For instance, only 22 percent of seniors are online,[9] but those who do go online are enthusiastic and often turn to their public libraries to learn about the basics of the Internet, such as

> How can I connect to the Internet?
>
> What is the World Wide Web?
>
> What are hypertext and hyperlinks?
>
> What is a URL?
>
> What is a Web browser and what does it do?
>
> What are protocols, what do they do, and how does each (e-mail, telnet, ftp, Usenet, http) differ?
>
> What is an ISP (Internet service provider) and how do I select one?

History of the Internet

Tutorials that cover the history of the Internet and the World Wide Web can help students understand that it is not a single entity, but rather a noncentralized global network of networks.

Internet Skills

There are many different skills that new Internet users need to learn to function efficiently on the Web.

Web Browser Navigation   As with any software application, people who are new to the Internet often find it helpful to receive instruction on how to function in a Web browser. The interfaces in the various available browsers are not always the most user-friendly. Highlighting the features and functions available will assist new users.

Communication on the Internet   One of the top uses of the Internet for many people is to communicate with others. There are multiple methods to engage in online communication, including e-mail, instant messaging, chat, and discussion groups.

Netiquette   Unique sets of social rules surround appropriate behavior while on the Internet. These come into play particularly when e-mailing, chatting, and posting to discussion groups. Although they may seem like common sense once they are introduced to a new user, a vehicle to learn them before making an online faux pas will be appreciated!

Research on the Web

Using Web Search Tools   New search engines, directories, and indexes are introduced regularly. There will continue to be a need to instruct people to use them as they are introduced.

Web Search Strategies   Without a solid understanding of the most efficient techniques to conduct searches, users easily are overwhelmed by the amount of information a Web search returns.

Evaluation of Web Resources   Because anyone can publish to the Web, it has never been so important to teach students the criteria required to assess the quality of information retrieved from the Internet.

WebQuests   The term *WebQuests*, coined in 1995, describes an "inquiry-based activity that involves students in using Web-based resources and tools to transform their learning into meaningful understandings and real-world projects."[10] It has become a popular tool for organizing Web searches by educators. There are six critical components to a WebQuest:[11]

> an introduction to set the stage and provide background information
>
> a task that is doable as well as interesting
>
> a set of information sources that will help with the task
>
> a description of the process the learners should go through in accomplishing the task. The process is broken down into clearly defined steps
>
> guidance on how to organize the acquired information
>
> a conclusion that brings closure to the quest, reminds students about what they've learned, and encourages them to extend the experience into other domains

Figure 2.10 shows a WebQuest designed for middle school library users to teach them about Web site evaluation. A large collection of examples by age group can be examined at the WebQuest Portal (http://www.webquest.org).

FIGURE 2.10
What's It Worth? A WebQuest about Website Evaluation

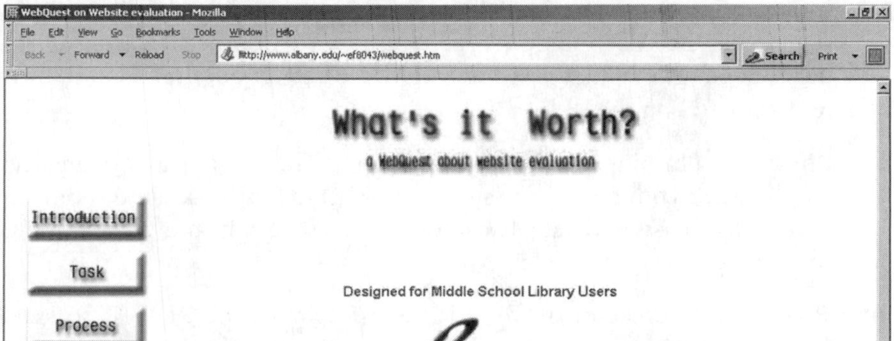

From Elizabeth Farquhar. Available: http://www.albany.edu/~ef8043/webquest.htm.

Invisible Web or Deep Web   The Invisible Web comprises the "text pages, files, or other often high-quality authoritative information available via the World Wide Web that general-purpose search engines cannot, due to technical limitations, or will not, due to deliberate choice, add to their indices of Web pages. . . . Sometimes also referred to as the 'deep Web' or 'dark matter.'"[12] Often this happens because the content is contained in dynamically driven databases. Increasingly, content is created in databases because it is more efficiently managed this way. There is danger of students being unaware of the Invisible Web's existence without instruction.

Making and Publishing Web Pages and Sites   There are a wide variety of topics that can be included in this category: creating basic Web pages, using specific HTML editors, Cascading Style Sheets, creating accessible Web pages, controlling access to pages and sites, creating Web graphics, design and layout principles, writing for the Web, and more. In fact, an online instruction could be created for almost every subject you will encounter in this book!

More Recent Internet Trends

File Sharing   File sharing has become a major issue in campuses across the nation. Electronic files (most often audio and video) are made available for download via the Internet. They are most often stored on individual users' computers and shared using a peer-to-peer model via services such as Kazaa. The difficulty arises because much of the downloaded material is copyrighted and is therefore illegal to share without permission. Educating people about the legal and moral aspects of file sharing has become, by necessity, an important topic.

Internet Safety   Internet safety is an important topic, especially with regard to children using the Web. Figure 2.11 is an example from the Chicago Public Library that illustrates a tutorial that prompts children to answer questions about the safety of various activities on the Web.

Phishing   Phishing describes hackers creating a replica of an existing legitimate Web page (often a commercial site such as a bank) to fool a user into submitting personal, financial, or password data. It is a scam that has become prevalent and that users need to be educated about.

RSS   RSS is an acronym for Rich Site Summary, or RDF (Resource Description Framework) Site Summary, an XML format for distributing news headlines and new content on the Web. It's also known as Really Simple Syndication and Webfeed. This technology can be set up to help stay abreast of new information by having it delivered to and constantly updated via a news aggregator, a piece of software freely available via the Web. Tutorials can be valuable to help users set up their own feeds or to instruct information providers to set up an RSS feed for their content. Figure 2.12 shows an RSS tutorial from LawLibTech that is posted on the Boley Law Library's legal research blog site for students.

Spam   Spam is unwanted, unsolicited, junk e-mail addressed to a large number of recipients. It has become so prevalent in the past few years that it has become more than just an annoyance. Learning how to minimize one's chances for attracting spam,

FIGURE 2.11
Internet Safety

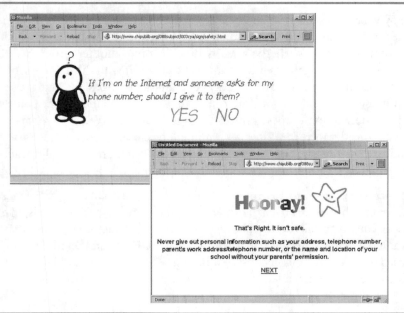

From Chicago Public Library. Available: http://www.chipublib.org/008subject/003cya/sign/safety.html.

FIGURE 2.12
RSS and Weblogs

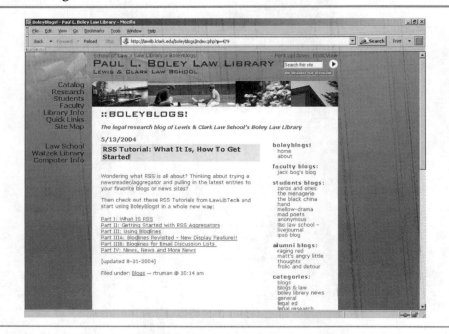

From Paul L. Boley Law Library, Lewis and Clark Law School, Portland, Oregon. Available: http://lawlib
.lclark.edu/boleyblogs/index.php?p=479.

how to filter it, and what to do with it when it is received are necessary skills in today's electronic world.

Spyware   Spyware is a technology that surreptitiously collects information about a person without his or her knowledge. A software program is installed on the user's computer, often when the user is downloading another program. Also known as adware, spyware gathers information and shares it with third parties, often advertisers who use the information to target their marketing. Besides being a serious concern over user privacy, this software can affect the performance of the computer on which it is installed, sometimes going as far as to hijack the Web browser and slow performance considerably. Tutt Library combined the closely related subjects of spam and spyware in its presentation "Spam, Pop-ups, Spyware, and Other Internet Annoyances" (see figure 2.13).

Voice over Internet Protocol (VoIP)   VoIP is a technology for transmitting ordinary telephone calls over the Internet. It takes analog audio signals, like the kind you hear when you talk on the phone, and turns them into digital data that can be transmitted over the Internet.[13] Because it bypasses the regular phone system, long distance calls are free. As this technology becomes more widely available, expect to see an increase in interest in learning about how it works.

FIGURE 2.13
Spam and Spyware

From Tutt Library, Colorado College, Colorado Springs. Available: http://www.coloradocollege.edu/library/instruction/spam.html.

Weblog   The weblog is a concept that has been around since the mid-1990s. Originally blogs were personal communication tools operated by individuals (bloggers) who compiled lists of links to sites of interest to them and intermingled this with information and editorials.[14] As the idea caught on, their purpose has expanded to more serious uses including politics, corporate communication with customers, and collaborative space.[15] Educators, including librarians, are exploring the value of blogs. Teaching students about blogs—their history, purpose, and potential—may become a component of information literacy instruction. Estep cites his experience teaching an information literacy class about weblogs by having students evaluate the information found on selected political weblogs.[16] Blogs will be discussed in greater detail in chapter 7.

Wi-Fi   Wi-Fi is short for wireless fidelity and is used commonly when referring to the IEEE 802.11 wireless networking specification. This is the technology that allows PCs and PDAs (personal digital assistant) to share a high-speed Internet connection over a distance of about 300 feet and connect a local network without wires. Many libraries are moving toward incorporating this technology into their buildings because it can be more cost effective than a wired network (especially in retrofitting an existing building) and can provide patrons with both mobility to connect throughout the building and access to difficult-to-reach areas. As more people become interested in having a wireless network in their homes, they will seek instruction on how the technology works.

Wiki   A wiki is a collaborative Web site comprising the perpetual collective work of many authors. It is similar to a weblog in structure and logic. However, it allows anyone to edit, delete, or modify content, including work of previous authors. The collaborative nature of a wiki has great potential in educational settings and for group projects. Wikis will be discussed in more detail in chapter 7.

General Library Orientation

Most academic libraries hold library orientation tours each semester when new students arrive on campus. Any library can be an intimidating structure to new patrons. Helping students learn where departments, services, and materials are located in the library is the first step to transforming them into independent information seekers. A virtual library tour can serve the same purpose. It provides the students with a map that they can use to become acquainted with the library building and its services.

Other types of libraries also see the value of offering a Web orientation to their facilities and services. Figure 2.14 shows a multimedia tour of the services offered by the Public Library of Charlotte and Mecklenburg County in North Carolina.

Information Literacy Courses

As the world of information becomes more complex, information literacy instruction has become an increasingly important part of the education process. Many higher education institutions include an information literacy class as a required part of the curriculum, often during a student's first year. It may be offered as a separate class for credit or may be incorporated into a survey course such as freshman English. These

FIGURE 2.14
General Library Orientation

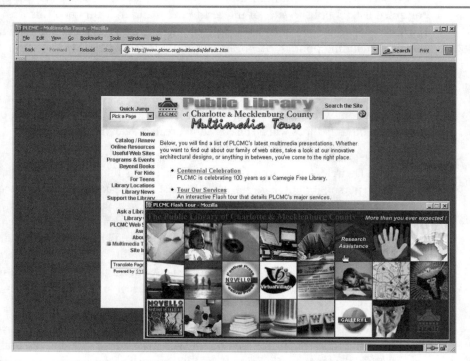

From Public Library of Charlotte and Mecklenburg County, North Carolina.
Available: http://www.plcmc.org/multimedia/default.htm.

courses allow concepts to be covered in an in-depth manner because the time constraints of a "one-shot" class are removed. In this type of forum, there are many opportunities for incorporating active learning, collaborative learning, multiple media to
present information, and the other characteristics of good library instruction. The
recognition of the need to educate people to be information literate is not limited to
academia by any means. A survey of information literature over a thirty-year period
indicates that school librarians and school media specialists have had to address this
need to teach information skills from kindergarten through high school. It also found
that, although user instruction traditionally was minimal in public libraries, current
demands for distance education support and from K–12 students have grown and
need to be tackled by public librarians.[17]

An example of a required information literacy tutorial can be seen in figure 2.15.
University of Wisconsin–Parkside requires that all students who enter the school with
fewer than 90 credits successfully complete this five-module course. Each module
includes a quiz on which students must score at least 80 percent to pass.

FIGURE 2.15
Information Literacy Tutorial

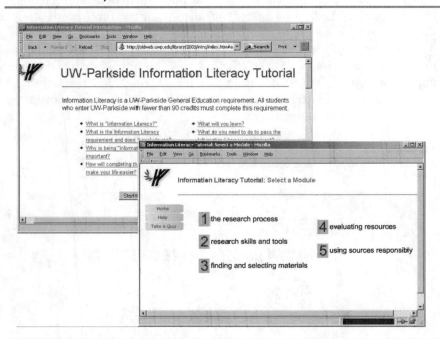

From University of Wisconsin–Parkside Library. Available: http://www.uwp.edu/
departments/library/ infolit/intro/.

The UW–Parkside modules include topics that are typical of those covered in information literacy courses:

The Research Process: Understanding the Assignment; Creating a Research Question; Finding Background Information; Creating Key Concepts; Identifying Related Terms

Research Skills and Tools: The Search Process; Search Results; What's a Record?; Boolean Searching; Search Tools: Phrase Searching, Wildcards, Truncation; Complex Searching; Subject Headings; Keywords vs. Subject Headings

Finding and Selecting Materials: Locating Information; Library Catalog; Periodical Indexes; Magazines vs. Scholarly Journals; Using the Web and Search Engines

Evaluating Resources: Why Evaluate?; What Gets Evaluated?; Evaluation Criteria; Evaluating Web sites; Evaluating Print Materials

Using Resources Responsibly: Plagiarism; Citing Sources; Citation Styles; Copyright; Fair Use

Academic Integrity and Intellectual Property

Although most information literacy courses include information about academic integrity and intellectual property, because it is a hot issue in education today, instructional units focusing strictly on this area have started to appear. These are issues that permeate all areas of the academic experience, but in many cases, the library is taking the lead on getting out the information to educate students about what is acceptable and unacceptable behavior. UCLA Library has developed an introduction to the issues that surround ethics and information: "Carlos and Eddie's Guide to Bruin Success with Less Stress" (figure 2.16). This interactive tutorial covers several important topics: intellectual property, file sharing, documentation and citing sources, avoiding disaster through organization and time management, and UCLA policies on academic integrity.

FIGURE 2.16
Academic Integrity and Intellectual Property

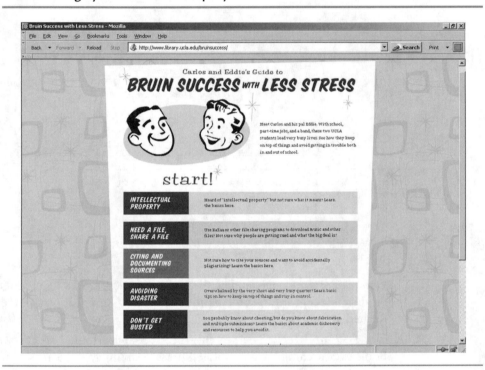

From University of California–Los Angeles Library. Available: http://www.library.ucla.edu/bruinsuccess/.

Productivity Software Applications

As the need for computing skills has evolved, many libraries—public ones in particular—have become the providers of training for productivity software applications. Tutorials have been developed to teach the use of applications such as word processing, spreadsheets, Web editing, multimedia, graphics creation, and, most recently, bibliographic management software such as EndNote and Reference Manager. Figure 2.17 shows one of the computer tutorials offered by King County (Washington State) Library.

FIGURE 2.17
Productivity Software Application Tutorial

From King County (Washington State) Library System. Available: http://www.kcls.org/comptutorials/publisher-1.cfm.

Notes

1. Nancy H. Dewald, "Transporting Good Library Instruction Practices into the Web Environment: An Analysis of Online Tutorials," *Journal of Academic Librarianship* 25, no. 1 (1999).

2. Association of College and Research Libraries. "Tips for Developing Effective Web-Based Library Instruction." *ALA Instruction Section*. 27 Oct 2004, http://www.ala.org/ala/acrlbucket/is/iscommittees/webpages/teachingmethods/tips.htm.

3. Kornelia Tancheva, "Online Tutorials for Library Instruction: An Ongoing Project under Constant Revision." Paper presented at the ACRL Eleventh National Conference, Charlotte, NC, 10–13 Apr. 2003. http://www.ala.org/ala/acrl/acrlevents/tancheva.PDF.

4. Lisa Denton, "Library Instruction in K–12 Schools," *Virginia Libraries* 45, no. 1 (1999).

5. John Bertot and Charles McClure, *Public Libraries and the Internet 2000: Summary Findings and Data Tables* (National Commission on Libraries and Information Science, 7 Sept. 2000). http://www.nclis.gov/statsurv/2000plo.pdf.

6. Michael Stephens, "Here Come the Trainers!" *Public Libraries* 43, no. 4 (2004).

7. Laura J. Haverkamp and Kelly Coffey, "Instruction Issues in Special Libraries." *Special Libraries Management Handbook: The Basics,* http://www.libsci.sc.edu/bob/class/clis724/SpecialLibrariesHandbook/instruction.htm.

8. Margaret Driscoll, *Web-Based Training: Creating E-Learning Experiences,* 2nd ed. (Jossey-Bass/Pfeiffer, 2002), 6.

9. Susannah Fox, "Older Americans and the Internet" (Washington, DC: Pew Internet and American Life Project, 2004), http://www.pewinternet.org/pdfs/PIP_Seniors_Online_2004.pdf.

10. Bernie Dodge, "WebQuest Page at San Diego State University," 2004, http://webquest.sdsu.edu.

11. Bernie Dodge, "Some Thoughts about WebQuests," 1997, http://webquest.sdsu.edu/about_webquests.html.

12. Chris Sherman and Gary Price, "The Invisible Web: Uncovering Sources Search Engines Can't See," *Library Trends* 52, no. 2 (2003): 283.

13. Jeff Tyson and Robert Valdes, "How VoIP Works." *Howstuffworks*. http://computer.howstuffworks.com/ip-telephony.htm.

14. Erik Sean Estep and Julia Gelfand, "Weblogs," *Library Hi Tech News* 20, no. 5 (2003): 11.

15. Will Richardson, "Blogging and RSS—the 'What's It?' and 'How to' of Powerful New Web Tools for Educators," *Multimedia and Internet@Schools* 11, no. 1 (2004): 10.

16. Estep and Gelfand, 11.

17. Hannelore B. Rader, "Information Literacy 1973–2002: A Selected Literature Review," *Library Trends* 51, no. 2 (2002): 243–44.

3

Design and
Development Cycle

As with any undertaking, setting up a systematic process that will guide you as the project proceeds is important. In the software industry, this is known as the design and development cycle. It incorporates the planning, development, production, and evaluation of a product from start to finish, and is a circular process rather than a linear one. By the time one version is released, the next one is already being worked upon. This chapter discusses the various components that make up a typical design and development cycle. You will find that the components don't always surface in the same place in the cycle, and they often overlap. In fact, the process can be fluid.

No matter what size project you are embarking upon, it is important to understand the different aspects of this cycle and to incorporate them into your process. Establishing a system will permit the project to be developed within a specified time and evaluated according to objective criteria. It will allow you to execute the project efficiently, saving you time overall. The four main stages you will deal with are preproduction, production, publication, and postproduction. In addition, two facets appear in all stages of the cycle: project management and evaluation. Figure 3.1 provides a graphical representation of the design and development cycle for Web-based instruction.

PREPRODUCTION

No matter how simple the project appears at first consideration, if you jump right in and start creating Web pages immediately, it is going to end up taking much longer than if you take the time up front to carefully plan each aspect of the project. This planning step is called the preproduction phase and can normally encompass about two-thirds of the entire cycle.

Needs Analyses

Preproduction starts with an idea. Maybe you and your colleagues have decided that an online tutorial is a good objective, or perhaps a faculty member who would like a

FIGURE 3.1
Design and Development Cycle

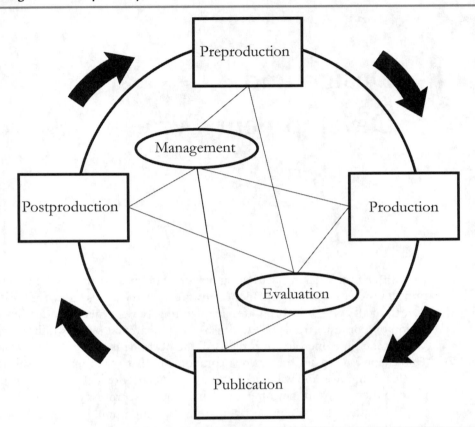

tutorial for a specific class has approached you. Whatever the origin of the idea, it has been formed in response to some perceived need. You must develop a good understanding of what that need is. Thus, the first step in the cycle is to perform needs analyses of the client, audience, stakeholders, information, and resources.

Client Needs Analysis

Start by interviewing your client (who may be a fellow librarian, an entire academic department, or a faculty member). You want to determine what the client hopes to accomplish with an online tutorial. Does the client have some specific goal in mind? What is it? For instance, will the tutorial replace face-to-face library instruction, or will it be a supplement to it? Is a Web-based tutorial really the best approach to provide the outcome the client is seeking? What resources does the client have for this project? Is there a departmental budget that will pay for the project, or does the client expect it to come from your library budget?

Audience Needs Analysis

Who is the audience you will be addressing in the tutorial? You will want to "get into their heads" before you design your tutorial. What are the characteristics of this audience—gender, age, ethnicity, socioeconomic level, educational background, learning style, and the degree of familiarity with the proposed subject matter? It is also essential to know the audience's level of computer competence. If you are dealing with an audience with mixed characteristics, you should recognize and factor that into your design.

Stakeholder Needs Analysis

Stakeholders are those individuals or groups external to your project who have an interest in the outcome of your endeavor. It will benefit your project to identify this group at the start as they can be important allies who can help ensure a successful outcome. Stakeholders for an instructional project can include other librarians, faculty, administrators, trustees, your organization's information technology department, or state and local government representatives. Most often they will not have a direct involvement with your project, but many times they are people who have control over your organization's budgets, technology, and politics. Identifying, establishing relationships with, and gaining the support from this group will help you reach your objectives.[1]

Information Needs Analysis

Determining information needs involves researching, selecting, and arranging the content that will be included in the tutorial. You will want to consult with the client or a content specialist to determine what is to be included and how to organize it for optimum retention. Often the client is not the person who understands the best way to present the content. For example, a faculty member who is the client probably knows the discipline but not necessarily how it relates to doing library research. Content to be included may also depend on the audience mix. For instance, if the targeted audience is made up of distance education students, the tutorial may want to emphasize online resources over print resources that require a trip to the library to use.

Resource Needs Analysis

What resources are available to support your project? Hardware and software resources need to be considered. Do you have what you need to produce the tutorial, or will you require additional applications or peripherals such as a scanner? What about the students' existing hardware and software? (Chapter 4 focuses in detail on hardware and software considerations.)

How much time is available to complete the project? What human resources are needed? Is there sufficient money in the budget to cover expenses? What delivery system is going to be used, and will your existing infrastructure support it? In the case of Web-based delivery, will it be delivered over a fiber-optic network or an analog phone line? The answer will shape what you decide to develop.

When you have worked through these analyses and have clearly outlined the results, you have the information you'll need to start on the next step in preproduction: design and prototyping.

Design and Prototyping

During the design and prototyping stage of the preproduction phase of the cycle, important preliminary work takes place. This is the time you will develop design ideas and instruction content and organize these into a detailed plan that sets the stage for production of your tutorial. In this section you will be introduced to brainstorming for design ideas, developing scripts, and creating visual tools that will become the blueprint for your tutorial.

Brainstorming

The beginning of the design stage is a good time to brainstorm. Assemble your project team (discussed later in this chapter under project management). Have each person contribute his or her ideas on what would be included in the perfect tutorial. Consider both content and functionality. With content, consider the message to be communicated. Start identifying what content can be included that will help develop the research skills the students will need to have. When discussing functionality, consider the level of interactivity that you will use to convey the content. When brainstorming, the sky's the limit, and no idea is too far fetched. This is particularly true when discussing functionality. Maybe you think that some interactivities that you might desire are beyond the technical capabilities of your team, but this isn't the time to reject anything out of hand. It's a time to see the range of ideas and expectations that each team member is bringing to the project and to establish the beginning of teamwork by learning about each other. You'll find that part of the fun of doing a project like this is that you will have the opportunity to further your knowledge and expertise as you meet the challenge of learning new technologies.

One tool that can help your team reach an agreement about what a good tutorial might consist of is to shop the competition. That is, visit sites and take a look at what other libraries or educational organizations have done on similar projects. Use the various sites to trigger conversation about what each team member likes or dislikes about a particular site. It will be helpful to compile a list of criteria or questions to consider that you have identified as being important to your project so that you have a basis for comparison (see figure 3.2).

A portal to library tutorial sites can be found on the LOEX tutorial page (http://www.emich.edu/public/loex/tutorials.html) or the ALA PRIMO Web site (http://www.ala.org/ala/acrlbucket/is/iscommittees/webpages/emergingtech/primo/index.htm). This exercise will serve to start the design process. You will discover your team's design and organization awareness. Which team member has a good eye for design? Who on the team understands content organization? As you proceed, the skeleton of your site's architecture will start to emerge, and each team member's role will become defined.

Once you have determined the basics of what you desire, the more detailed tasks of developing a script, planning the tutorial's progression through a flowchart or storyboard, and creating the interface design can begin.

Script

The script will become the nuts and bolts of the message you want to convey. It is a good idea to start with an outline that defines the main points to be made in the tuto-

FIGURE 3.2
Potential Comparison Criteria for Evaluation of Web-Based Instruction

EVALUATION CATEGORY	QUESTIONS TO ASK
Instructional design	Are the objectives clear?
	Is there provision for interactive practice?
	Is there a feedback mechanism in place?
	Are illustrations and examples incorporated into the instruction?
Subject content	Does it contain the right amount and quality of information?
	Is the material delivered in an appropriate manner for the targeted audience?
	Is the language jargon-free?
	Is the content presented in concise chunks, to facilitate easy recall by students?
Audience considerations	Will the material engage the students' attention?
	Is the material covered pertinent to students' needs?
	Does the site permit student control of movement through the tutorial?
Use of media	Do the graphics, sound, and other multimedia contribute to further the instruction?
	Do multimedia components download quickly?
	Do they require use of a plug-in; if so, are instructions provided?
Visual design	Is the screen design layout clearly organized and easy to understand?
	Is the layout consistent between screens?
	Is the interface aesthetically pleasing?
	Is the site easily identifiable as a cohesive unit?
	Does the color scheme used contribute to the tone of the site?
Ease of use	Is it intuitive to use?
	Is it easy to navigate?
	Do pages load quickly?
	Are frames used appropriately?
Evaluation	Are there evaluation mechanisms built into the tutorial?
Accessibility	Is the tutorial accessible to disabled users?

rial. Often the outline becomes apparent once the site architecture is determined. Site architecture is the design of the site, not in terms of artistic design elements, such as color or graphics, but in terms of the organization, navigation, and functional systems of the site. Figure 3.3 shows an example of a typical outline for a library instruction Web project. The script will include all aspects of the content: the wording for the text you want to include, media that illustrate the content (images, sound files, movie clips), activities to reinforce a concept, and skill checks to provide an assessment of retention of what has been taught.

FIGURE 3.3
The Script Outline for Research Tutorial
Z. Smith Reynolds Library: Putting the Pieces Together

1. Introduction
2. Selecting Your Topic
    i. Select a Topic?
    ii. Background Reading
    iii. State the Topic
3. Finding Library Materials
    i. Online Catalog
    ii. Searching the Catalog
    iii. Interpreting Catalog Search Results
        a. Call Numbers
4. Finding Journal Articles
    i. Periodical Databases and Indexes
        a. General vs. Subject Specific
        b. Electronic Databases vs. Print Indexes
        c. Citation Indexes vs. Full Text
    ii. Selecting a Database
    iii. Database Searching
        a. Building a Search Strategy
        b. Basic Search
        c. Advanced Search
    iv. Interpreting Results
    v. Locating the Article
5. Getting Materials from Other Libraries
6. Using the Internet
    i. Searching the Internet
        a. Search Indexes
        b. Search Engines
        c. Meta Search Engines
7. Citing Research
8. Getting Help
9. Glossary

Flowchart/Storyboard

Both a flowchart and a storyboard are tools to illustrate the step-by-step progression through the tutorial. A flowchart is a visual representation of the sequence of the content of the tutorial. It will show what comes first, second, third, and so on, as well as what pages link to each other, what actions your audience will take, and what will occur when each action is taken. It is a road map of your project. Figure 3.4 illustrates a simple flowchart created from the first several screens of the interactive tutorial "Falcon: An Interactive Web Tutorial," from Bowling Green State University Libraries.

FIGURE 3.4
Sample Flowchart Modeled from Falcon
An Interactive Web Tutorial

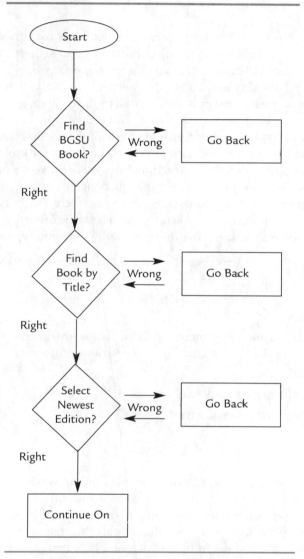

From Bowling Green State University Libraries, Bowling Green,
Ohio. Available: http://www.bgsu.edu/colleges/library/infosrv/
tutorial/tutor1.html.

The storyboard goes a step farther. It contains a sketch for each screen that includes text, information about the graphics (including placement, color, and size), design layout, color, font size and type, sound (including narration), and audience interaction. It should be detailed enough that team members know what happens on each screen, what will happen throughout the tutorial, and what each screen will look like.

Both the flowchart and storyboard are important tools of communication between the team and the client. It is the first visualization of what the project will become.

Mock-ups and Prototypes

The next step in the design process is to transform the design ideas contained in the storyboard to actual models of the site. A mock-up of the screen design illustrates how the interface will look to users. (Chapter 5 discusses the user interface design; we will look more closely at testing usability in chapter 8.)

Creating a prototype of the site design is a useful tool in the early stages to determine if the design is going to work before investing a great deal of time in producing the entire site. A prototype is typically a functional rendition of the site that is not necessarily fully developed but can be used for testing. One methodology for prototyping is called rapid prototyping, in which the instructional designers actively work with users to quickly build a series of prototypes rather than just one. In such a model, the evaluation and development activities are parallel processes where the two groups work together to decide which features will be kept and which will be discarded. It is an iterative process that has some advantages over the more traditional prototype model:[2]

- It encourages and requires the active participation of end users in the activities of design.
- It makes allowance for the natural reaction of users to change their minds during the design process.
- It facilitates users' understanding of their requirements for instruction products by engaging them in the implementation of the various prototypes.
- Errors can be detected early.
- It can increase creativity through quick user feedback.
- It accelerates the instructional development process.

PRODUCTION

The production phase of the cycle is the one most people think of when they decide to do a Web project. It is the part of the cycle where the actual site construction is done. Code is written, interactivity components are programmed, multimedia is produced, and your tutorial is brought to life. By waiting to start this stage until you have put in place detailed site architecture, thoroughly organized content, and a set page and site design, you will streamline the actual production of the site. Chapters 5 through 7 focus on different aspects of the production cycle in detail: user interface design, multimedia, and interactivity.

PUBLICATION

Once your tutorial has been produced, you will want to make it available to users. Publication of a Web product is a much simpler process than with other types of multimedia products. The HTML and image and sound files are transferred from the computer on which they were created onto a Web server where they become published.

Your tutorial is now ready to be accessed simply by pointing a Web browser to its URL (uniform resource locator, or Web address). Arrangements must be made with the Web site's system administrator to provide you with sufficient access privileges to maintain and update the files as needed.

POSTPRODUCTION

The postproduction phase of the cycle is as important as the planning phase. It includes such tasks as developing a marketing strategy, site indexing, site maintenance, and planning for the next version of the tutorial.

Marketing Strategy

If your tutorial is designed to be used by only a specific group of students, then it may not be necessary to do more than provide a professor with the URL of the site. However, if you are targeting a broader audience, it may be advisable to develop specific methods to get the word out about your tutorial so users can find and use it. Marketing strategies can range from simple to elaborate, but often such methods as notifying appropriate mailing lists, posting an announcement on your organization's home page, or sending out a broadcast e-mail announcement are effective. Your team can explore the best means for your particular situation.

Site Indexing

Site indexing is the process of indexing your tutorial on external Web search engines (as opposed to the indexing done on a search engine installed on your organization's Web server). To improve the potential for users to find your tutorial via the major search engines like HotBot or AltaVista, you will want to use available tools to describe your site accurately. The main way to accomplish this is to use <meta> tags to specify accurate descriptions in the <head> of your document. Also, use descriptive terms in the <title> tag because many search engines index from this tag. The process may also be speeded up by taking a proactive approach by submitting your site manually to various search engines rather than waiting for their automated indexing programs (called robots) to visit your site and find you.

Site Maintenance

Once your tutorial is published, it is important to take steps to ensure that it stays functional and current. For example, the Web is notorious for changing constantly, and you will want to make sure that you regularly check for broken links and update them.

Planning for the Next Version

Publishing a Web tutorial isn't a finite project. As you proceed through the postpublication evaluation process, you will start to gather information that will form the nucleus for revisions and improvements.

TESTING AND EVALUATION

Testing and evaluation are important components of the design and development cycle, but can't be neatly assigned into just one phase. Testing and evaluation are the primary vehicles you have to receive essential information to help ensure that your tutorial is effective. Because they are essential elements of a successful Web instruction project, this subject is covered in depth in chapter 8.

PROJECT MANAGEMENT

No matter whether your project is large or small, it will require management from start to finish. A large project may call for a dedicated project manager; a small project may have one of the team members also wearing a management hat. There are many facets of a project to manage: authoring a project proposal, obtaining funding, the timeline, the budget, the staff and team, resources, reports, client and stakeholder relations, and quality control.

Project Proposal

If you are part of a small organization, it might not be mandatory that you formulate a project proposal to proceed. But as the demand for digital services and increased information technology supports increases, some organizations have instituted a mandatory proposal process so that each project is carefully thought out and resources can be scheduled. An example of a proposal process can be seen in figure 3.5. Duke University Libraries (Perkins System) has codified the process required to propose a new digital service.

Even if this step is not required, it is a good idea to consider formalizing your proposal in writing. A succinct, well-thought-out document can be used to support your idea and sell it to stakeholders (who will appreciate a clearly outlined description including the project's impact, timeline, and resources requirements). If the potential funding source is from a grant, this document can serve as a basis for your grant application.[3]

A proposal may vary in length and complexity, depending on specific circumstances, but typically it will include

the goals of the project

a description of activities involved

its significance to and impact on its intended audience and the organization

a timeline

a budget

required resources

Timeline

Usually time is one of the constraints on a project. For example, a university's general research and reference tutorial needs to be ready at the start of the fall term, or a pro-

FIGURE 3.5
Project Proposal Process

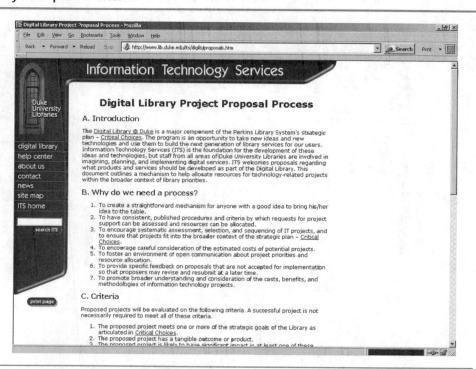

From Duke University Libraries, Durham, North Carolina. Available: http://www.lib.duke.edu/its/
diglib/proposals.htm.

fessor needs a course-related tutorial two weeks before the research assignment is due. Any project is more effective if there is a detailed timeline to follow. A timeline will include the project schedule that details tasks and activities, projected completion dates, and persons assigned to each task. Project management software is available to track timelines (for example, Microsoft Project), but one can be done without investing in expensive software. A spreadsheet will work well and a Google search will return links to free project management software.

To create a timeline, make a list of all activities involved in each phase of the project, put them in sequential order, estimate the time it will take to complete each task, and assign responsibility. You may want to set up different views of the timeline— weekly, monthly, and overall views. A good model that will work is a Gantt chart, also known as a bar chart. Figure 3.6 illustrates a simple Gantt chart of a Web project.

Budget

Managing the project budget can be a major task in a large-scale project. If you are starting with nothing, you may have to create a budget prior to your project's being

FIGURE 3.6
Gantt Chart for a Web Project Using Microsoft Project Software

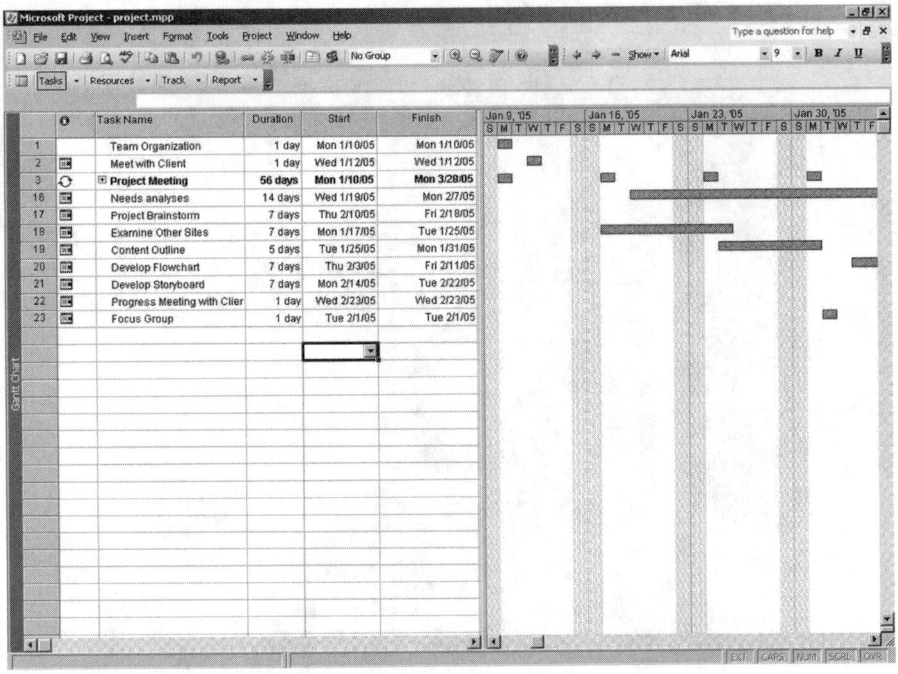

		Task Name	Duration	Start	Finish
1		Team Organization	1 day	Mon 1/10/05	Mon 1/10/05
2		Meet with Client	1 day	Wed 1/12/05	Wed 1/12/05
3		⊞ **Project Meeting**	**56 days**	**Mon 1/10/05**	**Mon 3/28/05**
16		Needs analyses	14 days	Wed 1/19/05	Mon 2/7/05
17		Project Brainstorm	7 days	Thu 2/10/05	Fri 2/18/05
18		Examine Other Sites	7 days	Mon 1/17/05	Tue 1/25/05
19		Content Outline	5 days	Tue 1/25/05	Mon 1/31/05
20		Develop Flowchart	7 days	Thu 2/3/05	Fri 2/11/05
21		Develop Storyboard	7 days	Mon 2/14/05	Tue 2/22/05
22		Progress Meeting with Clier	1 day	Wed 2/23/05	Wed 2/23/05
23		Focus Group	1 day	Tue 2/1/05	Tue 2/1/05

Screen shot of Microsoft Project used by permission from Microsoft Corporation.

approved. Using the results from the initial resource needs analysis, you may have to consider expenditures for hardware and software to produce the tutorial. If you don't have trained staff, application training may have to be factored into the budget. Human resources, even if you aren't paying an extra salary to someone on staff, are a major budget item since staff hours spent on the project will most likely be one of the largest costs for which you must account.

Funding the Project

The source of funds to support your project should be identified as early as possible in the planning stages because the viability of continuing may hinge on it. If your project is small and you already have appropriate facilities, hardware, software, and trained staff, funding might not be a real issue. But if this project marks your entry into the Web production arena, substantial funding may be necessary for you to be able to proceed. Communication with the administrators of your organization will provide a means to assess the situation. Is there flexibility in the current library budget that will permit funds to be available immediately or is it necessary to ask for funding from your governing body to be included in a future budget? Does the fact that library funding has declined significantly in recent years[4] mean that you will need to research possible grant programs that can pay for your project? If a grant is determined as the best way to approach funding the project, most application processes will extend the project implementation time because of the length of time required for application review and approval processes. The resources section at the end of this book cites various sources for locating and securing grants and funding.

Staffing and Teamwork

Forming the right team for your project and managing the resulting team dynamics may well be one of the most challenging aspects of the project. As you are forming your team, keep in mind the roles that may need to be filled:

Web author—creates the HTML pages for the tutorial

scripting programmer—adds interactivity into the tutorial through scripting or other technologies

instructional designer—determines the best way to present the content in an online environment to optimize retention

content specialist—determines the content to include (may be the library's bibliographic instructor or the subject specialist for the content being presented)

writer—writes the script and content

editor—edits the script and content

graphic/animation designer or videographer—understands user interface design and creates graphics and other multimedia

systems designer—designs how the tutorial will work from a technical standpoint, works with instructional designer on flowcharts and storyboard, manages authors, selects authoring tools

information technology specialist—provides the expertise on server and network issues

evaluation specialist—creates evaluation plan and tools

marketing specialist—handles the planning and execution of publicity

project manager—oversees the process and the team

It is important to define the roles and responsibilities for each team member and to associate these roles with the tasks to be accomplished. This ensures that all participants understand the team structure and expectations.

Depending on the skills of existing library staffers, there may be a need to go outside the library to locate people with the skills to produce the tutorial. Even with qualified staff, you will want to select people who will complement each other and "subordinate personal prominence to the efficiency of the whole" (*Webster's New Collegiate Dictionary* definition of teamwork). It is important to remember that, according to Tuckman's model of small group development, teams go through four stages of development on their way to becoming a cohesive unit:[5]

Forming is the stage in which group members learn about each other and the task at hand.

Storming develops as group members reach a level of comfort with each other and may start vying for status within the group and argue.

Norming is the stage in which the group structure is developed. Rules are established for achieving goals, roles are defined, and the group is ready to get down to the business at hand.

Performing is the stage in which the team begins to function as a system and focuses attention on the work or content. Emphasis here is on productivity and achievement. Collaboration and cooperation are incorporated to work toward the shared goal.

Coaching staff to put the good of the team before individual considerations is a skill that requires patience, maturity, and a good sense of humor.

Resource Allocation

Most organizations don't have unlimited resources. Even if you've determined that you have the necessary resources to complete your project, you may well be sharing those resources with others in your organization. For example, your content specialist may be the library's bibliographic instructor, the site designer may be the systems administrator, and the like. Most likely, your team members won't be able to devote 100 percent of their time to this project. Scheduling the time that team members can commit to a particular project is important to meeting the project timelines. You also may be sharing hardware and software resources with others in your organization (and with the public), and the project manager will have to become involved in allocating those resources so they are available when team members need them.

Reports

Depending on the scope of the project, it may be necessary to submit progress reports to your client and stakeholders at crucial points throughout the design and development cycle. In addition, regular reports can serve as an effective record-keeping method that will be a valuable tool for project evaluation. Reports can also be a good way to communicate the overall project progress to team members. If your project is grant funded, you may be sure that there will be a reporting component required.

Client Relations

If you are working with a client, you will want the client to stay informed and satisfied with the progress of the project. Therefore, you must make time to communicate regularly. Maintaining a good relationship with the client can make a world of difference if the project gets off schedule for whatever reason. The client is much more likely to be understanding of extenuating circumstances if he or she has been kept in the loop in a positive manner.

Quality Control

Overseeing the emergence of an exemplary product calls for quality checks at each step of the production cycle. You may incorporate both formal and informal methods for evaluating if your tutorial is meeting expectations of the criteria established in the pre-production stage. These methods will be discussed in detail in chapter 8.

It should be evident by now that even though the design and development cycle provides a structure to follow, it is a nonlinear process with more than one way to implement each phase. There is plenty of room for variations depending on the team you have assembled, the characteristics of your client, and the leadership style of the project manager. Keep in mind the main factors that will influence how you proceed: money (budget), time (scheduling), staffing (expertise), and facilities (hardware/software). Finally, remember that no matter how important it is to be systematic, it is just as imperative to provide space for creativity.

Notes

1. Clara S. Fowler, "Audience and Stakeholders," in *Developing Web-Based Instruction: Planning, Designing, Managing, and Evaluating for Results*, ed. Elizabeth Dupuis (New York: Neal-Schuman, 2003), 43–44.
2. Barbara Bichelmeyer, "Rapid Prototyping," in *Education and Technology: An Encyclopedia*, ed. Ann Kovalchick and Kara Dawson (Santa Barbara, CA: ABC-CLIO, 2004), 487.
3. Elizabeth A. Dupuis, *Developing Web-Based Instruction: Planning, Designing, Managing, and Evaluating for Results* (New York: Neal-Schuman, 2003), 257–60.
4. According to ALA Funding website at http://www.ala.org/libraryfunding/.
5. B. Tuckman, "Developmental Sequence in Small Groups," *Psychological Bulletin* 63 (1965): 384–99.

4

Selecting Project Development Tools

As discussed in the previous chapter, analyzing hardware and software needs is an important part of the preproduction stage of your Web project. There are three major areas to consider: constraints that may exist depending upon the hardware and software available to users, development hardware, and authoring software.

USER CONSTRAINTS

One of the main benefits of a Web-based delivery system is that it can be used across platforms. A platform is the underlying hardware or software for a system, commonly called the operating system. Customarily, software application programs were developed to run on a particular platform. A developer that wanted an application to run on multiple platforms would be forced to write separate programs. But with HTML, the language of the Web, it doesn't matter if your students are on PC-compatible, Macintosh, or Linux platforms. However, you do have to worry about what hardware and software your audience uses to access your tutorial.

So, what do you need to be concerned about? Your main concerns fall into three categories: hardware issues, browser issues, and access methods.

Hardware Issues

It is doubtful that you are in the envious situation where all of your users have late-model, identical computers. Therefore, you must take into account the range of hardware being used to access your instructional site.

Monitor Screen Size and Display Capabilities

Display capabilities can vary greatly. It is interesting to note that as of mid-2004, the majority of Internet users worldwide choose a screen resolution of 1024 × 768 pixels (the number of individual points of color; in this case, 1024 horizontally and 768 vertically). But 25 percent are still using 800 × 600.[1] This is a good indication that there are still older monitors in use with even lower resolutions. If your users have older monitors, they may be restricted to a resolution of 800 × 600, or possibly even 640 × 480. As you lay out the design for your user interface, you need to take care in selecting a display size. If you design your site at 1024 × 768 and your user's screen can display only 800 × 600, that user will not be able to view the entire screen and will have to scroll both horizontally and vertically to read the contents of the screen. This is tedious for the person focusing on the content of a site. The display resolution should be no larger than the lowest resolution a user may have. Browser.com offers a free screen size tester to help developers see how their pages will look on different sized screens (see figure 4.1).

FIGURE 4.1
Screen Size Tester

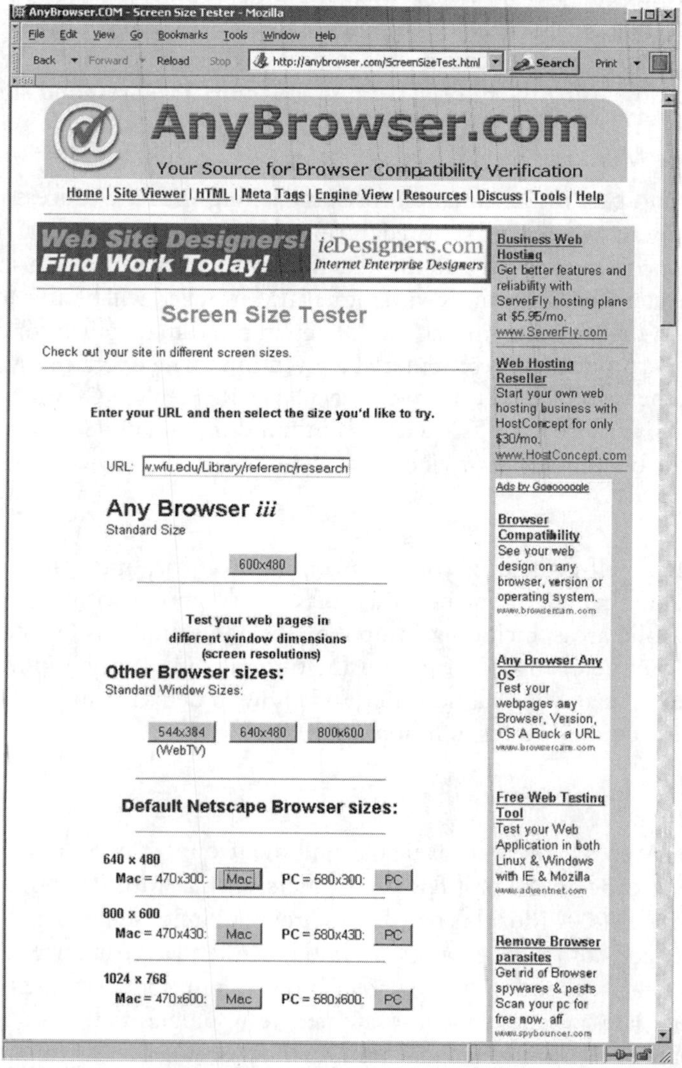

From AnyBrowser.com. Available: http://anybrowser.com/ScreenSizeTest.html.

Although color monitors are the norm today, most likely there are still monochrome or grayscale display screens in use, particularly with older notebook and smaller computers. If you know that some of your audience may be accessing your tutorial with noncolor screens, it's important for you to plan your color design to accommodate that.

Processor Speed

The clock speed of a processor, or central processing unit (CPU), determines how fast it interprets and executes program instructions (commands). This is measured in megahertz (MHz) or gigahertz (GHz), depending upon the age of the computer. A 3.6 GHz computer will execute 3,600 million cycles per second. Because every instruction requires a specific number of cycles, the clock speed helps determine how fast those instructions will be executed. Although computers produced since 2000 have GHz processors, there are still plenty of computers running on the slower MHz processors. If your audience members have lower computer CPU speeds and you create a tutorial that requires a great number of commands to be issued simultaneously, the audience will have a hard time using the tutorial because the tutorial will respond slowly.

Random Access Memory

RAM is the second part of the equation for speed, along with the processor. It is the place in the computer where data is stored during the short term for easy access. When RAM fills up, the computer must pull the data from the hard drive, which slows down the process considerably. Computers with more RAM installed will be able to run programs faster than those with minimal RAM. Keep in mind that your tutorial isn't the only thing that is running on a computer at a given time. The operating system, Web browser, and other applications are using available RAM also. Graphics intensive applications require more RAM, so keep this in mind if you are designing a tutorial that relies heavily on animation or video.

Sound

Although it seems self-evident, if you are planning to incorporate audio into your tutorial, make sure that your audience has access to a computer with sound capabilities. In many public areas, including computer labs, the sound has been disabled so that others will not be disturbed. If part of the tutorial will convey important information in audio format, you will need to decide how to deliver it in public environments (perhaps providing access to headphones).

Browser Issues

Several different Web browsers are available, and the two most prevalent are Internet Explorer and Netscape. In the past few years others, such as Mozilla and Opera, have gained popularity. In 2004 Mozilla's bare bones browser Firefox appeared on the scene. But different versions of these browsers are in the marketplace concurrently. Because users don't necessarily abandon their current browser and update to the newest version and because latest versions incorporate new technologies that have been developed since the previous update, you may find you have browser-compatibility issues. If you decide to incorporate a certain type of scripting to provide interaction or use some of the more recent markup language elements, in older browsers your page may not function as you had planned. Some features that are not supported in aging browsers include cascading style sheets, layers, frames, and JavaScript. These are defined and discussed in later chapters. At this point, it is important only to know what browsers support the features you plan to use. As shown in figure 4.2, Webmonkey provides a

FIGURE 4.2
Browser Chart

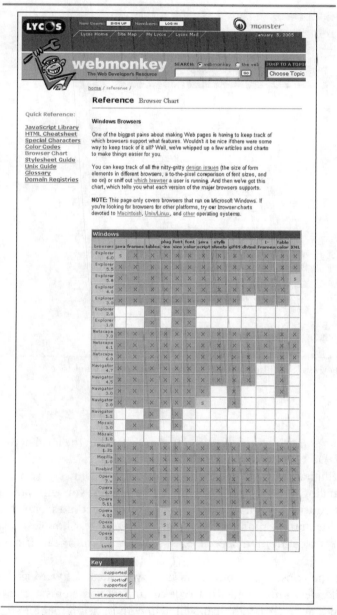

From Webmonkey, The Web Developer's Resource, a subsidiary of Lycos (a registered trademark of Carnegie Mellon University). Available: http://webmonkey.wired.com/webmonkey/reference/browser_ chart/.

browser chart that specifies which features are supported by various browser types and versions. In addition, there are utilities available on the Web that you can use to test the compatibility of browsers with your pages. For example, NetMechanic.com offers a fee-based service that will scan your site's pages and report on coding that may cause problems in different browsers (see figure 4.3).

FIGURE 4.3
Browser Compatibility Check

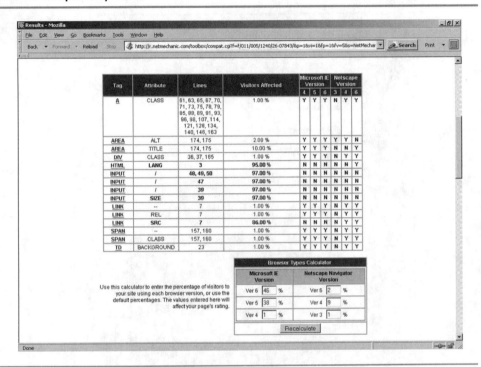

From NetMechanic.com. Available: http://www.netmechanic.com/toolbox/html-code.htm.

Access Method

How are your users going to access the tutorial? Are they all on the local network using fiber optic cable? Do they subscribe to an ISP (Internet service provider) via cable modem or DSL (digital subscriber line)? Do any of them connect to your site via a modem over an analog phone line? If there are modem users, you will want to be able to gauge how fast your pages will load under different connect rates. Figure 4.4 shows a tool from WebSiteOptimization.com that can be used to test how fast a Web page downloads under six connection speeds. Slow load times can mean frustration for your users.

Determining the constraints your users have with their software and hardware will help you make decisions about what type of authoring systems are required for graphics, video, and audio. That, in turn, will help with decision making on selecting development hardware.

FIGURE 4.4
Web Page Speed Report

DOWNLOAD TIMES	
Connection Rate	*Download Time*
14.4K	17.31 seconds
28.8K	8.85 seconds
33.6K	7.65 seconds
56K	4.75 seconds
ISDN 128K	1.73 seconds
T1 1.44Mbps	0.52 seconds

From WebSiteOptimization.com. Available: http://www
.websiteoptimization.com/services/analyze/.

DEVELOPMENT HARDWARE

Having the appropriate development hardware to create a multimedia project will make the project move along much more smoothly. Nothing is harder than trying to create multimedia programs with substandard equipment. However, budgets can vary enormously and concessions may have to be made. This is a general discussion of items that need to be considered when selecting the hardware to be used. For help in researching specific hardware and selection criteria, refer to the resources section at the end of this book.

Computer Selection

Before you design and produce your Web-based tutorial, you will need to select the computer workstations to be used. You may decide to have one central computer where the entire production will take place, or you may choose to do different portions of the production on different computers. Deciding which workstations to use must be done in conjunction with the choice of authoring software (discussed later). Software is developed according to what platform it will run on, so if you decide on an application that is available only on a Windows operating system, then you clearly need a computer that runs Windows. Similarly, each software application has minimum system requirements for it to perform properly. These include processor speed, operating system type, amount of RAM, available hard disk space, color display capability of the video card, and availability of a CD-ROM drive, sound card, and a network interface card (NIC) or modem. Normally, the software manufacturer lists both minimum requirements and recommended specifications. Don't be surprised if you discover that running a certain application on a computer with the minimum specifications results in less than satisfactory performance. As mentioned, any application you run will be competing with other programs for system resources. It is always a good idea to configure a computer to exceed the minimum requirements listed. The good news is that computer prices have continued to plunge quickly as capacities for storage, processing speeds, and memory have increased. Powerful computers are more affordable than ever.

You will also want to investigate the input/output capabilities available on a computer before making your selection. Most computers now come equipped with a CD burner, which plays and creates CDs, and more and more with DVD burners, which will also write to CD. Such a drive is critical if that is the method you have chosen to back up your data or provide an alternate delivery mechanism. One important specification to be aware of is the speed at which the drive records. Specifications will tell you three rates: how fast it records, rewrites, and records (in that order). These specs will be indicated in this format: 4×, 4×, 20×. How fast it records can be an important element in workflow. For instance, it will take twenty minutes to fill a 650 MB CD using a 4× drive and barely three and a half minutes using a 24× drive.

For years, most computers automatically included a parallel port (used to connect a local printer) and a serial port (used to connect other hardware devices). In the late 1990s a new connector was introduced, USB (Universal Serial Bus) that standardized the connection of peripherals (see the next section for a discussion of peripherals) to a single port, simplifying the entire issue. USB connectors are now common and have almost completely replaced the serial port. Most peripherals are manufactured with USB interfaces. You need to make sure that the computer you use in your project has the connector ports you need. There is nothing more frustrating than buying a new piece of equipment and discovering there isn't a way to connect it to the computer!

Peripherals Selection

A peripheral is any external device that attaches to a computer. Although you might not know them by this term, as a computer user you are familiar with many computer peripherals. Typically their purpose is to input or output data; some do both. Common input peripherals are the keyboard and the mouse. One of the most common output devices is the printer. Peripherals that serve both functions include hard disks, floppy disks, and modems. Several devices that you will want to consider for a Web project include monitors, video adapters, sound cards, scanners, cameras, camcorders, video cards, and removable file storage systems.

Monitor

The monitor is the most common output device, and it is not one you can choose to do without. However, as briefly described previously, there are considerations that should be made in selecting the appropriate monitor for a multimedia project.

CRT vs. LCD Not too many years ago, the biggest decisions to make when selecting a monitor were choosing display size and resolution. Now, however, there are two distinct monitor types that are affordable to typical computer buyers: CRT (cathode ray tube) and LCD (liquid crystal display). Each has its advantages and disadvantages as a development tool.

The monitor that most users have been familiar with for years is the CRT. The technology used in CRT monitors is the same as used in your television. They work by firing beams of electrons at phosphor dots on the inside of a glass tube. This is why they are so bulky, often deeper than they are wide. They are a proven, reliable technology, however, and are cost effective. These monitors are capable of displaying multiple resolutions, which can be very helpful for testing how pages display at different resolutions and for providing flexibility on display for the computer operator. Some CRTs are advertised as being flat screens. This may cause confusion as this is different from flat panel. This flat screen feature is designed to reduce the glare that is typical with the traditional rounded CRT screen. They also give better performance than LCDs in playing full color motion video and have better color calibration control. Both of these advantages may be good enough reasons to stick with the proven CRT monitor.

LCD panels have become very popular as the prices have come into a more affordable range. This is the technology that has been used for some time in laptop computers and is now available for desktop configurations. In an LCD monitor, each pixel is produced by a tiny cell that contains a layer of liquid crystal. It's a more sophisticated version of the display technology you see in digital watches.

The biggest selling point for LCD monitors is their thin profile and light weight. They take up about 70 percent less space and weigh about 50 percent less than a comparably sized CRT monitor. For many, the real estate that can be reclaimed on the office desk is well worth it. LCDs also consume half the power of a CRT. Another benefit of the LCD is that, unlike the CRT, the display size specification is a real indicator of the viewable area. What is the downside to LCD monitors? The view angle we have become accustomed to with a CRT is a true 180 degrees, which the LCD does not have. If a person sits at an odd angle to the computer screen, the picture may be hard to see and the color will be skewed. This becomes an issue if working with another person on a single monitor. Another significant shortcoming of the LCD in a Web development environment is that its technology entails a fixed number of pixels being hardwired, which means that it has a fixed native resolution, and whatever that is, is the optimal one. Changing the resolution to seen how pages display at different ones will be difficult to accomplish. At lower resolutions the screen is redrawn into a smaller area or all the pixels are blown up to fit the screen, resulting in a jagged image.

Screen Size   The second factor to consider in choosing a monitor is its size. In general, the larger the screen size, the more pixels it can display horizontally and vertically. The size is measured in the same manner as a television screen—diagonally from one corner to another. The size specified for a particular CRT monitor may be misleading because there is always an area around the edge of the screen that can't be used. Look for the "viewable area" size to determine how much screen is actually available. Today, seventeen-inch screens are the most common and prices are low enough to make them very popular. The extra screen space in a larger display makes work with multiple windows at the same time much easier. Even the prices for nineteen- and twenty-one-inch monitors have dropped, making them viable options as well. When working on a multimedia project, aim for the largest screen size you can afford.

Resolution   The higher the resolution—the number of pixels (squares) per inch—of the monitor, the sharper the image will be. It is useful to have a monitor that can display multiple resolutions so you can test your page design in the different resolutions your audience will use. CRT and LCD monitors that specify a maximum resolution number (for instance, 1280 × 1024 pixels) also support lesser resolutions (1024 × 768, 800 × 600, and 640 × 480).

Color Capacity   Over the years, monitors have been developed in different display modes that have evolved from monochrome to millions of colors. The term display mode refers to the maximum number of colors and the maximum image resolution.

VGA (Video Graphics Array), an older mode, displays 256 colors (also known as 8-bit color) at a resolution of 320 × 200, or sixteen colors at up to 640 × 480.

SVGA (Super Video Graphics Array) supports resolutions up to 1600 × 1200 and colors up to 16 million.

XGA (Extended Graphics Array) can display more than 16 million colors (known as true color or 24-bit color) in an 800 × 600 resolution or 65,536 colors at a 1024 × 768 resolution.

SXGA (Super Extended Graphics Array) and UXGA (Ultra Extended Graphics Array) are the newest specifications to come along. SXGA is generally used in reference to 1280 × 1024 screen resolutions and UXGA to 1600 × 1200.

Color Depth   Color depth, also called bit depth, describes the number of bits used to describe a pixel. A bit (short for binary digit) is the smallest unit of data in a computer. One bit has a value of either 0 or 1. Depending on the capability of the display mode and video adapter, a pixel can be described by one bit (monochrome), up to 24 bits (true color). The chart in figure 4.5 shows the bit depths used to display different numbers of colors.

FIGURE 4.5
Bit Depth and Number of Colors

BIT DEPTH	NUMBER OF COLORS
1	2 (monochrome)
2	4 (CGA)
4	16 (EGA)
8	256 (VGA)
16	65,536 (High Color, XGA)
24	16,777,216 (True Color, SVGA)
32*	16,777,216 (True Color + Alpha Channel)

*Special graphics mode used by digital video to achieve certain effects.

One important point to remember when you are relying on the colors displayed on a monitor is that different monitors display the same colors differently. It's not a good idea to get your mind set on a particular hue because it will not necessarily look the same on another display. In addition, there are only 216 colors that display consistently in Web browsers on older 8-bit color monitors. In chapter 5 we will discuss issues in selecting Web-safe colors to ensure the color you intend is the one your audience sees.

Video Adapter

The performance of your monitor depends partly on the video adapter (also called a graphics card), which is usually installed in an expansion slot on the system board, and is sometimes integrated. Its primary component is a video controller that sends data to the display and provides digital-to-analog conversion (converting strings of binary zeros and ones to output that is meaningful to humans, in this case a picture). Video adapters contain their own memory: the computer's RAM isn't used for storing displays. Higher resolutions require more video RAM. The memory in the video adapter relates directly to the capacity of the display modes discussed in the previous section. When you are working on a multimedia project, the computer you use should have the highest quality video adapter possible within budget.

Sound Card

To include audio in the project, a sound card is required. A sound card serves as both an input device (from a microphone, radio, tape deck, CD player, or CD-ROM) and output device (via speakers, headphones, or CD-R/DVD-R). It will be used in both capacities to capture audio and play it back. Sound cards are available in both analog and digital format, or with both capabilities.

Analog technology is used when inputting sound from a microphone or outputting to a speaker. The card takes normal analog (electronic transmission via signals of varying frequency) signals and converts them to digital ones (electronic technology that stores and processes data as zeros and ones) and copies it onto the hard drive or another storage device. This part of the card is called the analog-to-digital converter (ADC). To hear what's been recorded, the sound card works in reverse, converting the digital information back to analog and feeding to a speaker that generates the sound. This part of the card is known as the digital-to-analog converter (DAC).

The newer digital sound card technology is practical for applications that need digital sound, because no conversion is required. Digital cards have provisions for digital input and output so you can transfer data directly from the source (for instance, a CD) onto your hard drive.

Most late-model computers include a sound card as part of the basic configuration. A basic sound card should have a line in and a line out, but it may go beyond that and have additional I/O (input/output) connectors for things such as CD audio and video. Your sound card should support the two digital audio standards: MIDI (Musical Instrument Digital Interface), a standard for representing music electronically, and Sound Blaster, which is the de facto standard for PC sound. If possible, choose a PCI (Peripheral Component Interconnect) sound card over an ISA (Industry

Standard Architecture) because the PCI card is faster. PCI connections allow data to flow at 32 bits at a time versus the 16 bits that ISA supports.

You will find that some sound cards come as a chipset right on the motherboard of the computer (the part of the computer that contains the computer's basic circuitry and components).

In addition, don't forget to acquire a microphone and speakers so that you can input and play back the audio you create. Headphones can also be a useful tool for working on an audio digitization project.

Scanners

Scanners come in a variety of types and price ranges. A flatbed scanner is the most popular format and will serve well for most Web projects. It can be used to scan photos, pictures, and pages from books. It consists of a flat surface where the document or image is placed. When a light passes over the document, the scanner converts the light to a computer-readable format. A color scanner has three light sources, one each for red, blue, and green.

Today, you will find two different technologies available for flatbed scanners: the newer CIS (contact image sensor) and the traditional CCD (charged-coupled device). CIS scanners are much smaller, sometimes only a few inches thick. This is possible because these devices gather light from red, green, and blue LEDs (light emitting diodes) that are directed at the original document. The LEDs take up much less space than the CCD technology, which relies on a system of mirrors and lenses to project the scanned image. CIS scanners also require less power than CCD scanners and often run from a battery or through a USB port on the computer.

The term you see most often in discussions of scanners is resolution. You will see scanner specifications that talk about 600 × 600 dpi (dots per inch) or 1200 × 1200 dpi. For Web projects, it's not necessary to use a scanner capable of the higher resolutions. Web images display at a maximum of 72 or 96 dpi, depending on the operating system. To ensure small file size for faster downloading, you want to scan your graphics at 72 or 96 dpi. Other features to consider when choosing a scanner include mode of connectivity to the computer, maximum scan size, and scan speed. Most scanners come bundled with imaging and OCR (optical character recognition) software, so that may become a factor in choosing a particular brand or model.

Cameras

You may choose to work with either a conventional camera or a digital camera. With a conventional camera, you can develop your film into prints or slides and then digitize them using a flatbed scanner.

Digital cameras have become increasingly popular as their image quality has improved and the prices have dropped. Good quality digital cameras are now affordable and may soon be a standard peripheral for most systems. A major benefit for a Web project is that a digital camera removes the step of having to scan an image into digital format. With a digital camera, the image is captured in a digital format that is immediately ready for transfer into the computer, which can then be manipulated with graphics editing software. In a digital camera, the imaging is performed by a charge-coupled device (CCD) or CMOS (complementary metal-oxide semiconductor) sensors. The CCD or CMOS replaces both the shutter and the film found in traditional cameras. For an in-depth discussion of digital camera technologies, refer to the HowStuff Works article on digital cameras at http://electronics.howstuffworks.com/digital-camera.htm.

There are four fundamental issues to consider when selecting a digital camera: computing platform, image quality, memory storage, and connectivity. In addition, there are several other features to check such as lens type, battery life, flash capability, and file formats. Whether they are critical depends on the parameters of your project.

Computing platform. The platform used was more of an issue a few years ago than it is now because most digital cameras today interface with both Windows and Macintosh. Make sure you get a camera that is packaged with the software that works with your platform. It can be discouraging to end up with a camera that you can't interface with your computer without investing in additional software.

Image quality. The quality of the image depends on many things, but the most important determinant is the resolution of the CCD. It wasn't too long ago that the typical resolution for a digital camera was 640 × 480 pixels. Resolutions are now being talked about in megapixels with resolutions going over 3500 × 2300, thanks to the advent of 8+ megapixel CCDs. For a strictly Web project, where printing capability is not an issue and pricing is, a camera that has 640 × 480 will usually suffice.

Memory storage. Today's digital cameras use removable storage, which comes in a variety of formats. The main advantage is that when a memory card is full, it can be removed and another inserted in its place without having to stop and load the images onto a computer. A second advantage is that the cards can be inserted directly into a computer (with the correct accompanying hardware) and treated as a disk.

Types of storage systems available include built-in fixed memory, which is found in older or inexpensive cameras; SmartMedia cards, which are small Flash memory modules; and CompactFlash, which is slightly larger than SmartMedia.

The amount of storage on each varies because different storage capacities mean different retail prices. The memory capacity of the card must be coupled with the resolution of the images being captured to determine how many images will fit on one card. In a typical example found in the listed specification of a 6-megapixel camera with a 256 MB memory card, 950 images fit on the card in standard resolution, but only 44 when set to its highest resolution. The higher resolution capability is very important if the desired output is a large sized print. For Web projects, lower resolutions are preferred.

Connectivity. Once the images are on the camera, they need to be transferred to a computer for editing. Some cameras provide the option of connecting directly from the camera to a computer port and into an image-download software application. However, this requires power from the camera, is a slow procedure, and can drain batteries very quickly. If you are going to download in this fashion, use the AC adapter that normally comes with the camera, and save your batteries.

Most commonly, your computer recognizes the camera's storage device as another drive. This enables you to use the features of your operating system to copy or move the files from the camera to a folder, independent of any image management software (which will be discussed in the next section).

Different devices, known as card adapters or readers, are available that work like a bridge between the camera and the computer. You insert the memory card in the reader, which is connected to the computer, to download the images. The most popular digital camera cable connection today is the USB. It has almost replaced the older serial, parallel, and SCSI ports because it is more efficient and faster. A USB connection can transfer data three times faster than a serial connection, an important feature when moving large image files. An even faster connection option is becoming more common: FireWire, originally developed by Apple, is the standard referred to as IEEE (Institute of Electrical and Electronic Engineers) 1394 and is even faster than USB. A major benefit of both USB and FireWire is that they are hot pluggable, meaning that they can be connected and used without having to first turn off the computer.

Camera Features   Almost every digital camera has an LCD (liquid crystal display) panel, which allows you to preview and arrange pictures without having to transfer the images to a computer. It also is the interface to adjust camera settings, such as resolution selection, and it can serve in place of the viewfinder as well. You will want to examine how the LCD works because it is different on each model. If the LCD is the only viewfinder (and not just a supplement to the customary one), you should also consider that LCD panels are hard to see in the direct sunlight.

Check to see if the camera has a fixed- or auto-focus lens. With a fixed-focus lens everything from a few feet on will be in focus. This won't help if you need to photograph something close up. Most cameras have some kind of zoom capability, which might be either two or three predefined settings or gradual zoom action. If the ability to take close-up pictures is critical to your project, you will want to be sure that this feature is included. Two different types of zoom are available: optical and digital. Optical zoom is similar to the type of zoom in a regular 35mm camera; when you zoom, the physical lens moves in and out. With a digital zoom there are no moving parts and the camera's "brain" digitally zooms in, simulating the optical zoom electronically. This process essentially crops the image and then fills in pixels to enlarge the image back to the specified size—a negative effect overall. You can accomplish the same effect using imaging editing software. The most important zoom to consider, then, is the optical capacity.

Battery life is an important component. There is a wide variation in how long a camera will last with one set of batteries. A single camera can vary depending on whether you leave the LCD in preview mode or do most of your image selection and arranging within the camera rather than after the images are transferred to the computer. Different cameras use different modes of transfer, and some of these are memory hogs. If you are going to use batteries consistently, then invest in rechargeable ones, which, although more expensive up front, will save you money in the long run. There are different rechargeable battery technologies, and the more you are aware of these, the better off you will be. NiCad (nickel cadmium) batteries are those whose performance suffers if not charged properly (making sure the charge is completely drained before recharging). NiMH (nickel metal hydride) is a more current technology that does not have memory problems. LiOn (lithium ion) batteries are the longest lasting of the rechargeables and don't have memory problems, but are the most expensive. Some cameras use proprietary batteries rather than standard sizes, such as AA. Whether to buy a camera with nonstandard batteries is an important consideration. Even if using rechargeable ones, if the charge gives out at an inopportune moment, it will be much more convenient to locate regular alkaline batteries to use in the short term until you can recharge yours!

Another feature is the flash capability. Find out what the range is, whether there is red-eye reduction, and if you can override the flash if you choose to do so. Many cameras also have a self-timer that allows you to get yourself into a picture you're taking.

Many digital cameras are now available with the capability to capture short video clips. The type of format captured varies depending on the manufacturer. Common file formats available include MPEG (Moving Pictures Expert Group), AVI (Audio-Video Interleave), and QuickTime, which are discussed in more detail in chapter 6. If you just need a few seconds of video, this can be more cost effective than purchasing a digital camcorder.

Audio capture, another option featured in many digital cameras, can be used to annotate information about the picture being taken. It also allows audio to be captured with the video clips if the clips are also a camera feature.

What image format choices does the camera offer? If you are going to use the camera for Web projects, then it is very handy to have JPEG (Joint Photographic Experts Group, also discussed in detail in chapter 6) as one of the choices because this format is supported on the Web and will save you the step of having to convert it. Fortunately this format is the de facto standard. If the camera captures images only in its native format, how easy is it to export it to the format you require?

Accessories   Depending on the types of images you want to create, you may also want to consider acquiring a tripod to ensure that your images are sharp. A tripod is beneficial when photographing things such as architecture. It will be essential for making a virtual reality tour, where you would be photographing a 360° view of a room. There are specialized accessories to help with a panoramic photographic project. One example comes from Kaidan (http://www.kaidan.com/products.html), which manufactures panoramic tripod heads that permit capturing a 360-degree view with a single snap of the shutter. Finally, although many cameras come equipped with a case and strap, don't forget to ask about these essential accessories also.

Video Camcorders

If you are planning to incorporate video into your project, you must realize that video editing is the most resource-hungry computer task. Video production requires a fast computer with plenty of RAM and hard disk space. In addition, you will probably need to install an expansion card to provide a way to input the video from a camcorder into the computer. This card is known as a video capture card.

Most of today's camcorders come equipped with features such as LCD monitors and zoom lenses. The main distinctions to be made between models are compatibility with a video cassette recorder (that is, the tape can be directly played in a VCR), maximum recording time, and (this should come as no surprise) resolution. The main decision to make is whether to use an analog or a digital camcorder. Most people are familiar with the traditional analog camcorder, and you may have one already available for use. However, you should be aware that you'll never have 100 percent accuracy when transferring from analog to digital. Just as with a photocopy, the quality of each reproduction is reduced.

Several different analog formats are available in camcorders. Analog camcorders include the tape format with which most people are familiar, Standard VHS (which can be played on a VCR but has low resolution). Other formats include VHS-C (compact VHS, which plays in your VCR with an adapter), S-VHS (Super VHS with better resolution than VHS), S-VHS-C (compact Super VHS), 8mm (is more compact than VHS, has a longer playing time, but can only be played from the camcorder), and Hi-8 (higher resolution than 8mm, more expensive tapes). The most common format used in analog camcorders in today's market is Hi-8; VHS-C and Super VHS-C use is declining.

Each of these formats has features and limitations, but because they all need to be converted from analog to digital, a chief consideration is how effectively you can convert the video into a digital format. Selecting the right video capture card is one factor in how well your conversion will work. When converting analog video to digital, it must be compressed to reduce the size of the file. An algorithm, or specialized computer program, known as codec (compressor/decompressor) controls the amount of compression. Basically, a video codec is used to compress the video data to reduce file size, and also to decompress it for viewing. When a video is compressed with any particular codec, that same codec must be installed on the machine that is going to view the video, because the video must be decompressed with the same codec that it was compressed with. Common codecs are M-JPEG, MPEG-1, MPEG-4, WMV (Windows Media Video), Real Video, and DV (digital video). Different codecs are more appropriate for some tasks than for others. For instance, M-JPEG is best used when you are outputting the file back onto a tape for playback, but is not a good choice for multimedia on the Web. MPEG-1, which is designed to pack a large quantity of video into a small file and is a low-loss compression technique, is used primarily with CD-ROMs but also found on the Web. The newer MPEG-4 is a codec standard that is designed for the delivery of interactive multimedia on the Web. It includes specifications for video, audio, and interactivity. WMV and Real Video are also good choices for the Web because many computers already have these codecs installed.

Some of the codecs are "lossy," meaning that frames (the individual still images in a video sequence) are dropped to decrease file size. This can result in a choppy looking video. If you are using a high-quality tape, the loss may not be as evident as if you use a low-resolution one (such as VHS). Some capture cards are more liable than others to drop frames, so it is worthwhile to locate reviews that rate different cards. Other factors that can cause frames to drop include whether your computer's processor can digitize fast enough or if its hard drive can spin fast enough to record at the rate selected.

When you consider which analog video capture card to select, be aware of the input/output ports you have. You will want to make certain that the card you choose has an input port that is compatible with the type of analog camcorder you are using. Also determine what codecs the card supports so that you get a card that will use the type of compression you have selected.

Clearly, there are many challenges to overcome when you work with analog tapes—a good reason to consider using a digital camcorder. Importing digital video into your computer is a much easier undertaking and will result in a higher quality video, as there is no loss of video or audio quality during the transfer. Most digital camcorders record images digitally on a mini-DV cassette tape. (Sony offers a similar format, digital8, which uses standard Hi-8mm tapes.) Digital formats have better resolution than analog—500 lines versus a maximum of 400 for the Hi-8 format (pushed to 500 when used in digital8) or 250 for VHS. A digital camcorder has built-in compression before images are written to the tape. The DV codec is a lossless algorithm, which ensures high quality images. Digital video doesn't suffer, of course, from the conversion deterioration that occurs with analog tapes. Importing a digital video into a computer for editing is just like copying files from a peripheral over a high-speed connection.

The latest trend in digital camcorders is the DVD format. Instead of recording magnetic signals on tape, these burn video information onto small discs. Two DVD formats are supported: DVD-R and DVD-RAM. Both are three-quarters of the size of a movie DVD disc. An advantage of the DVD-R is that it can be played in a DVD player but it can be used for recording only once. DVD-RAM discs can be used over but can't be used in your DVD player. One major caution about DVD camcorders: video recorded on DVD uses the MPEG-2 codec and cannot be edited on your computer. This type may thus not be the best choice for use with a Web project!

Another new development in digital camcorders is the memory card feature in some models.

The most common high-speed digital connection that is used to transfer video to your computer is the IEEE 1394 interface known most commonly as FireWire. You may also hear it referred to as i.LINK (Sony). Digital camcorders come equipped with this port. You will need to add a digital capture card that supports IEEE 1394.

Other features should be considered in making a digital camcorder selection. If the digital camcorder will be used to record from older analog camcorders, be certain additional ports are included, such as S-video. Investigate the microphone that is included. A front-mounted microphone will get better results than a top-mounted. An external microphone is the best option. The size of the LCD screen can be important; a larger one makes it easier to see what's being recorded and facilitates playback.

Dazzle Video Creator

An inexpensive, easy-to-use alternative to installing a video capture card is a device called Dazzle. It is easy for the novice because it has an all-external setup. It plugs into the USB port of your computer and you connect your camcorder or VCR to it. Dazzle comes bundled with all the software needed to produce digital files in several formats including MPEG-1, RealVideo, and Windows Media. The minimum requirements to use this device are a 500 MHz processor and 128 MB of RAM, a much more cost-effective solution than would be needed for traditional video digitization. The quality and sophistication level are not going to equal a professional video production setup, but it may be a very appropriate solution for your needs. Find out more about this device at Dazzle (http://www.dazzle.com).

Removable File Storage

You will want to take into account how you are going to share and store your files as your project progresses. It may be that you have access to a network file server where files can be shared with everyone on your team, but usually there will be some need to transport files between computers, make backups or archives, or store large files. As you are deciding on which type of storage to select, consider the following features:

capacity (how much data it will store)

media costs (for the drive and the disks)

durability (of the storage media)

portability (ability to be moved from one computer to another)

speed (how fast the data transfers)

interface (how the device connects to your computer)

The most common storage technology is magnetic, which includes floppy disks. Unfortunately, these have limited storage capacity (usually 1.44 MB), so you may want to consider removable mass-storage options. A variety of choices are available, but be aware that most are not interchangeable with each other and that prices can vary by thousands of dollars. One well-known magnetic removable storage device is the Iomega Zip drive. It is available in a variety of interfaces: external with USB or FireWire connection and internal with ATAPI (AT Attachment Packet Interface) or SCSI (Small Computer System Interface) connectivity. Storage capacity choices for Zip disks are 100, 250, or 750 MB. The benefits of using a Zip drive are that it is affordable, easy to use, and widely used. The external version is portable, and the USB connection allows it to be attached to any computer.

If you are incorporating video into your project, you may require a greater mass storage capacity than a disk that holds less than a gigabyte of files. High-capacity removable storage devices are available that store many gigabytes (GB) of data. Iomega also manufactures the Rev Drive, a new high-capacity storage choice that can store up to 35 GB of data.

Another increasingly popular magnetic storage choice is the portable hard drive. It is like an internal drive found in your computer, comes in a sealed case, and connects to your computer via a USB cable. Another type of portable hard drive is the microdrive, built into PCMCIA cards that can be plugged into laptop computer slots.

One technology that has become common and affordable is optical storage. The most common medium is CD-R (CD-recordable) and CD-RW (CD-rewritable), providing a storage capacity of over 700 MB. CD-R allows you to write data to it one time, while CD-RW drives allow you to overwrite data previously written to disk. DVD-R and DVD-RW storage functions much like CD-R/CD-RW, but offers up to 4.76 GB of storage capacity.

Media storage cards, like those used in digital cameras and discussed earlier, can also be used for storage of all types of data, in addition to images. Called flash memory, this is solid-state storage, meaning that the devices have no moving parts. Cards with capacities of up to 4 GB are available.

Yet another popular portable storage choice has developed with the advent of USB flash drives. They are very useful to transfer data between computers and are about the size of your thumb or a car key. Because of their size, you will also hear them referred to as key drives, jump drives, thumb drives, and pen drives. As with other types of removable storage, flash drives come in a range of capacities, usually from 8 MB to over 1 GB.

AUTHORING SOFTWARE PROGRAMS

There are many different types of software applications that may be needed to produce a multimedia, interactive Web tutorial. This section presents an overview of the most common categories of authoring software. Examples of each type of tool are highlighted, but be sure to refer to the resources section at the end of this book for links to comprehensive sites to use to research each category. Your selection will depend on the platform you have chosen for your development hardware, the minimum system specification required, and the types of multimedia and interactivity you have decided to incorporate into your project.

Many software applications are available for evaluation at no charge. You can find demo versions on company Web sites and can test-drive them before you make a purchase decision. Also, many companies offer significant price cuts to educational institutions and students. Always check to see if there is academic pricing if your organization qualifies as such!

HTML/Web Editors

There are different ways to approach authoring Web pages for your project. How you decide to do it should depend upon the types of interactivity you plan to use, your team members' levels of expertise, and their preference for working either directly with the source code or using a visual method.

HTML can be written without using a Web editor. With the most basic text editor, Notepad (Windows) or TextEdit (Mac), you simply write the HTML markup code manually. This is probably not the most practical approach for the novice, however, because it is quite time consuming, is prone to error, and requires in-depth knowledge of HTML coding and other scripting languages. At the other end of the spectrum are simple visual editors that require no knowledge of HTML and operate like a word processing application. An example of this is Netscape's Composer, which is part of the Netscape suite of components. It works well for authoring very basic pages but does not include the functionality that will support the integration of higher-level features, which are discussed in later chapters. Word processors such as Microsoft Word also have built-in functionality to save documents as Web pages, but here again, you will sacrifice the capability to control the editing to the level that is optimal in authoring Web pages.

It is best to select an application that has been developed specifically for authoring Web pages. Today these applications have matured to the point where they provide all the features necessary to build complex and advanced Web pages. Prices range from zero to several hundred dollars—but don't assume that the most expensive is the best.

The two main types are code-based and visually based (WYSIWYG, for what you see is what you get, pronounced "wizzywig"). Both perform the same functions, but are very different in how the author works to build a page.

With a code-based editor, the code is in plain view (see, for example, figure 4.6). You can see exactly which tags and attributes you are using. Unlike a plain-text editor, however, a code-based editor can automate the creation of tags and often also can automate generating the higher-level features that will bring interactivity to the page.

FIGURE 4.6
Web Page Viewed in Code-Based Editor NoteTab Pro

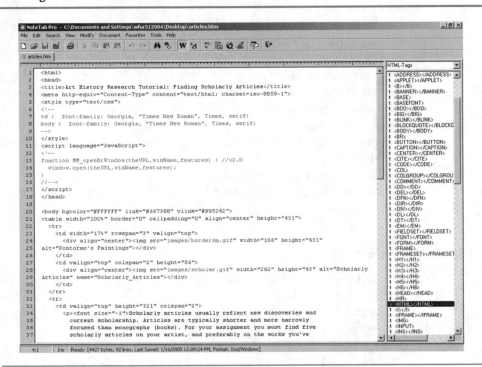

From Fookes Software, Charmey, Switzerland. Available: http://www.notetab.com/html.php.

Code is generally color-coded so that it is easy to distinguish from the page text. Traditionally, this type of editor has been considered to be the choice for power users who don't want to give up control of the code. Two examples of this type of editor are Macromedia HomeSite (for PC, http://www.macromedia.com/software/homesite/) and Bare Bones Software's BBEdit (Mac, http://www.barebones.com/products/bbedit/index.shtml).

The visual-based editor has typically been considered more user friendly for most Web authors. When using a visual or WYSIWYG interface, the author is shielded from the HTML coding and sees only how the page will display to a user. This method allows the author to concentrate on how the content should appear, but sacrifices control of the author's ability to fine-tune the source code. Another obstacle to be aware of is that WYSIWYG code is often bloated, meaning that unnecessary code is generated. This generally will not make any difference in how your page displays, but may become an issue if you need to troubleshoot or want to reformat the page. Two examples of a WYSIWYG editor are Macromedia Dreamweaver (for PC and Mac, http://macromedia.com/software/dreamweaver/) and Adobe GoLive (for PC and Mac, http://www.adobe.com/products/golive/main.html). In April 2005, Adobe announced an agreement to acquire Macromedia, so it will be interesting to see which direction is taken with their competing software applications.

Most of each type of editor provide a bridge between the two methods. For instance, a good WYSIWYG editor will have a source inspector in which the author can view and edit the code directly. Similarly, a well-designed code-based editor will have an interface so the author can view the page layout in a browser (see, for example, figure 4.7).

No matter which style of editor you decide on, you will want to look for certain features that will help you achieve advanced designs and interactivity. Look for an editor that includes support for the features listed below and that can help with advanced features, which are discussed in later chapters:

site management

checking the integrity of source codes

cross-browser compatibility check

spell check

link check

global find-and-replace

support for scripting languages such as JavaScript, Perl, and PHP

support for standards including XHTML, XML, and XSL

CSS (cascading style sheet) support

FIGURE 4.7
Web Page Viewed in Dreamweaver WYSIWYG Editor with Code Editor View

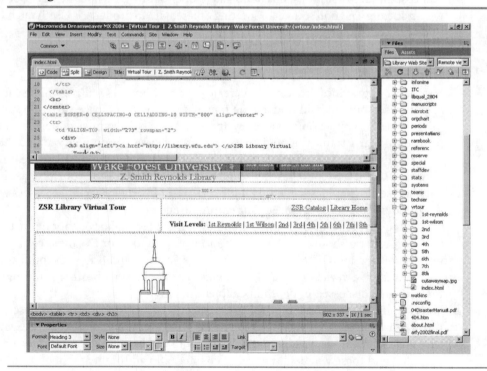

From Macromedia, Inc. Available: http://macromedia.com/software/dreamweaver.

support for team collaboration

multiple document display

design templates

Content Management Systems

If yours is a small-scale project, a simple Web editor may suffice. Some offer features that help manage content to a certain extent with the inclusion of design templates and collaboration features. However, if you are embarking on a large-scale creation of Web instruction modules or courses, you may want to investigate investing in a content management system (CMS).

As the name implies, CMS is a system designed to streamline the management of content on a Web site by permitting the separation of content from presentation. It consists of two parts: a content management application (CMA) and a content delivery application (CDA). The CMA portion allows dispersed subject specialists to manage the creation and modification of content without needing to be versed in HTML authoring. The CDA side of the system can be managed centrally by staff members who have Web design expertise. Typically, the systems operate through the use of templates set up centrally with defined areas that are either restricted or available for content addition or editing. Of course, features vary by system (and price!), but typical ones include format management, revision control, indexing, and search and retrieval.

As might be expected, a CMS is available in different levels, from enterprise systems that cost hundreds of thousands of dollars to open source software such as Zope (http://www.zope.org). A good source for locating different CMS products is CMSWatch (http://www.cmswatch.com).

Graphics Applications

Some sort of graphics program that creates and manipulates images will be a must for your project, but you will find a wide range of choices (and price variations). As with other types of applications, graphics applications have been developed for both the professional artist and the novice. In making a decision, you will want to take into account the expertise and artistic talent of the team member who will be creating your graphics. If you have purchased a scanner or digital camera for your project, it probably had some graphics software bundled as part of the package. If so, assess whether the bundled software will meet your editing needs.

Because you will be creating graphics for display on the Web, one of the basic selection criteria should be that the application provides for the most common supported file formats: GIF (Graphics Interchange Format) and JPEG. It should also allow you to import a variety of graphic formats. These, along with other multimedia formats, will be discussed in depth in chapter 6.

Graphic applications can be divided into two major categories that describe how the graphics are created and stored: image editors and illustration software. There are advantages and disadvantages to working with either bitmapped images or vector graphics, and these will be discussed in chapter 6. In addition, an integration of these two types is available, called an object-based editor.

Image Editors

Image editors are programs that create raster graphics, often called bitmap images because they are created as a series of dots on a grid. Common raster file formats are BMP (bitmap), TIFF (Tagged Image File Format), GIF, and JPEG. Bitmap image editors are the most commonly used graphics software. The industry standard is Adobe Photoshop, the high-end editor used by most professionals with a steep learning curve to go along with its powerful, complex capabilities. Many other programs are also available that can produce satisfactory graphics and that require a much lower investment of time to master. Any image editor you consider should include the ability to scan in images as well as to enhance, resize, and retouch them.

Illustration Software

Illustration software includes those applications where you create drawings using lines and curves, known as vector graphics. Vector graphics are created through a series of mathematical statements that place lines and shapes in a two- or three-dimensional space. Common vector formats are AI (Adobe Illustrator), WMF (Windows Metafile), CDR (CorelDRAW), and SVG (Scaleable Vector Graphic). Representative applications include Macromedia Freehand, Adobe Illustrator, and CorelDRAW (see figure 4.8 for an example).

FIGURE 4.8
Adobe Illustrator Software for Vector Graphics

From Adobe, Inc. Available: http://www.adobe.com/products/illustrator/main.html.

Object-Based Editors

A third category of graphics software, object-based editors, integrates raster and vector capabilities into one package. This category is becoming popular for creating Web graphics and animations. Object-based editors have greater flexibility because they enable you to combine images with text and line art to streamline the creation of Web objects such as navigation bars, banners, buttons, and rollovers. An example of this integrated approach is Macromedia Fireworks (PC and Mac, http://www.macrome dia.com/software/fireworks/).

There are issues to consider when creating graphics for the Web (see chapter 6), and these should be kept in mind when selecting a graphics program. Beneficial features that should be included to streamline the creation of Web graphics include

> image optimization (to reduce the size of a graphic)
>
> image slicing (to enhance the download of a larger image by slicing it into several smaller images)
>
> color management and support for Web-safe color
>
> batch processing of objects
>
> built-in templates (particularly valuable for nonartists)
>
> 3-D effects
>
> support for building interactivity

There are so many choices for graphics applications that the selection task can be overwhelming. About.com's topic site on graphics software (http://graphicssoft.about .com/od/findsoftware/) is a good resource to use to find the appropriate applications for your project. Its section on finding graphics software includes a list of programs for both PC and Macintosh platforms and identifies free and shareware programs as well as those available commercially.

Animation Applications

Your choice of an animation authoring application will depend on the type of animation format you have selected. There are a variety of types of animation, but there is no one tool that can be used to create all of them. Just as with regular graphics, animations can be either raster or vector objects. The various animation formats mentioned here are discussed in depth in chapter 6.

Raster Animation Tools

One of the most common animations on the Web is the animated GIF. Your graphics software may already be capable of producing animated GIFs. For instance, Adobe Photoshop includes ImageReady, which has animation building functionality. There are stand-alone applications designed to create this type of animation also. Examples are GIF Construction Set Professional (PC, http://www.mindworkshop.com/ alchemy/gifcon.html) and VSE Animation Maker (Mac, http://vse-online.com/anima tion-maker/index.html). Some animation is possible by scripting to manipulate page elements. Some HTML editors (Dreamweaver is an example) have this functionality incorporated into their programming.

Vector Animation Tools

Similarly, your illustration software may have built-in functionality for creating vector-based animation, so check its features before investing in a separate program. The best-known application to create this type of animation is Macromedia Flash (http://www.macromedia.com/software/flash/), an industry standard for creating animations on the Web. Its increase in popularity has resulted in the development of third-party authoring tools that also allow you to create Flash animations or to export a file to the SWF (Shockwave Flash) format. Full-featured, it can be used to create rich interactive content.

Streaming Animation Tools

Another major trend in animation on the Web uses streaming media, a technology that allows users to hear or view large multimedia files without having to wait for them to download onto their computers. RealNetworks (http://www.realnetworks .com) has been at the forefront of developing this technology. To produce real media you may want to select its product, RealProducer. A basic version is available at no charge. Apple also has an authoring tool, QuickTime Pro (http://www.apple.com/quicktime/), which you may want to consider. Both of these programs also support SMIL (Synchronized Multimedia Integration Language), which is a protocol for synchronizing the timed playback of multiple independent media files. A good resource for the latest information on streaming technology, including authoring software, is Streaming Media (http://www.streamingmedia.com).

Screen Recording Animation Tools

A popular method to teach students to use a particular application or database is to make a video screen presentation that shows the desktop activity or construct a simulation that permits the student to interact as though in a live session. Available features often include support for narration, creation of call outs and hot spots, import of audio and video files, and the use of transitions. Figure 4.9 shows a screen movie project authored with Camtasia Studio by TechSmith (for PC). A full-featured application will support saving the presentation in the most popular file formats including SWF, RM, WMF, and MOV. A similar product for Mac is Snapz Pro from Ambrosia Software (http://www.ambrosiasw.com/utilities/snapzpro/), although the only format save is QuickTime.

Virtual Reality Animation Tools

Are you considering creating an interactive three-dimensional world using VRML (Virtual Reality Modeling Language)? VRML was the original language to create 3-D image sequences and possible user interactions within the scene. It has been superseded by X3D, an XML (Extensible Markup Language) open standard for 3-D content delivery. As is expected with a new standard, authoring and editing tools are being developed. A good source to see what is available for all platforms is the Web 3D Consortium (http://www.web3d.org/applications/tools/authoring/).

If a virtual walkthrough tour of your library is high on your list to produce, you'll need to obtain specialized software to do the authoring. The industry standard tech-

FIGURE 4.9
TechSmith Camtasia Screen Recording Animation Software

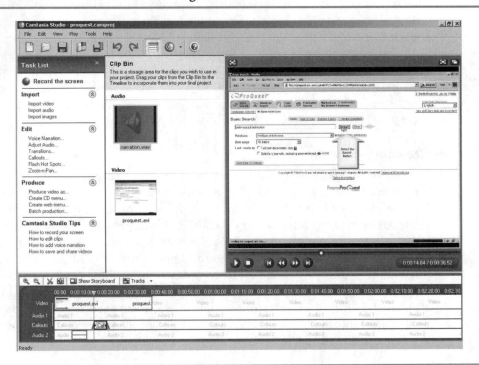

From TechSmith. TechSmith product screen shot reprinted with permission from TechSmith Corporation. Available: http://www.techsmith.com/products/studio/default.asp?lid=CamtasiaStudioHome.

nology for this type of interaction is VR, which is short for virtual reality. A wide variety of software choices are available depending on what type of project you are creating and on your level of expertise. These include Apple QuickTime VR Authoring Studio (Mac, http://www.apple.com/quicktime/resources/tools/qtvr.html), Realviz Stitcher Express (PC, Mac, http://www.realviz.com/products/stx/index.php), iSeeMedia PhotoVista Virtual Tour (PC, http://www.iseemedia.com/virtualtour/productinfo.html), and VR Toolbox VRWorx (cross-platform, http://www.vrtoolbox .com/vrthome.html).

Audio Software

Introducing small incidental sounds into a Web project may require nothing more than the sound recording software that is included in your operating system. However, if you plan to incorporate audio into your tutorial to any extent, you will want to explore using specialized audio editing software to record and edit sound. You can turn to RealProducer (http://www.realnetworks.com) to handle your streaming audio needs. Sound Forge is another well-regarded digital audio editor (http://mediasoft ware.sonypictures.com/products/soundforgefamily.asp). There are reasonably priced editors available that are full featured: Adobe Audition, formerly Cool Edit (PC, http:// www.adobe.com/products/audition/main.html) and SmartSound SonicFire Pro (Mac, http://www.smartsound.com/sonicfire/index.html) are just two examples. You should make certain that whichever audio editor you select supports a wide range of sound files (see chapter 6 for more information on sound files).

If you already have sound files and just need to convert them to a different format, a stand-alone format converter (called batch encoder) is a more cost-effective solution than purchasing audio editing software. Batch encoders are normally included as a part of a full-featured editing program. You can find shareware encoders for all platforms available for download from Hitsquad (http://www.hitsquad.com/ smm/cat/FORMAT_CONVERTERS/).

Video Editing Applications

Once you import video into your computer, you will need software to manipulate it. It's very probable that video production software will be bundled with a digital camcorder or video capture card. If this is the case, you should make that part of your purchasing decision making. Many integrated hardware and software packages are on the market, with prices ranging from under $100 to $1,000. Well-known manufacturers include Pinnacle Systems (http://www.pinnaclesys.com) and Matrox (http://www .matrox.com). Adobe's Premiere (http://www.adobe.com/products/premiere/) is the industry standard for digital video production, but because it is designed for the professional, expect a steep learning curve. If you are new to video editing, look for software that is intuitive or that guides you through each step. Microsoft includes a very nice entry-level video editor, Movie Maker, as part of Windows XP (http://www .microsoft.com/windowsxp/downloads/default.mspx).

The editing process involves putting video segments in the order you want and then adding transitions, text, background music, and perhaps narration. With most software, this is a drag-and-drop process, using either a timeline or a storyboard metaphor. A storyboard approach is more straightforward because each frame is represented by one thumbnail image and includes all the elements. In a timeline, each separate component (audio tracks, text, video clips, or transitions) has its own track, so the author has more control. Some software packages provide both ways to deal with editing—a good solution, so that a beginner can evolve as he or she gains skill as an editor. As with other applications, you want to make sure that your video editing software supports the file format you have chosen (see chapter 6 for more information on video file formats).

Presentation Tools

Presentation software applications, such as Microsoft's PowerPoint, may not be your top choice to author a library instruction tutorial. Many people choose presentation software for instruction because it is easy to learn and to incorporate multimedia. The format for presentation authoring is slide creation, which lends itself to a linear progression through materials. Although most presentation software incorporates various levels of multimedia and interactivity, those features are often either lost when the presentation is converted to a Web-viewable format or do not work identically across all browser types and versions. However, some presentation software now incorporates support for Web interactivity. RealNetworks has developed a slide show product that works well to incorporate images and animated text into a streaming video slide show. If you decide to use presentation software, make sure it supports the various Web file formats, and be prepared to settle for interactivity that may include only the user's ability to select a link to continue.

Authoring Systems

Most of the authoring tools presented so far are designed to handle one aspect of a multimedia project, such as the creation of graphics, animation, or sound. To combine these into an interactive multimedia program, some sort of programming is needed to make it all work together. However, a type of software called an authoring system has been developed so that people can develop interactive multimedia programs without having to know a programming language. This type of application allows authors to use a graphical approach to tell the program what to do by placing items in a timeline, manipulating objects on a flowchart, or organizing screens into stacks (best known from Apple's Hypercard program). Although the author looks at a graphical interface, the graphical objects are composed of underlying preset programming modules. By having preprogrammed modules, actions that might take hours to write using a programming language can be created in minutes. A few of the applications discussed under a specific category, such as Microsoft's PowerPoint, can be considered an authoring system, but usually you will hear this term used to describe more sophisticated applications like Macromedia Director and Authorware. Having an authoring system greatly reduces the learning curve for nonprogrammers because it requires less technical knowledge to master. However, it is a mistake to think that most of these programs are so intuitive that you can sit down and be productive right away.

In addition to its relative user-friendliness over raw programming, one of the main advantages of an authoring system is its ability to quickly prototype an application. This feature can be very helpful for making quick mockups to be shown for feedback prior to producing the site in detail.

The major disadvantage of most authoring systems is the limitation that results from having an application with predetermined programming. It reduces the flexibility to go beyond what is built into the system. Many systems allow for flexibility by including external scripting functionality for the power user. Another limitation is that programs developed on proprietary authoring systems often require a specialized plug-in so they can be played on the Web. For example, Macromedia's Authorware requires Web Player. Finally, high-end programs like Authorware can be very expensive (more than $2,900).

Course Management Systems

Course management systems (CMS), as they are known in the education field, are systems that are designed to facilitate the development, delivery, and management of learning environments on the Web.[2] In the business world they are known as learning management systems (LMS). Many institutions are turning to these to provide a way for professors to build interactive online courses or supplement traditional classroom teaching quickly and easily. Courseware software does not reside on your computer, but instead on a server. With an institution that already has a courseware product selected and in use, it may be a simple matter to initiate a course for your library instruction. For those that do not have their own servers, courseware companies exist that will host your course on their server, some at no charge. Figure 4.10 shows a course being created on the hosted Blackboard.com site. This service is free for sixty days, after which a reasonable yearly charge per course applies.

If you decide to select a course management system, there are many companies to choose from and many features available. A good tool to help compare features of many course management systems can be found at EduTools (http://www .edutools.info/course/). You should look for a system that includes the following features:

asynchronous communication (threaded discussions and e-mail)

synchronous communication (real-time chat and whiteboards on which users can write or draw)

FIGURE 4.10
Blackboard's Hosted Course Service

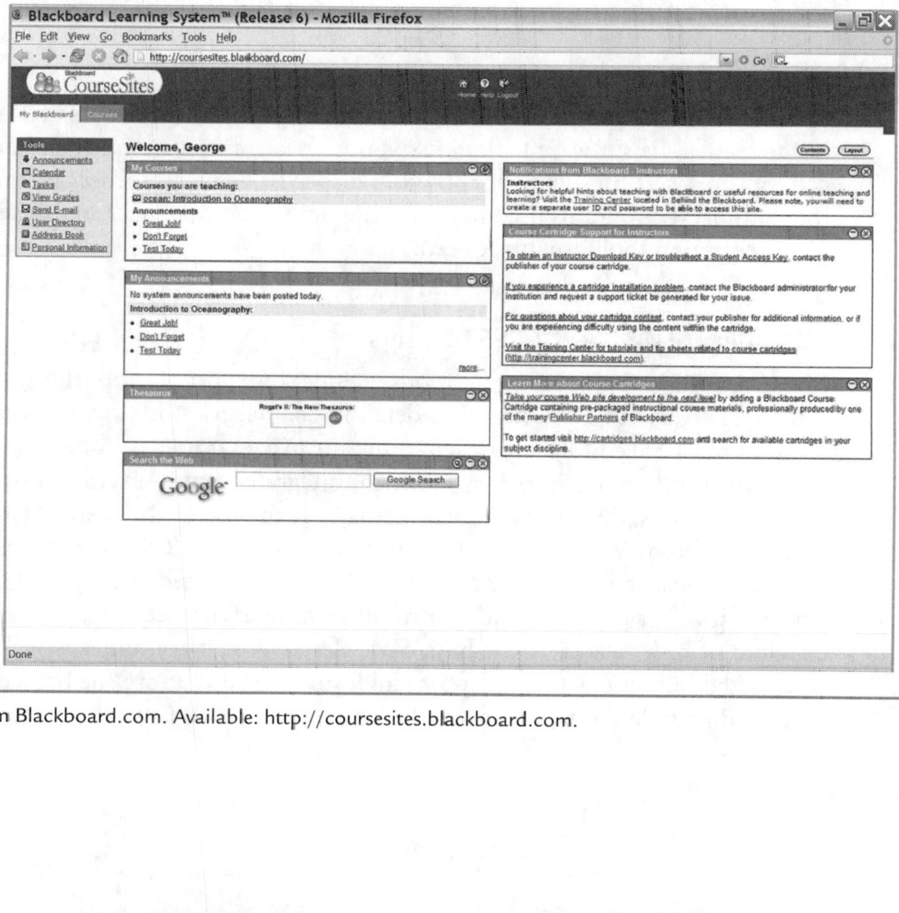

From Blackboard.com. Available: http://coursesites.blackboard.com.

user authentication

collaboration via group formation

survey and testing capabilities

content creation

online journal

file exchange

grading tools

course statistics

A new framework that will become more common in CMS and LMS is SCORM (Shareable Content Object Reference Model), a new XML-based standard designed to ensure interoperability among systems. It is used to define and access information about learning objects so they can be easily shared between different systems. This standard was developed in response to a U.S. Department of Defense initiative to promote e-learning standardization to facilitate moving course content and other related information cross-platform. As CMS and LMS evolve to newer updated versions, look for SCORM compliance.

Some of the major players in this market are Blackboard.com (http://www.blackboard.com), WebCT (http://www.webct.com), and TopClass (http://www.wbtsystems.com).

Specialty Tools

Specialty tools are programs that serve to create specific components of a Web site. For instance, there is software that allows you to create an online quiz, and another type can capture a screen from your computer display. (Chapter 7 focuses on many specialized authoring programs used to create interactive components.) In this section, a few of the common tools are introduced.

Cascading Style Sheet (CSS) Editors

Most Web editing software applications include some sort of support for working with cascading style sheets (discussed in detail in chapter 5). Additionally, some integrate stand-alone CSS editors into their program. An example is TopStyle (http://www.bradsoft.com/topstyle/index.asp), which integrates with several third-party Web authoring tools, including Macromedia Dreamweaver MX, and NoteTab Pro. However, if your Web authoring program doesn't have a CSS component, or it isn't exactly full-featured, you may find that a program focused strictly on CSS may give you much better guidance and control in creating style sheets. Figure 4.11 shows an example of a dedicated CSS editor, StyleMaster Pro. It combines a WYSIWYG and code-based interface with many powerful features. The W3c.org site has a good section on cascading style sheets, with a long list of authoring tools (http://w3c.org/Style/CSS/).

FIGURE 4.11
StyleMaster Pro for Authoring CSS

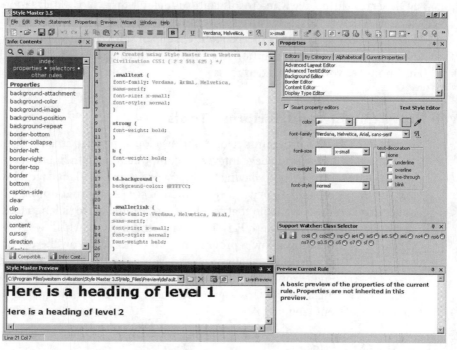

From Westciv. Available: http://www.westciv.com/style_master/.

Database Applications

If you decide to develop a dynamic rather than static educational instruction site, you will be including a database of some sort. Potential uses for databases will be covered in more detail in chapter 7, but it is important to include consideration of a particular database application as you are determining your required development tools. Whether a database is appropriate depends on many factors, but once you decide to use a database, the next step is to choose the appropriate one for your needs. Questions to ask include

What database software (if any) is in use in your organization?

If there is software in use, is it available to you for your project?

How large is the database?

What volume of traffic to the database do you expect?

How sophisticated are your database requirements?

Does your staff have expertise in database development?

What will your budget support?

What hardware requirements exist?

The needs that you determine will help you decide whether you require an enterprise level database solution such as Oracle (http://www.oracle.com) or Microsoft SQL Server (http://www.microsoft.com/sql/default.mspx), or a more modest solution such as Microsoft Access (http://office.microsoft.com/en-us/FX010857911033.aspx). Do you have the internal expertise to use an open source (software that is freely available to use and modify) solution like MySQL? Which database is best for the scripting technologies you have decided to use?

Web Programming and Scripting Tools

If you don't have a programmer on your development team, many of the authoring tools discussed previously have integrated components into their products that permit you to write scripts without having to know a programming language. However, if you are fortunate enough to have a team member with a programming background, authoring tools are available that facilitate writing the various languages of the Web (examples include XML, Java, Perl, JavaScript, and Python, which will be discussed in chapter 7). These tools allow a programmer to concentrate on the development task rather than the underlying language syntax. Much like the HTML editor, these scripting tools automate much of the process of code creation. Cnet's download.com (http://www.download.com) is a good resource to use to find links to development tools for different languages.

XML/XSLT Editors

As XML (Extensible Markup Language) and its corresponding styling language XSLT (Extensible Stylesheet Language Transformation) become more prevalent on the Web (both will be discussed in detail in chapters 6 and 7), software to facilitate easy XML/XSLT authoring and validation has been developed. Like HTML, XML and XSLT can be authored by hand, but an editor is preferable to streamline coding and minimize coding errors. Web Developer's Virtual Library has a list of links to XML editors (http://www.wdvl.com/Software/XML/editors.html). Two popular XML editors are Altova XML Spy (http://www.xmlspy.com) and SoftQuad XMetal (http://www .xmetal.com). As has happened with other technologies, expect in time to see major Web editors add support for authoring XML.

Integrated Application Server and Authoring Tools

Another avenue to pursue if you are planning to incorporate dynamic delivery of information assembled on the fly into your tutorial via a database is a Web application server. An application server is a program that handles transactions between a Web browser on a client computer and an institution's back-end applications that reside on a server. For example, it processes data contained or referenced in a database and delivers that content to the user's browser in HTML. Supplying many of the same functions that you can achieve with manual scripting, this fairly recently developed tool is designed to tightly integrate several components in a single development interface. With a Web application server, the developer does not have to reinvent the wheel to build a robust interaction with a database. A familiar example of an application server is Macromedia's ColdFusion (http://www.macromedia.com/software/cold fusion/). Information, including links to reviews, on various application servers is maintained on TheServerSide.com (http://www.theserverside.com/reviews/matrix.tss).

Because application servers can be very expensive, their use may be overkill if your database access is low. Check with your information technology department. One may already be installed at your institution.

Notes

1. OneStat.com, http://www.onestat.com/html/aboutus_pressbox31.html.
2. Nada Dabbagh, "Web-Based Course Management Systems," in *Education and Technology: An Encyclopedia*, ed. Ann Kovalchick and Kara Dawson (Santa Barbara, CA: ABC-CLIO, 2004), 622.

5

Designing the
User Interface

The user interface, the graphical link between the student and a computer program, encompasses every aspect of a user's possible interaction with a computer. To the students who use your Web instruction, the interface is the tutorial. Without a doubt, designing and creating your library instruction user interface is one of the major challenges in the preproduction and production stages. Your goal in creating Web instruction is to produce an instrument that will engage students and motivate them to actively learn in an independent environment. The successful creation of the interface requires that a wide variety of elements be brought together so that they mesh to present the instruction in the most effective manner, requiring the least explanation.

The subject of what constitutes good user interface design has been well studied and discussed. Many of the themes that are being presented here are the result of work accomplished by prominent researchers in the field of human-computer interaction; in particular the work of Ben Shneiderman (http://www.cs.umd.edu/~ben/) and Jakob Nielsen (http://www.useit.com). These pioneers have been instrumental in establishing best practices for making computers and the Internet more usable for all of us.

The purpose of this chapter is to examine the important usability factors to consider and incorporate into a winning interface. We will take a detailed look at

>   user-centered design
>   instructional design and content
>   basic guidelines and principles for user-interface design (adapted for the Web)
>   navigation
>   screen layout and presentation aids
>   visual design considerations
>   multinational design considerations
>   user accessibility
>   page optimization

USER-CENTERED DESIGN

From the beginning, the design process should be focused on your users, or audience. You are going to be creating a teaching tool for a population that traditionally does not have a high level of comfort in the library world. To many students, the library is a mysterious place, organized with puzzling numbering schemes and a foreign language of library jargon. Acquiring a thorough understanding of the user is a must.

One of the first steps to be taken in the preproduction phase is the audience needs analysis discussed in chapter 3. The results from this analysis will be the starting point for involving the user in the design process. From the analysis you should know

who will be using the tutorial

their preferred learning styles

their previous experiences using libraries

their prior exposure to library instruction

their base of knowledge in the specific subject area being taught

the level of their computer competence

what type of hardware and software they have at their disposal

their skill using the Web

what their expectations are from the instruction

Involving the user doesn't stop with what you discover from the initial needs assessment. To ensure maximum usability of your program, users should be drawn in throughout the development process. How can users' preferences and opinions be gathered? Assembling a focus group as you begin the design process is one way to hear from users about what they like or don't like about Web site design in general, previous library instruction experiences, and various instructional methods. The one drawback to this sort of user encounter is that users can give opinions only about what they already know. If they have not experienced innovative library instruction methods or engaging interactive Web instruction, they won't realize what is possible. Nevertheless, a focus group can provide a basic picture of what your audience thinks it wants.

Next you will want to develop a wire-frame prototype and have users try it out and provide feedback. A wire-frame prototype is a simple preliminary model of the site, without artwork, that identifies the main navigation and content. Adopt an iterative design process, and use testers' reactions about each updated version to make design adjustments. Several methods that work well for testing usability are discussed in depth in chapter 8.

INSTRUCTIONAL DESIGN AND CONTENT

When initiating a discussion about interface design, it's not uncommon to think primarily about screen layout and visual elements. This is important, of course, but it shouldn't be separated from the main goal of the project—to deliver instruction effectively. The instructional design of the tutorial is the place to begin.

Instructional Design

Instructional design is more than filling a page with content and throwing in a few hyperlinks. We are all used to this model of the Web: pages full of information with links that allow us to follow nonlinear paths. However, providing information isn't the same as delivering instruction. Instructional design is defined as the systematic process of translating general principles of learning and instruction into plans for instructional materials and learning. Ritchie and Hoffman identified the following sequences that are considered essential to the instructional process:[1]

> *Motivating the learner.* Visual and multimedia elements can contribute to the motivation factor, but incorporating such components as problem-solving opportunities, critical-thinking exercises, and an established relevance to the learner's needs are strong stimuli.
>
> *Identifying what is to be learned.* Establish clear objectives at the beginning. Let the students know what outcomes are expected.
>
> *Reminding learners of past knowledge.* Many students have had some exposure to libraries in their past or to the subject being studied; offer a review to establish their existing knowledge.
>
> *Requiring active involvement.* Active involvement is more than clicking on a hyperlink to move through the site. Interactive exercises that relate to a specific assignment that the students must submit let them actively engage in the learning process.
>
> *Providing guidance and feedback.* Incorporate ways to let the students know if they are on the right track. Skill checks at crucial points throughout the instruction can give students a tool to assess their understanding of the material.
>
> *Testing.* Testing is still the most common way for the instructor to know if students have learned what has been taught.
>
> *Providing enrichment and remediation.* Offer a way for students to revisit parts of the instruction if they have a problem and to contact the instructor for help.

Open versus Closed Structure

One goal of instructional design is to keep the student focused on what is being taught. The nature of the structure of the Web tends to work against this goal. The Web is an open system that can take students on a tangent with the click of a mouse. Keep this in mind as you design an instructional site. For example, you may wish to illustrate points or show examples by taking students to an external site. You want to offer this flexibility to the student, but in a controlled manner. You don't want to provide links in your instruction that will take students away from your site so that they have difficulty finding their way back. Proper planning of navigation and window structure is important to keep your instruction contained. Using frames is one way of maintaining control over the Web environment. The advantages and disadvantages of using frames will be covered later in this chapter in the navigation section. Controlling window placement and appearance is another appropriate way of making sure that your users can return to where they left off in your tutorial. Two approaches are prevalent.

Opening a Second Browser Window

Many Web users have become accustomed to having second browser windows open to take them to a new site but leaving the original window open so it can be returned to easily. It's simple to make a second window open when a user clicks on a URL: add the attribute target="_blank" to the end of the URL. For example, <a href="http://zsr .wfu.edu/" target="_blank">Online Catalog</a> takes the user to a second window. A second full-sized window will open and display the new site. For users who are comfortable moving back and forth between windows via the taskbar, this can be an easy solution. However, if a user is oblivious to new windows opening (and many still are), the new window can cause confusion. This method is one that Nielsen discourages in his 2004 update of the Top Ten Mistakes in Web Design (http://useit.com/alertbox/ 9605.html), noting that people usually don't notice what has occurred. If you decide to use this method, be certain to provide instruction on what to do so that the user knows how to return to the tutorial and doesn't end up with multiple browser windows open.

Opening Smaller Pop-up Windows

Most Web surfers are familiar with the little pop-up windows that often appear superimposed over the browser interface. Typically they are advertising or a survey request. In that context they can be annoying, but when used properly they can be an effective way to give access to external sites or additional information without having users leave the tutorial page. Figure 5.1 shows a pop-up window that takes users to additional information without leaving the tutorial.

FIGURE 5.1
Pop-up Window to Present Additional Information

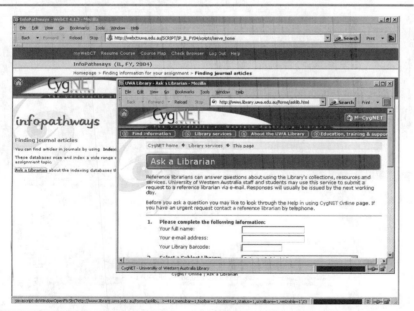

From InfoPathways, University of Western Australia Library. Available: http://www.library .uwa.edu.au/training/infopathways.html.

Many Web editor software programs can create these pop-up windows without having to know a specific script. If your software doesn't have this capability, it is easy to find window-building utilities on the Web. Figure 5.2 shows an example of one. You copy and paste the generated script into the body of your HTML document. It allows you to control how the window will appear, including if it will have a menu or tool bar, a location field, or scroll bars or be resizable. The size and placement of the window can be configured also.

Writing for the Web

Writing content for the Web requires a different mind-set than writing for print. Morkes and Nielsen's research has shown that on the Web reading is 25 percent slower than from paper, most users scan text rather than read word-for-word, and Web content should be 50 percent of the length of its paper equivalent.[2]

How should this influence how content is written? Morkes and Nielsen offer the following guidelines:

Be concise. People are not as comfortable reading from a computer screen as they are reading from a print source. Reading from a screen can be tiring to their eyes, and although screen readability is improving as monitor resolutions become enhanced, it will be a long time before everyone has access to high-

FIGURE 5.2
Pop-up Window Building Utility

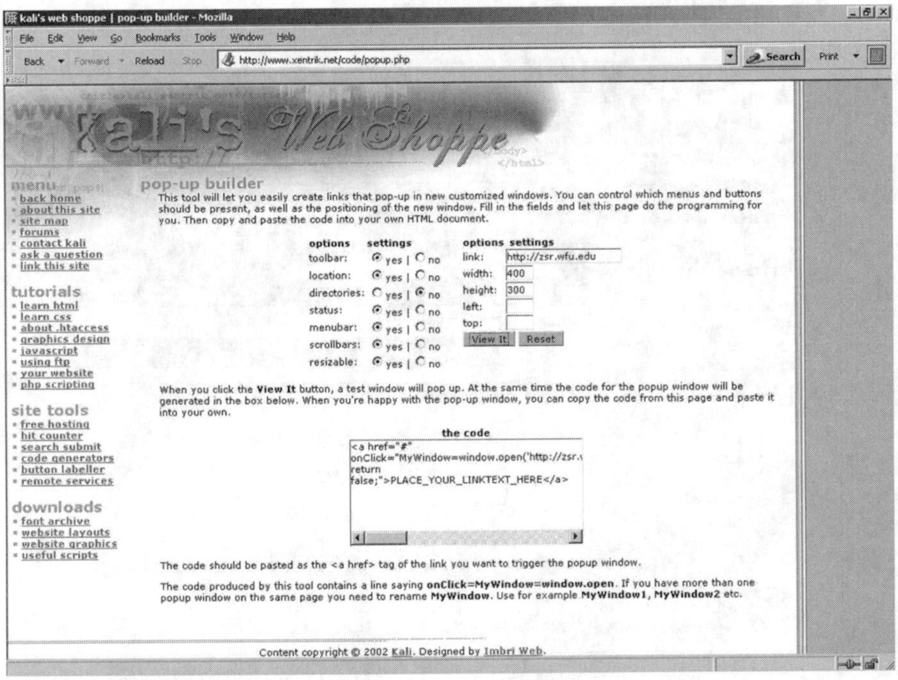

From Kali's Web Shoppe. Available: http://www.xentrik.net/code/popup.php.

resolution screens. Also, users don't like to scroll down a page to read text. By keeping the text succinct, a page of information can be restricted to fit on a screen so scrolling is unnecessary.

Write for scannability. Because people don't like to read text on a screen, they tend to scan a page to pick out key words and ideas. By planning to present content so that it is scannable, you will ensure that students will have a better chance to encounter the most important points. To enhance scannability

> use meaningful headings that will tell the reader what content is to be covered
>
> highlight keywords via hyperlinks, color, or making the type bold
>
> incorporate bulleted lists
>
> restrict each paragraph to one idea
>
> restrict each page to one topic
>
> use graphics to illustrate key points and provide a distinctive caption
>
> include a table of contents or site map

Notice in figure 5.3 that scannability has been increased by using headings, bold text, highlighted keywords, and bulleted lists.

FIGURE 5.3
Page Optimized for Scannability

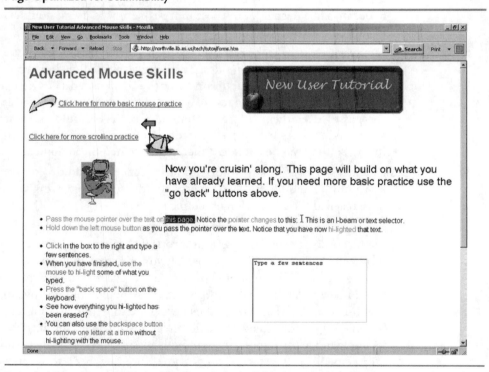

From the Library Network's Technology Committee. Available: http://tech.tln.lib.mi.us/tutor/welcome.htm.

Use an inverted pyramid style via hyperlinks. Using a concise writing style doesn't mean that in-depth content has to be sacrificed. By using an inverted pyramid organizational style, users can start with the main points, the conclusion in essence, and use hyperlinks to continue deeper to secondary pages for more detailed information.

BASIC USER-INTERFACE DESIGN

Many of the best practices for user interface design (UID) on the Web have evolved from Ben Shneiderman's eight golden rules of interface design.[3] These principles apply to most interactive systems, and Web designers have adapted them to relate to the Web environment.

Strive for consistency. Consistency can mean many things. There is consistency of actions, navigation, screen layout, and terminology. Providing consistency helps the user to know what to expect and to learn the interface more quickly. Consistency can also be discussed as it relates to other Web sites. Experienced Web surfers have come to expect certain functionality from Web sites and recognize certain objects as having particular meanings. Straying too far from the consistency of how a typical Web site works may frustrate and disorient the user.

Enable frequent users to use shortcuts. Experienced users have different expectations than do novices. A person who has previously worked through a tutorial may want to quickly get to specific sections—for remediation or to follow hyperlinks to a deeper level. These more experienced users should have access to shortcuts to get what they want efficiently.

Offer informative feedback. For every action, there should be some sort of response. This may be as modest as having a third color designation for the ALINK (Active Link) in addition to ones for unvisited (LINK) and visited (VLINK) links. Some graphics are designed to give visual feedback as the cursor passes over them. More substantial feedback should be programmed when asking users to complete more complex activities, such as submitting forms, so they can be confident that they executed the action correctly.

Design dialogs to yield closure. Information sequences should be grouped to have a beginning, middle, and end. Users shouldn't be left guessing whether they have reached the conclusion of a topic.

Offer error prevention and simple error handling. Any system should be designed so that users don't experience serious errors; if that is not possible, users should be able to "fail gently." This means that your design should anticipate potential error-causing incidents and provide corrective measures. Error correction should be worded in a straightforward, constructive, and positive manner so that users don't feel as though they have done something wrong. If a link has become outdated, provide specific directions for handling it. If higher-end technologies are being included, provide instructions for system and plug-in requirements at the start so users know what they need to use the tutorial;

don't make them wait until they try to access an unconfigured file type on the introductory page. Provide links to the sites where additional software can be downloaded.

Permit easy reversal of actions. Users should be able to undo any action without dire consequence. In a Web form, include a reset button. Navigation should allow users to back out of a screen and return to the previous one.

Support internal locus of control. Skilled users of the Web want to feel that they are in control of their experience. Program in enough flexibility so that these users don't feel they are being held back. One simple tool for freeing savvy Web users is to provide a search engine or site map to allow them to move through the tutorial more freely.

Reduce short-term memory load. Humans can process only a limited number of chunks of information in short-term memory. (Seven plus or minus two is the rule.) Concise content, short screens, and real-world metaphors can help minimize information overload. This style of writing lends itself to the concept of *chunking*, or dividing material into small segments that can be more easily digested. Chunking can be directly related to the concept of learning objects, discussed in chapter 1.

NAVIGATION

Navigation in an instructional site is second only to content in importance to the success of the instructional design. In fact, navigation can be an organizational tool for designing your content delivery. Without effective navigation, users can become lost, and content may become inaccessible. This section looks at various types of navigation and related issues.

Qualities of Successful Navigation Systems

Research shows that successful navigation shares certain qualities.[4] Effective navigation should

be easily learned

be consistent

provide feedback

appear in context

offer alternatives

require an economy of action and time

provide clear visual messages

offer clear and understandable labels

be appropriate to the site's purpose

support user goals and behaviors

With a good navigation system, the site's users will always know where they are, where they can go next, and where they have been. Always highlight the current location so that it tells the user "You are here." Use a visual placement marker to highlight the present position of users. For example, the tutorial shown in figure 5.4 has as a location marker the title across the top of the screen, "Analyse Your Assignment." Indicators of the current location should also include such information as your organization name just in case the user has entered your tutorial from a back door instead of at the top level.

Types of Navigation Systems

Depending on the size of the site that the navigation is designed to serve, setting it up can range from straightforward to complex. A site with breadth (many pages at the same level) and depth (multiple levels) may require more than one navigation system. Let's take a look at the types of navigation systems that might be appropriate.

FIGURE 5.4
Tutorial with Location Marker

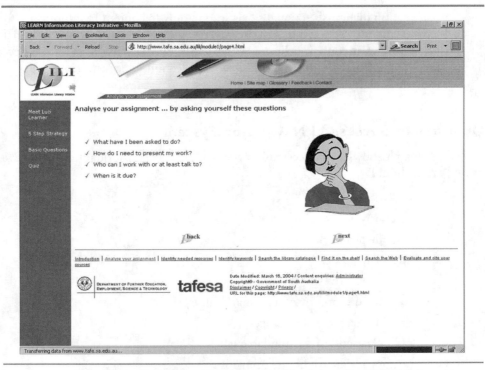

From LEARN Information Literacy Initiative, LEARN Network of South Australian TAFE Libraries.
Available: http://www.tafe.sa.edu.au/lili/index.html.

Introductory Splash Screens

Although not a navigation system in its entirety, a splash page provides an introduction to a site and sets the tone. Often it is used to highlight main sections of the tutorial, and as such, can be considered to be a navigational aid. An example of this can be seen in figure 5.5. Splash screens should be used with care because users may find them a barrier to the content. If you decide to have a splash screen, be sure to include a text link option to bypass it.

Hierarchical Systems

The information structure hierarchy for your tutorial can be a principal navigation system. It can supply a picture of the information contained in your site in the context in which it was organized. Keep in mind that a hierarchical method of organization is familiar to most people because they have used similar systems that start at the top level and move down the line to more specific details. A typical way to translate the hierarchy of your site into a navigation tool is to use a table of contents. A basic site map can also provide a hierarchical view of the content.

FIGURE 5.5
Splash as Introductory Navigation

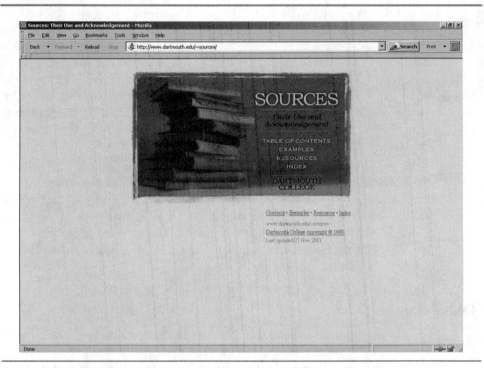

From Dartmouth College, Copyright © 1998 Trustees of Dartmouth College.
Available: http://www.dartmouth.edu/~sources.

When you are planning your hierarchical navigation in terms of your information structure, don't go overboard with too much breadth (number of options at each level of the hierarchy) or depth (number of levels in the hierarchy). Remember the rule of seven plus or minus two, and don't overload the user with too many choices from any one menu.

Global Systems

A global system is a sitewide navigation device. It provides access to areas of your site beyond the specific tutorial or module you are using. This type of navigation device can be useful if you have a number of instructional modules available for students or if your current tutorial is multimodular in structure with each module or topic standing as a self-contained unit.

Local Systems

If you consider your overall tutorial the main site, think about each individual topic or module as a subsite. Local navigation systems provide a way to maneuver through the subsite. Because users prefer to have information delivered one screen at a time and to read scannable text, it may be necessary to present one element of a particular topic on each screen. With a local navigation mechanism present, users can see what additional elements are included and can get to them efficiently.

Local navigation systems should be used in tandem with global systems. There should always be a way for users to return to other areas of the site. Most likely you will find that a combination of navigation systems gives users the best navigation experience. Figure 5.6 is an example of a multiple navigation system. The buttons across the top of the screen serve as a global navigation system with links to other modules in the tutorial. The text menu down the left side of the screen acts as a local navigation system within the current module. The link to the site map at the bottom of the screen will take the user to a hierarchical view of the content. Other links at the bottom of the screen also return the user to the main list of other available tutorials.

Ad Hoc Systems

Sometimes links to additional information on your site do not fit nicely into any of the previous three systems. Often you will find these links embedded into the text of the page. Because they are not overt navigation tools, they can easily be missed as users scan through the text. If the link is going to an incidental piece of information, then this may be an acceptable solution. If you are trying to emphasize the importance of the link, however, figure out a way to bring it into prominence, perhaps by creating a bulleted list, so that it stands out for the reader.

Navigation Methods

There is no single way to create the various navigation systems. Limited only by their imagination, Web designers have produced different methods that serve the same purpose. Following are some of the most popular methods and their advantages and disadvantages.

FIGURE 5.6
Multiple Navigation Systems

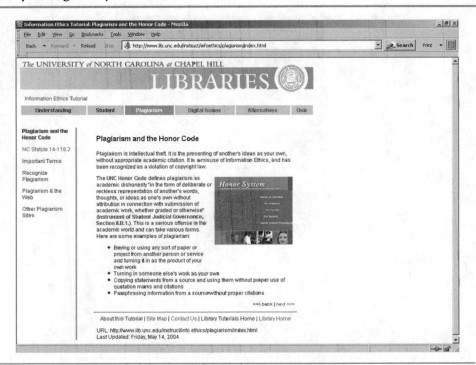

From UNC–Chapel Hill Libraries. Available: http://www.lib.unc.edu/instruct/infoethics/plagiarism/.

Text

Using text links as navigation is simple to do and can be read by any browser. If you decide to go with text, keep the text length concise so that the link doesn't overlap into a second line, and devise a visual clue so that users will know they are looking at a navigation tool. Successful methods include highlighting each menu item with a small graphic or offsetting the menu by highlighting it with a different color background. Such visual clues set the navigation text apart from the rest of the content on the page. Tables of contents and site maps are typically text based. The text for the navigation system in the Open University's Safari tutorial in figure 5.7, for example, is set apart as a numbered list, placed within a table cell that has a different highlighted background color when the item is displayed.

Tool Bars: Image Maps, Tabs, and Icons

Many Web designers build graphical navigation tool bars, which take many different shapes. (Using graphics effectively will be discussed in greater detail in chapter 6.) Using graphics for navigation ensures that the system will stand apart from the text content of the page. A few popular permutations of the graphical toolbar that you may come across include image maps, tabs, and icons.

FIGURE 5.7

Text, Tabs, and Frames for Navigation Systems

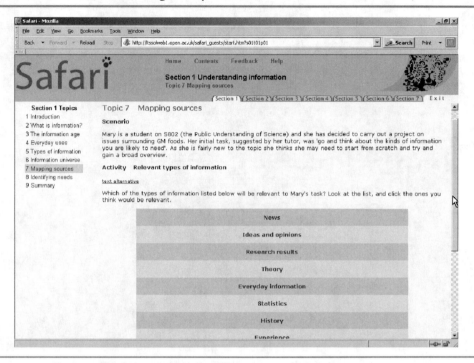

From Open University Library. Available: http://www.open.ac.uk/safari/.

An image map is a graphic object that is subdivided into areas, each of which takes users to a different destination. The splash screen shown in figure 5.5 is an image map. The clickable areas (or hot spots) of an image map are defined by specifying coordinates in the HTML coding and attaching a URL destination to that area.

Tabs have become a popular way to separate content into different categories. See the top right of figure 5.7 for an example.

Icons are small graphics that are meaningful representations of particular topics, functions, or actions. Users today are comfortable with icons as navigation devices because icons have become pervasive in computer and Web environments to represent common actions, such as print or return home.

Menu Trees

A menu tree, or nested navigation, is a way, through scripting, to display a collapsible menu, that is, one that can contain several levels. When completely closed, the user sees only the top level of the site hierarchy. Clicking a link displays the next level down. To close a particular menu, the user clicks any other link, which collapses the previous branch of the tree just expanded. Figure 5.8 shows an example of navigation using a menu tree. Many menu trees use a folder metaphor of plusses (+) and minuses (−) to allow the user to open and close the menus. An example of this type of tree can be seen in figure 5.9.

FIGURE 5.8
Collapsible Menu Tree for Navigation

From Z. Smith Reynolds Library, Wake Forest University. Available: http://www.wfu.edu/Library/ITC/training/index.html.

FIGURE 5.9
Folder-Style Collapsible Menu Tree for Navigation

Drop-down Menus

Drop-down menus illustrate a way to supply navigation without taking up much real estate on the screen. Most users are familiar with these and know to click on them to get a list of options. Drop-down menus are fairly easy to assemble by using a script. Many script libraries (which will be discussed in chapter 7) have free scripts you can adapt to use for your menu. Many Web editing programs now include this type of scripting functionality with a user-friendly interface. The example in figure 5.10 shows a simple drop-down box displayed in a browser and screens of the steps in Dreamweaver to create it.

Breadcrumb Trails

A breadcrumb trail shows the hierarchical structure of a site so that users know where they are in relation to the overall site. In figure 5.11, look at the arrow pointing to the breadcrumb trail at the top of the content area. It tells users where they are in the hierarchy of the instruction. It pinpoints their location in the context of the entire site, showing the path from the top layer to the current page. Breadcrumb trail navigation is best suited for a large, complex site and so may have limited applicability in a tutorial setting where a guided navigation may be more appropriate. However, if you are planning an intricate instructional site, breadcrumb trails are a simple-to-construct, space-conserving way to show navigation to the user.

FIGURE 5.10
Creating a Drop-down Menu with Macromedia Dreamweaver

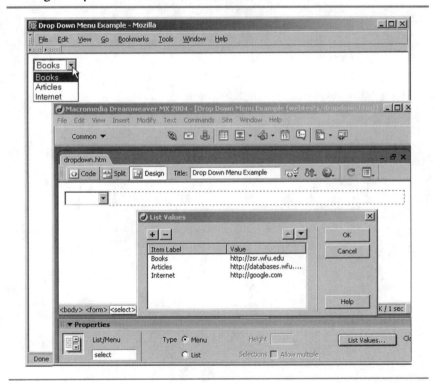

FIGURE 5.11
Breadcrumb Trail Navigation

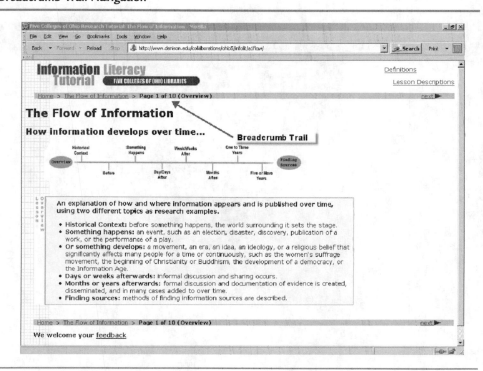

From Five Colleges of Ohio Libraries. Available: http://www.denison.edu/collaborations/ohio5/
infolit/a1flow/.

Arrows

Users associate an arrow on a screen with the action that will move them forward or backward one screen. Including arrows on the screen of your tutorial permits users to move sequentially through a section of the tutorial in a linear fashion. In figure 5.6 the arrows at the bottom right of the content area of the screen allow the user to move sequentially through the module screen by screen. Including arrows to proceed through a subsite supplies an extra level of navigation.

Site Maps

Site maps are used to provide a visual ready reference of a site's structure or organization. Typically site maps are text links that display the hierarchical order of the site's content. If done correctly, site maps can help users orient themselves to the information contained and can provide a level of access that permits them to choose the path of their instruction. Figure 5.12 is an example of a site map for a library research tutorial. Successful site maps allow users to see the various levels of the entire site in one glance without being so big the map becomes overwhelming.

FIGURE 5.12
Site Map

From Z. Smith Reynolds Library, Wake Forest University. Available: http://www.wfu.edu/Library/referenc/research/map.htm.

Search Engines

Although normally the instructional design for a tutorial will be planned to proceed in a particular sequence, a search engine that locates terms on Web pages can be useful in helping users who return to the tutorial to revisit a particular point or concept. They can search for something specific without having to proceed step by step through the entire instruction. This type of flexibility passes some control to the user.

Placement of Navigation Tools on the Screen

Navigation tools are incorporated into most Web sites today. Because most people read from left to right and from top to bottom, the left and top of the screen are the areas that are most suited for navigation. If you place your navigation tools down the right hand side of the screen, unless you configure the layout to adjust to the resolution that a user has chosen, there is a distinct possibility that the navigation may be hidden. For example, if a screen is designed for a 1024 × 768 resolution and the navigation tool is in the last 100 pixels of the screen, a user who has set his computer at 800 × 600 will not see the navigation tool without scrolling over to the right side to bring it into view. The same is true of navigation tools that appear at the bottom of the screen. If the content pushes the size of the screen below the fold, or bottom edge of the initial screen, users have to scroll down to see the navigation tool. If a designer wants to ensure that what is placed on the right of the screen shows for everyone, then the design should be set to adjust by percentage if the interface will take up the entire screen. Instead of designating a specific number of pixels for the screen by width and height, screen layout should be designated to be a percentage of the screen width and height. Because screens are drawn top to bottom and from left to right, it is preferable to locate navigation tools in the top or left areas of the screen to be confident that they are viewable to all.

Linear versus Nonlinear Navigation

Linear navigation takes students from point A to point Z in a step-by-step progression that guides them through the instruction in a structured way. Students start at the beginning and progress only as they make the correct choices to show they have grasped the concept being taught. This may be appropriate for those with no previous exposure to the subject being covered or if you intend that the tutorial be completed in one sitting or class period. A linear approach helps ensure that students stay on task.

However, there are risks with offering only a linear progression. If the instruction is of any length, students may want to stop for a while, come back later, and pick up where they left off. If they have to enter through the first screen and work through every subsequent screen to get back to where they stopped, they'll rapidly become frustrated. What about students who want to return to the tutorial to review a particular section or concept? They will want quick, easy access to just that information. If you intend for your tutorial to be used in this fashion, then a nonlinear navigation scheme is more appropriate. Figures 5.6 and 5.7 are examples of ways to provide a nonlinear navigation. Users can enter the tutorial from any of the topic areas in these menus.

You Quote It, You Note It! from Vaughan Memorial Library, Acadia University, has a linear navigation design. As shown in figure 5.13, students move through the instruction by clicking on the arrows at the top left of the screen to move forward or backward or to restart from the beginning. The instructional module takes only about 10 minutes to complete and covers a single topic, plagiarism. If you choose a strictly linear start-to-finish approach, it's a good idea to follow this model of designing a session that can be easily complete in a distinct session.

One nonlinear approach to instructional design in Web instruction is branching. Branching is a concept where the sequence of progression of the tutorial depends on the learner's response to questions and activities. Branching allows a student to skip over what he or she already knows, or to be directed to remedial instruction if found to be weak in a certain subject area.

Frames as a Navigation Device

Frames are used to subdivide the browser window to display multiple, independently controllable pages simultaneously. One of the most popular uses for frames is to provide a stationary navigation page that stays in view while new pages load in the second frame. This provides a uniform navigation tool without having to re-create the tool bar or menu on each page.

FIGURE 5.13
Linear Navigation

From You Quote It, You Note It! Vaughan Memorial Library, Acadia University, Wolfville, Nova Scotia. Available: http://library.acadiau.ca/tutorials/plagiarism.

Whether to use frames is a subject that initiates passionate discussion. Web usability guru Jakob Nielsen's recommendation is "frames: just say no." [5] Why does he think that frames should be avoided?

First, the URL that displays at the top of the browser is actually the address for the frame set, the document that specifies the size and location of each frame. The URL for the pages that are actually displayed does not appear to users. If a page from an external site is displayed in one of the frames and users try to bookmark it, they will end up with a bookmark to the original frame set document.

Second, printing a page from a frame can be difficult for users. They need to know to click on the desired document to activate the frame for printing. If they have used the navigation frame to pull up content in the second frame and simply issue the print command, the navigation page will print because it was the most recently activated frame.

Third, to ensure that important information is displayed in full, most frames are normally specified to be a particular size. This can work well if users can accommodate a large display, but can also cause difficulty for users with small screens because there often isn't enough room for the navigation frame and the content frame. When this happens, the content frame is the one most likely to be cut off.

These reasons for being concerned about the usability of frames may apply more to a regular Web site than to a contained tutorial. The need to bookmark a specific content page within a tutorial is not as pressing as it may be in a general site, and most users will probably want to set the bookmark to the starting page of the tutorial. Printing may not be a concern, but if it is, providing an easy-to-print version of the site is one option to solve this potential problem. In an instructional setting, frames can serve the function of becoming a way to provide access to external resources without having students stray away from the tutorial. The static navigation menu stays in view at all times, providing a simple way for students to return to the instruction. Frames can work very nicely within a well-designed self-contained tutorial. Figure 5.7 uses invisible frames to anchor its navigation schemes in place. The content, when longer than the screen, is scrollable as can be seen by the partial scroll bar on the right, to which the cursor is pointing.

If you do decide to go with a frames format, include a nonframes version if there is any possibility that your audience might use a browser that doesn't support frames. You also want to provide a <noframes> section within the frameset document that displays alternative content to viewers who are using a browser that doesn't support frames. This content can include a link to the nonframe version of your tutorial.

SCREEN LAYOUT AND PRESENTATION AIDS

This section discusses tables and cascading style sheets. These are two of the main tools that are valuable to help you structure the layout of your tutorial so it displays and formats optimally. Traditionally, it has been difficult to overcome the limitations of HTML for content presentation. HTML is a markup language, not a page layout and formatting language. Tables were identified early on as a work-around to this problem. Cascading style sheets (CSS) were developed as a specification to describe the presentation including both layout and formatting, such as colors and fonts that traditionally have been embedded in HTML code tags.

Layout Tables

It didn't take long for Web authors to turn to using tables as a way to gain some control over page layout and formatting. Each individual table cell has the ability to support distinct formatting independent of other structural elements. By putting content inside table cells and specifying that the borders be invisible, it became possible to produce a page that had a complex design. When you look at the top screen in figure 5.14, you don't notice the tables because the borders are hidden. The view of the same page from within a Web editor (bottom of figure 5.14) shows how table cells have been used to arrange the content.

If you decide to use tables for page layout, be aware of how you size the table. You can choose to size it to a certain width of the screen, so that it will adjust to different resolutions. A table sized to 90 percent width will take up 90 percent of a 640-pixel screen and 90 percent of a 1024-pixel screen. Using this method may work well, but as resolution capability increases, the block of text that looks good in a table cell on a 640×480

FIGURE 5.14
Using Tables as a Layout Device/Using Styles for Formatting

From Appalachian State University Libraries. Available: http://www.library.appstate.edu/
tutorial.

screen will probably look like a one-line paragraph on a 1280×1024 screen. To ensure that the text is displayed the way you intend it within a table cell, you should specify
a fixed width. Because there are still many lower resolution monitors in use, the safe maximum width for a table is about 750 pixels. (You want to allow for pixels lost to the
browser window frame, page margins, and user taskbars.) Align the table in the center
of the page so that the extra screen space is the same on the left and right of the table.

If you are using tables, be aware that the content of any given table will not appear
until the ending table tag </table> is downloaded to the browser. This means that if
you are using nested tables (tables within tables) to control page layout, the user will
see a blank page until the final tag of the container table is read. One approach is to
specify widths. Most browsers can start to render the content with this information.
An alternate approach is to use a series of individual tables that consist of one table
row each. The page will start to display as soon as the first table is completed.

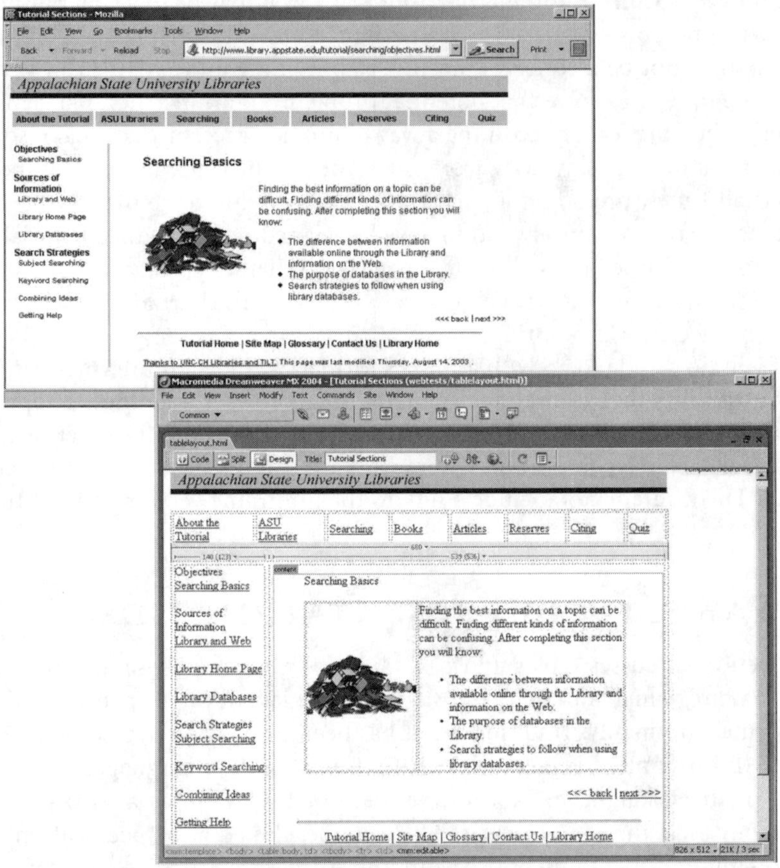

As support for cascading style sheets to control layout increases, there are many good reasons to consider discontinuing the use of tables for layout and turn instead to CSS for presentation solutions:

Tables can be slow to load because of the difficulty of rendering tables (as mentioned).

Tables increase the size of files unnecessarily.

Table widths specified to help the page load more quickly can cause layout problems in different resolutions.

Tables are less accessible to disabled users. Tables were developed to hold tabular data, not to format a page. To ensure that content is easily accessible by those using screen readers, the content in the left column needs to precede that in the columns to the right.

Tables make a site less accessible to viewers using cell phones and PDAs.

Tables don't always print out as well as they show on the screen.

Tables make redesigns of existing sites labor intensive.

Cascading Style Sheets

Tables may have helped work around the problem of page layout in the past, but they aren't really the officially sanctioned solution. Tables have been put to use in a way not originally intended in an effort to address a problem that had no solution at the time. The need for more sophisticated control has been recognized for some years and the original cascading style sheets (CSS) specification was developed to handle the presentation of Web documents.

Background of CSS

CSS is a style-sheet language that separates presentation (format and style) from the content and structure provided in an HTML, XHTML, or XML document. The World Wide Web Consortium (W3C), a group of more than 350 member organizations, made its first style sheet recommendation, CSS1 (Cascading Style Sheets, Level 1), in 1996 (revised in 1999). CSS1 addresses style using common desktop publishing terminology. CSS2.1 (CSS Level 2, version 1) became a W3C Candidate Recommendation in February 2004. It contains all of CSS1 and addresses layout, including content positioning, layout, automatic numbering, page breaks, and right to left text and has features for internationalization. In addition, it supports media-specific style sheets so that authors may tailor the presentation of their documents to visual browsers, aural devices, printers, Braille devices, handheld devices, and so forth. At this writing, CSS3 is still under development. It will contain all of CSS2.1 and will extend it with new selectors, fancy borders and backgrounds, vertical text, user interaction and speech, and much more. With CSS3, the W3C is taking a modular approach so that added functionality can be implemented and tested as they are ready without having to wait for all items to be completed.

How CSS Works

With CSS, a Web author can control style and layout elements such as font, type size and color, margins, indentations, line spacing, and more. CSS provides separate style rules that are used to format HTML elements. Instead of trying to control formatting from within an HTML element, which has to be specified each time the attribute is used, CSS allows the author to specify the style once, and it is automatically applied to the HTML element each time it is used. For instance, using the customary formatting in HTML (which has now been deprecated), if you wanted the headline for your page to be an Arial font that is green and in italics, you would code your headline tag like this every time you used a headline:

```
<h1>
<font face="Arial, Helvetica, sans serif" color="#009900">
<i>Headline</i>
</font>
</h1>
```

A style sheet allows the attributes for an element (or selector) to be specified by the author three ways. First, in an external file (ending with the file extension .css) that resides on the Web server. In this case, you enter the path to that file in the head of your document:

```
<head>
<link rel="stylesheet" href="../tutorial.css">
</head>
```

Second, embedded in the header of the document:

```
<head>
<style type="text/css">
<!--
h1 {font-family: Arial, Helvetica, sans serif; font-size: x-large; font-style: italic;
    line-height: normal; font-weight: bold; color: #009900}
-->
</style>
</head>
```

Third, expressed inline, to override the general style for one occasion:

```
<h1 style="color: #ff0000; font-family: Times, Times New Roman, serif;">
    A New Headline Color and Font with Inline CSS</h1>
```

The obvious benefit of using an external file to store your styles is that you have to make changes in only one document to execute sitewide modifications.

It's not necessary that you pick just one way to apply styles. Cascading style sheets are called this because more than one style sheet can be used on a document, with different levels of importance assigned depending on the location of the style designation. If you define different styles for the same element, the style that is closest to the HTML tag prevails. For example, the style specified in the tag takes precedence over one designated in the head of the document. The style in the head of the document is more important than the one located in the external .css file. This comes in handy when you want to make one-time adjustments to an element on a particular document or a section of a document but prefer that the original style stay in place over the rest of the site.

To look at a basic example of how applying styles changes the display in a browser, study figure 5.14. The document is shown being authored in Dreamweaver (lower right screen). No styling is evident. But when it is displayed in a CSS-supported browser (upper left screen), dramatic visual enhancements are evident. This is accomplished with an external style sheet referenced in the <head> tag of the document:

<link REL="stylesheet" HREF="libtutorial.css" TYPE="TEXT/CSS">

CSS Syntax

CSS is expressed in easy-to-understand scripting. As mentioned, standard desktop publishing terminology is used, so if you understand setting up styles in that environment, it shouldn't be too difficult to learn CSS. And, as discussed in chapter 4, many development tools are available to automate the process. A specific syntax is used to construct statements that define the rules being set.

A CSS statement consists of a selector and a declaration block. The declaration block consists of a list of semicolon-separated declarations in curly braces. A declaration consists of a property, a colon (:), and a value.

Take a look at this rule for a Heading 1:

```
h1 {
position: absolute;
top: +50px;
left: +50px;
color: #008080;
font-family: Verdana, Helvetica, Arial, sans-serif;
}
```

The selector is *h1* and there are five declarations in the declaration block: position, top, left, color, and font-family. In each declaration, the text to the left of the colon is the property (for example, position). The text to the right of the colon is the value (for example, absolute). CSS information can come from a variety of sources, which include the author (as discussed), the user (a local file controlled at the browser level, to override the author's styles), and the user agent (that is, the browser's default presentation of HTML elements).

The main advantages of using CSS are that presentation information for an entire site can be contained in one document, allowing swift and easy updating, different users can have different styles to serve their particular needs (large print, for example), HTML code is reduced in size and complexity, and it can be used with XML.

Browser support for CSS is increasing, but don't expect to see support in versions older than 4.0 of Internet Explorer and Netscape Communicator. If you implement style sheets for your design control, be aware that users whose browsers don't support CSS will be able to see the content, but not the styles, which the browser will ignore. This can affect the presentation of your content, so you may want to postpone using styles until you are certain that everyone in your audience uses a browser that can handle CSS. In 2005, there is good support for CSS1 by most current browsers. Support for CSS2.1 is best in standards-compliant browsers such as Opera, Mozilla, and Firefox. Some of these even provide partial support for CSS3.

Detailed information about cascading style sheets can be found on the W3C's Web site (http://www.w3.org/Style/CSS/).

Extensible Stylesheet Language (XSL)

An additional language for styling pages, XSL (Extensible Stylesheet Language) is used to describe how data from XML documents are presented to the user. XSL can be used only in conjunction with XML, and in fact is XML. However, CSS can be used with XML as well. This can be somewhat confusing to authors who are new to CSS and to XML/XST. Under which conditions should one be used over the other?

CSS is easier to learn and use. But because it is simple, it has limitations that XSL can handle. CSS is widely implemented but is only a formatting language. It attaches style properties to elements found in a source document. It cannot transform data from the source into human-readable format. It assumes that this process is handled by an external program. The power of XSL lies in its capability to transform XML data into HTML/CSS documents (known as XSLT, XSL Transformation)—such as ordering lists, replacing words, and replacing empty element with text. The W3C provides a helpful chart that outlines the basic attributes of each (see figure 5.15). For detailed information on XSL/XSLT visit the W3C Web site (http://www.w3.org/Style/XSL/).

FIGURE 5.15
When to Choose CSS or XSL

	CSS	XSL
Can it be used with HTML?	Yes	No
Can it be used with XML?	Yes	Yes
Transformation language?	No	Yes
Syntax	CSS	XML

From W3C. Copyright © 14 June 2004 World Wide Web Consortium (Massachusetts Institute of Technology, Institut National de Recherche en Informatique et en Automatique, Keio University). All Rights Reserved. http://www.w3.org/Consortium/Legal/. Available: http://www.w3.org/Style.

VISUAL DESIGN CONSIDERATIONS

Visual design involves the artistic or aesthetic considerations of designing a site. A visually appealing tutorial will attract more interest from your audience. Guidelines for designing a visually appealing site exist, of course, but because of the wide spectrum of tastes and creativity, they are open to a much more flexible interpretation than UID guidelines are. This section presents some of the main visual design elements to bear in mind when you are designing your tutorial.

Simplicity and Clarity

No matter what other choices you make, your final product should be characterized by visual simplicity. You have seen Web sites that are so cluttered that the intended message is lost; you want to avoid this at all costs. Your goal is to get the meaning of the instructional content across to your audience as clearly as possible. If users have to wade through excessive text, links, and graphics to find the main focus of the screen, the instruction won't be successful. Include only what needs to be there, and take out the rest.

White Space

The proper use of space can help achieve a simple, clear design. Known as white space, this is the open space on a page between design elements. In figure 5.16 white space works to emphasize the different visual elements on the page. In this tutorial, Research 101, the white space that separates the navigation, banner, and content helps users easily differentiate between the different components of the page. On a Web page, white space isn't necessarily white, of course, but whatever color or texture the background has been designated. Well-designed white space can help guide the users' eyes from one screen element to the next. The space helps define the different elements on the page by acting as a cushion between them. On a computer screen, white space also provides a rest area for our eyes. Reading from a computer screen is more visually demanding than reading from print, and white space provides us space to absorb what is on the page before proceeding further.

Color

Color is one of the most powerful visual elements that you will have in your design. It can be used to help your design in a variety of ways. Color can accentuate, highlight, and guide the eye to essential points or links; identify recurring themes or be used to differentiate between elements; and trigger feelings and associations.

People respond immediately to color, and the scheme you choose will set the mood for the tutorial. Color will elicit some sort of response even before users begin to read the content. You want to ensure that the colors you select will draw them into the learning experience.

FIGURE 5.16
Effective Use of White Space

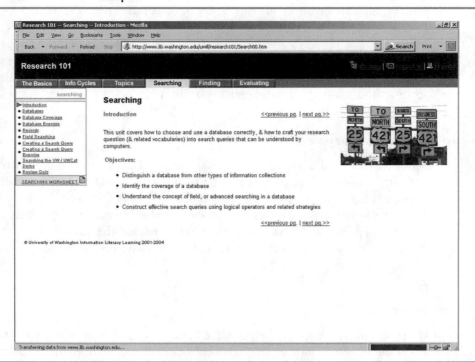

From University of Washington Libraries, Seattle. Available: http://www.lib.washington.edu/uwill/research101/index.html.

Color Symbolism

Because colors mean different things to various populations, it is important to consider your target audiences before you decide on the color palette for your tutorial. You should be cognizant of the different meanings of colors between cultures and of the various psychological responses that colors bring out. Figure 5.17 lists common color meanings and perceptions around the world.

Our response to color is strongly influenced by our cultural background. For example, the color green in the United States indicates both *go* (safe) at traffic lights and environmental awareness, but in some tropical countries is associated with danger. In Western cultures black is associated with death and mourning, but in Eastern cultures white is. In the United States white is associated with purity, but in India red is. Understanding these differences will ensure that your tutorial doesn't send the wrong message to diverse audiences on the basis of its color.

Color also evokes emotional responses (see figure 5.17). We are all familiar with the concept that red connotes warmth and that blue connotes cold. Red, orange, and yellow hues can induce excitement, aggressiveness, and stimulation. Blues and greens can suggest security and peace.

FIGURE 5.17
Color Meanings and Perceptions

COLOR	PSYCHOLOGICAL RESPONSE	NOTES OF INTEREST
Red	Power, energy, warmth, passions, love, aggression, danger, excitement, desire, speed, strength	Changes meaning in the presence of other colors: with green, it becomes a symbol of Christmas; when combined with white, it means joy in many Eastern cultures; in China it is a symbol of celebration and luck
Blue	Peace, tranquility, calm, harmony, cold, trust, conservatism, security, technology, cleanliness, order	Used in the United States by many banks to symbolize trust. It is often considered to be the safest global color
Green	Nature, health, good luck, jealously, envy, renewal, environment, fertility, spring	Doesn't do well globally: problems are associated with green packaging in China and France
Yellow	Joy, happiness, imagination, hazard, illness, optimism, hope, philosophy, dishonesty, cowardice, betrayal	A sacred color to Hindus
Purple	Spirituality, mystery, royalty, transformation, cruelty, arrogance, mourning, wisdom, enlightenment	Appears very rarely in nature
Orange	Vibrancy, flamboyance, energy, balance, warmth	Signifies an inexpensive product
Brown	Simplicity, earth, reliability, comfort, endurance	Food packaging in the United States is often colored brown with success; in Colombia, brown discourages sales
Gray	Intelligence, futurism, modesty, sadness, decay, staidness, maturity, conservative	The easiest color for the eye to see
White	Purity, cleanliness, precision, innocence, sterility, death, youth, simplicity	Signifies marriage in the United States, but death in India and other Eastern cultures
Black	Wealth, formality, evil, anger, remorse, power, sexuality, sophistication, death, mystery, fear, unhappiness, elegance	Signifies death and mourning in many Western cultures; in marketing, conveys elegance, wealth, and sophistication

Combining Colors

The combination of colors you choose can also have an effect on your audience. Some colors complement each other, others contrast. The use of a complementary color scheme may create a mood very different from a contrasting scheme. Deciding on the most effective color scheme is a process that can be a career in itself. However, many resources on the Web can teach you the basics of color theory so that creating an effective color scheme doesn't become an overwhelming task.

If you are like many people, you last studied color in elementary or high school. Before you start to work out your color scheme, you should reacquaint yourself with some color basics. One Web site you can visit to read about basic color theory is Worqx (http://www.worqx.com/color/).

There are three primary colors on the color wheel: red, yellow, and blue. When you combine two of the primary colors, your result is a secondary color: violet (a combination of red and blue), green (blue and yellow), or orange (red and yellow). A primary color combined with an adjacent secondary color produces an intermediate color: red orange, red violet, blue violet, blue green, yellow green, and yellow orange. These make up a basic twelve-color wheel (see figure 5.18). To complete the picture, include the neutral shades: white, black, and gray. White reflects all light and black absorbs all light. Gray is an impure white.

With just these twelve hues and the three neutral ones, you have an almost unlimited choice of colors. This is possible with variations to the basic group of tint, shade, tone, value, and intensity:

Hue is color with no black, white, or gray added.

Tint is a hue plus white.

Shade is a hue plus black.

Tone is a hue plus gray or a hue plus a complementary color.

Value is how light or dark a color appears.

Intensity is how bright or dull it appears.

Figure 5.18 also shows a few proven approaches to take when deciding on a color scheme:

Monochromatic is a scheme that uses one color in combination with some of its tints, tones, and shades.

A *complementary* color scheme is one that begins by using two colors that are opposite each other on the color wheel and then incorporates tints, shades, and so on, to finalize the colors.

A *triadic* color scheme is made up of three colors that are selected by drawing an equilateral triangle within the color wheel.

An *analogous* scheme uses two or more colors side by side on the color wheel.

For those who might be challenged when it comes to selecting colors, utilities are available to help choose a harmonious color scheme for a Web site. One is Color Wheel Pro (figure 5.19), which uses examples created in Flash that allow you to preview potential color schemes by rotating a color wheel. Once you find a scheme that

FIGURE 5.18
Color Wheel and Color Schemes

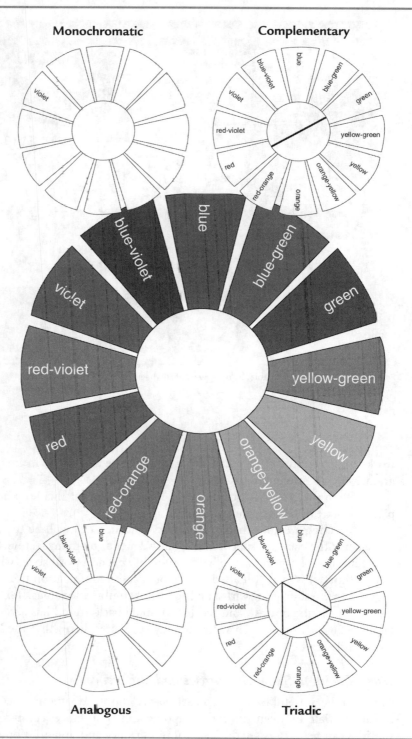

Monochromatic

Complementary

Analogous

Triadic

FIGURE 5.19
Utility to Aid Color Scheme Creation

From Color Wheel Pro. Available: http://www.color-wheel-pro.com.

works for your project, you can export the palette and use it in image editing programs, such as Adobe Photoshop.

Refer to the resources section on color at the end of this book for several good places to start or renew your color education.

In selecting a color scheme, a primary consideration will be the legibility of the text against the background color. Legibility depends on many factors, but color is one of the important aspects, along with font, font size, and word style (which will be discussed shortly). When you are deciding on a color combination to increase readability, you are safest in going with a high-contrast combination. Black text on white background has high contrast, and red text on blue background has a very low contrast. Figure 5.20 illustrates (even with the gray scale used here) that the high contrast is more easily read.

Using Colors to Show Similarities and Differences

Color can be a useful tool to help users see relationships among screen elements and to differentiate between tutorial components. For instance, color-coding titles and subtitles can help users see the levels of importance and organization of information.

FIGURE 5.20
High and Low Color Contrasts and Legibility

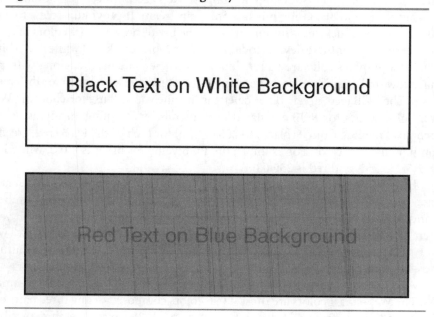

Navigation systems can also be enhanced with the proper use of color. The key to using color coding effectively is to use these visual clues consistently throughout the site. A cautionary note, however: don't rely strictly on color for providing visual clues. You may have users who are color blind or have other visual impairments that make color coding useless to them!

Browser-Safe Colors

In the early years of Web design, the issue of how to ensure colors displayed consistently across all types of monitors was a big one. Color capability among monitors varied; most only had 8-bit video cards that would display 256 colors. There were obvious display inconsistencies between Macintosh and PCs. (For more discussion on monitor color capabilities, refer to chapter 4.)

To address this problem, a 216-color palette was developed using colors that appeared to display the same across platforms and in all browsers. Why were only 216 used instead of 256? The forty colors that were discarded were those that varied on Macs and PCs. But by restricting the number of colors to 216, designers were able to be certain that colors would not dither. Dithering is the attempt by a computer program to approximate a color from a mixture of other colors when the required color is not available.

Monitors today typically support millions of colors, so the need to use the browser-safe palette has diminished. If you know your users are using up-to-date computer systems, don't be as concerned about the issue.

Development of Web pages for other form factors than computers is still in its infancy. However, the technology to support Web access to cell phones and PDAs is moving along and becoming much more mainstream. If providing access to your site on those types of devices is important, then the use of browser-safe colors may remain a concern. Most of these devices today are either 1-bit (black and white) or 8-bit color.

Most graphics software will include the browser-safe palette, along with palettes that allow millions of choices. There are different palettes developed for different purposes. The RGB (red, green, blue) palette is the one you will use for choosing Web colors. Color values for RGB are stated in numerals by assigning an intensity value to each pixel ranging from 0 (black) to 255 (white) for each of the RGB (red, green, blue) components in a color. For example, the RGB value for black is 0 0 0, white is stated as 255 255 255, and red is 255 0 0.

HTML uses hexadecimal numbers for color coding. Hexadecimal refers to the base-16 number system, which consists of sixteen unique symbols: the numbers 0 to 9 and the letters a to f. You will need to convert your colors from their RGB values to their hexadecimal values. A Google search for "RGB hexadecimal converter" will link you to an assortment of these tools (see, for example, http://page.mi.fu-berlin .de/~boethin/pub/coca/).

Another concept in managing color choices for the Web is that of Web-smart colors. The Web-smart colors are those 4,096 colors composed of any three pairs of identical hexadecimal digits (0–9 and a–f), such as #dd1188. To see the difference between browser-safe, Web-smart, and unsafe colors, visit the 4096 Color Wheel (http://www .ficml.org/jemimap/style/color/wheel21.html) (see figure 5.21). As you pass your cursor over the wheel, the hexadecimal value is displayed for all three choices. As is the case with browser-safe color palettes, need for Web-smart may be waning. But it is useful to be aware of the choices.

How Many Colors?

Although it may be tempting to include many colors, using too many can be distracting and overwhelming to users. You'll do best if you stick to Ben Shneiderman's guidelines, "use color conservatively" and "limit the number of colors."[6] Many design guides suggest limiting the number of colors to four. Like other visual-design guidelines, this is not set in stone, but is a good basis to work from.

Link Colors

The first hyperlinks were all blue that changed to purple once they had been visited. As the art of Web design evolved, many Web authors began to tie their link colors in with the overall color scheme of the site. Just a few years ago, some usability experts felt strongly that the only appropriate colors for links are the original blue and purple because these colors are recognized and understood by most Web surfers. There is little confusion by users on this point. If the link is blue, they haven't been there yet. If it is purple, they have.

However, this concern has lessened in the past few years. Users are becoming savvier about surfing the Web and know to look for colored, underlined text. Current usability guidelines for the use of color for links are updated to recommend

FIGURE 5.21
Color Selection Utility for Web Colors

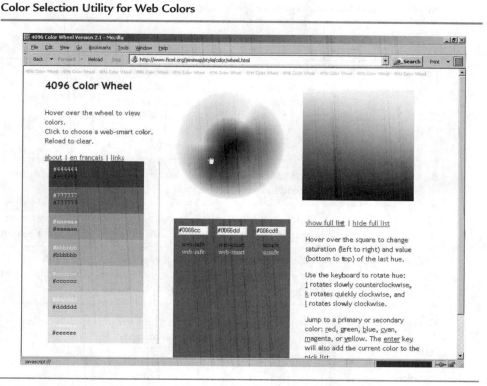

From Jemima's Chevron. Available: http://www.ficml.org/jemimap/style/color/wheel.html.

that different colors may be used for links but that visited and unvisited links should remain different. "Colors for unvisited links should be more vivid, bright, and saturated than that for visited links, which should look 'used' (dull and washed out)."[7]

Highlighting

Highlighting refers to various methods used to make critical information prominent to users. In Web design, colors or patterns are often used to bring attention to text or objects, but they are not the only way to highlight information. Figure 5.22 shows several highlighting techniques that you may consider and lists their advantages and disadvantages. It's important to use highlighting judiciously. You want to use highlighting to bring something to the user's attention but not overpower other objects on the page. One highlighting possibility that CSS2 has made feasible is the ability to designate a background color behind an element in the page.

Backgrounds

Page backgrounds are used to create a mood for the site. A background should contribute to the purpose of the site and enhance the content. Be conscious that it can have a positive or negative effect based on how it is designed and used.

FIGURE 5.22
Advantages and Disadvantages to Highlighting Techniques

HIGHLIGHTING TECHNIQUE	ADVANTAGE	DISADVANTAGE	USE
Color coding	Shows relationships among screen elements	Some people have difficulty distinguishing colors. Use redundantly with another highlighting system	See section on color
Blinking	Gets users' attention	Distracting, illegible, annoying	Don't use
All uppercase characters	Easily recognized as a headline	Not as easy to read as mixed case	Table labels and some headings
Underlining	Along with color, an indication of a hyperlink	On a Web page, underlining means a hyperlink	Only in conjunction with a hyperlink
Oversized characters	Gets attention easily	Takes up a great deal of screen space	Headings
Center and right alignment	Gets attention quickly	Difficult to read long blocks of text	Headings and accents

Backgrounds can be either a color or an image. If you decide to specify a color as your page background, select it using the color issues discussed earlier in this chapter.

If an image is your preference, there are some additional considerations to think about. A background image is a .gif or .jpg file (see chapter 6) that is tiled across and down the screen by default. Because of this, you should consider the following factors:

File size. Keep the file size small because the browser will have to download it to display the image. Think in terms of pixels. A background image that is 50 pixels by 50 pixels will be small enough to download efficiently at most connection speeds.

Pattern. Select a pattern that will tile seamlessly horizontally or vertically so that it seems to be one continuous pattern.

Readability. Choose a subtle pattern that won't interfere with the readability of the content.

Image dimensions. Try not to use one large image as your background. Since backgrounds tile, if you design your image to display on an 800 × 600 screen, it will tile on a large screen and not be viewable in its entirety at a smaller resolution. An image of that size will also be very large.

If you are using style sheets (and you should!), CSS2 includes a specification that increases the ways you can use backgrounds. Instead of an image automatically tiling across and down the page, CSS2 allows an author to specify whether the image should repeat or not, or tile horizontally or vertically for one row, and it allows placement and positioning of a single image on the page. Here are the values for repeating and their meanings:

repeat: horizontally and vertically.

repeat-x: horizontally only.

repeat-y: vertically only.

no-repeat: only one copy of the image is displayed.

Value statements for positioning an image on the page are similar and can be seen on the W3C site (http://www.w3.org/TR/CSS21/colors.html#q2).

Figure 5.23 shows four implementations of a single image using background specifications in CSS2. On each screen, in addition to the image, the coding that would reside in the style sheet is displayed here to show its syntax. With a single image (see lower left screen), variations in coding (shown on each screen) enable an author great flexibility in composing a background to create the best feel for the page.

FIGURE 5.23
New Background Capabilities Using Cascading Style Sheets

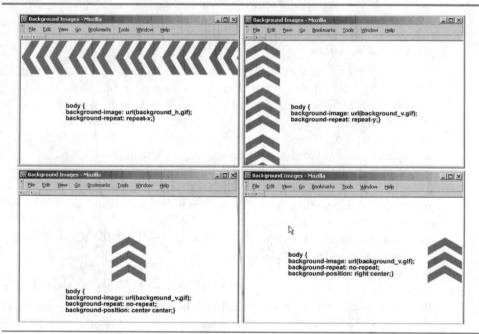

Linking

As HTML coding sophistication has evolved, choices on how to show hyperlinks have expanded. In the early days it was straightforward—if you saw a blue, underlined block of text, you knew that that was the place to click to be taken to a different location. Now, however, links can be displayed a variety of ways. Links are shown in all the colors of the rainbow, in different fonts, and often are not underlined. Users have also become more sophisticated. Nielsen compiled a list of usability guidelines for showing textual links:[8]

> To maximize the perceived affordance of clickability, color and underline the link text.
>
> If link text is colored, underlining is not always necessary. Two examples are navigation menus and other lists of links. Green and red can cause problems for color-blind users.
>
> Don't underline any text that isn't a link.
>
> Use different colors for visited and unvisited links.
>
> Never show text in your chosen link colors unless it's a link.
>
> Don't use tiny text for links and don't place links too close together. This causes usability problems for older users

Typography

Type has always been an important component of graphic design because it contributes greatly to setting the tone or mood of a design. However, it has typically been a frustrating experience to effectively control type on a Web page. The following subsections discuss typography on the Web and some of the issues you will encounter. Let's start by reviewing some of the common terms you will hear.

Fonts and Typefaces

You will see the terms font and typeface used interchangeably many places. They really have different definitions, and it helps to understand these. A font is a complete set of characters in a particular style and size. Times New Roman in 12 point is a font. A typeface contains a series of fonts. An example of a typeface would be Times New Roman in 8-point, 10-point, 12-point, and so forth. Additionally, within each typeface there can be many variations, such as normal, italic, and bold.

You should be aware that type sizes aren't standard: a point size in one typeface is not necessarily the same dimension as the same point size in another typeface. Figure 5.24 shows that different typefaces of the same point size are not actually the same size. This is because the point size is the distance between the bottom of the lowest

FIGURE 5.24
Comparison of Typefaces at Same Point Size

This is 14-point Arial.
This is 14-point Futura Light.
This is 14-point Verdana.
This is 14-point Times New Roman.
This is 14-point Garamond.

descender (for example, *j* or *y*) to the top of the highest ascender (for example, *l*, *d*, or a capital letter) with a little bit added on. This ensures the prevention of lines of type touching each other when set with no additional space.

Typeface Categories

There are four categories of typefaces:

> *Serif.* These have little strokes that decorate the letters. Times (Times) and Garamond (Garamond) are examples of serif typefaces, a more formal style of type. Serifs are helpful in providing a visual barrier to the tops and bottoms of letters, creating a horizontal emphasis that moves the eye as it travels along the line of text. For this reason, many feel that a serif typeface is the most readable.
>
> *Sans Serif.* These letterforms have no strokes and are more contemporary in style. Popular sans serif typefaces are Helvetica (**Helvetica**) and Avant Garde (Avant Garde). Some experts believe that a sans serif typeface is easier to read on a computer screen than a serif. Because of the low resolution on many computer screens, there aren't enough pixels to give the detailed definition to the serifs on each letter form.
>
> *Monospace.* In monospace typefaces, each letter takes up the same amount of space, similar to the old typewriter fonts. In other words, an *i* is as wide as an *r*. An example of a monospace typeface is Courier (`Courier`).
>
> *Decorative.* This category includes just about everything that doesn't fit into the other categories. Decorative type can evoke a wide range of moods and works best for titles and other accent text. These typefaces shouldn't be used in body text because they are often more difficult to read. Zapf Chancery (*Zapf Chancery*) and Bauhaus Bold (**Bauhaus Bold**) are good examples of decorative type.

Combining Typefaces

A combination of typefaces makes a more appealing visual design, but just as with color, it's not a good idea to overdo it. Pick two typefaces, one serif and one sans serif, to use. If you use the serif for your body text, then select a sans serif for the headings. And if you decide on a sans serif for your text, use a serif for its companion. Using two different serifs or two different sans serifs tends to look careless and indistinctive.

Text Alignment

Text should be left aligned because it is easier to read. This doesn't mean that center and right alignment shouldn't be used, but they should be reserved to accent and highlight.

Text Case

Mixed uppercase and lowercase letters are much easier to read than are all capital letters. According to Nielsen, it takes readers 10 percent longer to read a block of text that is in all capitals.[9]

Text on the Web

When text is transported from the printed page to a computer screen and the Web, challenges arise. What holds true in print isn't necessarily so on a screen display. How to handle text on the Web also depends on whether your users have the latest versions of the browsers they use. If they do, you will want to turn to cascading style sheets to control your text. If they have browsers that don't support CSS, then some of the following solutions may be helpful.

Font Sizing   Controlling font size on Web pages has always been a challenge. Originally, font sizes were specified using 0 to 7. If no font size is specified, the default size was 3. The browser developers decided what point size 3 equaled. As of version 4.01 HTML specifications, these controls have been deprecated, meaning that they have been outdated by newer concepts and have steadily become obsolete. For now, they are still interpreted, but the use of controls through CSS is being recommended. Cascading style sheet specifications for fonts are accomplished through setting a series of font properties that include family (for example, Helvetica, sans serif), style (for example, normal or italic), variant (for example, normal, small caps), weight (for example, normal, bold, bolder, lighter), stretch (for example, normal, wide, narrower), and size (for example, small, medium, or large).

In regard to size, there is still plenty of room for author confusion. Figure 5.25 shows the most common different units of measurements used in CSS2. Some are absolute, meaning they can't be adjusted by the user (through the browser). This may be an attractive option to some designers who want to guarantee their pages display exactly as designed. Others are relative, meaning that they are scaled based on the font-size preference set in the user's browser. It is preferable to use a relative size to increase accessibility to users of your site; also relative units scale better from one medium to another (screen to printer). Most savvy designers who want accessible sites use either the "em" or "%" measurement.

For detailed information on CSS2 specifications for fonts, visit the W3C Web site (http://www.w3.org/TR/REC-CSS2/fonts.html#font-specification). If you find this a bit more technical than you like, a helpful resource you might visit is the Wiki css-discussion list (http://css-discuss.incutio.com/?page=UsingFontSize).

Browsers and Fonts   Older browsers don't interpret instructions about which font to display. If a browser can't interpret the instruction, it will display the default font for the browser. For most browsers this is Times Roman (Times on a Macintosh) at a 12-point size. The HTML <font face> attribute was developed several browser versions ago to give designers some control over what font is displayed to the audience. By tagging text with

<font face="Arial, Helvetica, sans serif">

Text Here

</font>

the author could tell the browser to display in Arial, or in its absence, to look for and display in Helvetica. If neither of those is installed, the browser is instructed to use any available sans serif font. This attribute was just an interim solution, however, and has

FIGURE 5.25
Common Font-Sizing Options in CSS2

UNIT	DESCRIPTION	TYPE	NOTES	EXAMPLE

em	Unit of measurement equal to the current type size	Relative	1 em in 10-point type is equal to 10 points. When used in conjunction with percentage base sizing set in the body style, works well
			
			Relative to a parent element
				p {
				font-size: 1.2em;
				}

px	Stands for pixels. Defines a measurement in screen pixels	Absolute	Consistency across browsers, but ignores user preferences	p {
				font-size: 18px;
				}

%	A percentage relative to another value	Relative	Based on the size of a parent element	p {
				font size: 70%
				}

pt	Point. A point is 1/72nd of an inch	Absolute	Good for print style sheets, can be inconsistent on different browsers and ignores user preferences	p {
				font-size: 12pt;
				}

pc	Pica. Equivalent to 12 points; 6 picas = 1 inch	Absolute	Standard unit for print publishing	p {
				font-size: 10pc;
				}

keyword	Includes xx-small, x-small, small, medium, large, x-large, xx-large	Relative	Are relative to users' preferred "medium" settings in their browsers
			
			Limited choices, only 7 sizes
				p {
				font-size: x-small;
				}

been deprecated. As you might expect, CSS is the preferred recommended method for specification of font family. The property used to specify fonts in CSS is font-family. A declaration would look like this: *h2 {font-family: Verdana, Helvetica, Arial, sans-serif;}*.

User-Controlled Font Display No matter what text typeface you decide to use, most browsers allow users to override your choice and select their own font style and size. This may not be what you had in mind, but it is an important bit of user control that allows your audience to get to your content using their browser's preferences.

Font Availability Whatever font you designate, if that font is not installed on the user's computer, it will not appear. For this reason, it is wise to use fonts commonly found on most computers. Common Windows fonts are Arial, Verdana, Helvetica, Times New Roman, Georgia, Courier New, and Comic Sans. Common Mac fonts include Arial, Geneva, Helvetica, Chicago, and Times. Because you have no way of being sure what fonts are on users' computers, you should always specify more than one font when coding using {font-family:} in your stylesheet. If your first choice of font is one found commonly on one platform but not the other, then make sure your second choice is a font commonly found on the opposite platform. The final choice should always be either of the generic font designations, serif or sans serif, so you give the browser some indication of the kind of font you want displayed.

Platform Display Differences Text is rendered 33 percent larger on a Windows computer than on a Macintosh. The Mac OS uses 18 pixels to render 18-point text, and Windows uses 24 pixels. This is because Macintosh assumes a display at a resolution of 72 dpi, but Windows assumes 96 dpi. The result is that the same size text will appear much smaller on a Mac than on a PC.

Text and Screen Resolution It should come as no surprise that screen resolution affects text size appearance. When you are selecting a typeface size, test it at different resolutions. What is legible on a 640 × 480 screen may be more difficult to read at a higher resolution. The first display in figure 5.26 shows the text at a 1024 × 768 resolution. The second display is 800 × 600.

FIGURE 5.26
Comparison of Resolution and Text Size

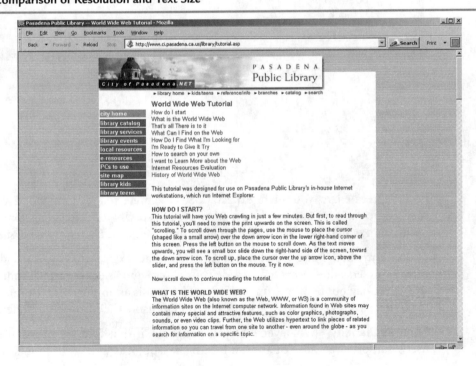

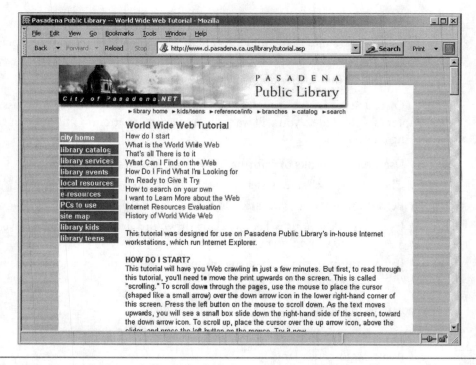

From Pasadena Public Library, California. Available: http://www.ci.pasadena.ca.us/library/tutorial.asp.

Images as Text

Because of the limitations of rendering typefaces on the Web, Web designers often turn to graphics to guarantee that the style of type they have chosen displays exactly as intended. By creating a text graphic, you can introduce more personality into your design. However, the downside to this solution is that your audience will experience a longer download time to display the graphics (see chapter 6 for a detailed discussion). If you decide to use graphics for some of your text, be sure to include the ALT attribute so that the text is accessible to those who turn off graphics or are visually impaired.

MULTINATIONAL AUDIENCE DESIGN CONSIDERATIONS

As it becomes more common to see cases where students for a specific online class can be located in highly dispersed locales, including different countries, there are issues that should be addressed to ensure a good learning experience to all. It is best to take a global approach to instructional design. Loring provides a useful checklist of issues to consider:[10]

languages used by your targeted audience

hardware, software, and infrastructure available

cultural variables that could affect instruction (political, economic, social, religious)

the role of the teacher and expected instructor/student interaction

Of course, although using the design guidelines that have been discussed in this chapter is a good idea, you will want to pay particular attention to some of the details Loring cites:[11]

Use smaller chunks of information in each screen's presentation.

Choose color schemes wisely (see the discussion on color earlier in this chapter).

Be certain the sounds you use don't have meanings other than what you intend.

Use images cautiously. People, their dress and even animals can have different meanings in different cultures.

Pay attention to the sequencing of images used to depict a concept as some languages read right to left.

When working with text

Use short concise sentences.

Avoid jargon and slang.

Position words correctly to accommodate right to left and vertically read languages.

Leave room in tables and graphics for translations. The space taken is different depending on the language.

Be aware of expressions that have a distinct meaning when put in a certain order.

USER ACCESSIBILITY

An integral part of your tutorial's design should address ensuring that it meets standards for access by disabled users. Unfortunately, as the Web has become more graphical and multimedia laden, it has become less accessible to those who have visual, auditory, motor, and cognitive impairments. If you are mindful of this need as you plan your project, it really isn't hard to design an accessible site. As part of its Web Accessibility Initiative Standard, the W3C has compiled its Web Content Accessibility Guidelines 1.0 (http://www.w3.org/TR/WCAG10/).[12] To make content more available to all users, the consortium developed fourteen guidelines with sixty-six checkpoints that have each been assigned one of three priority levels. Those that have been assigned a priority 1 level are considered to be essential for accessibility to a document. As you begin the construction of your tutorial, it will be valuable for you to visit the preceding link and become familiar with this guide. The fourteen guidelines follow:

Provide equivalent alternatives to auditory and visual content. Provide a text equivalent for every nontext element, including images, graphical representations of text, image-map regions, animations, applets, ASCII art, frames, scripts,

FIGURE 5.27
Providing Text Alternative to Audio and Visual Content

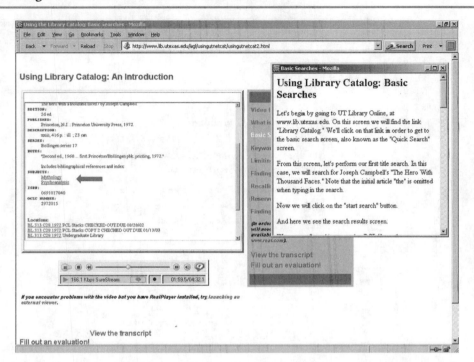

From University of Texas Libraries. Used by permission of the University of Texas Libraries, the University of Texas at Austin. Available: http://www.lib.utexas.edu/ugl/usingutnetcat/usingutnetcat1.html.

sounds, audio files, and video. Figure 5.27 illustrates a tutorial that provides a transcription to accompany a real media video. Doing such things as using ALT attributes for all graphics and image maps and providing transcripts for video clips make the content available through assistive devices such as screen readers or talking Web browsers. Providing nontext equivalents of text can also be beneficial to some users.

Don't rely on color alone. Ensure that text and graphics are understandable when viewed without color. Approximately 5 percent of Web users experience some degree of color blindness. Many have problems distinguishing shades of color. If your site depends on color solely to provide visual clues or uses low-contrast colors, it may be inaccessible to many users. To test your site for color accessibility (see figure 5.28), try Vischeck (http://www.vischeck.com/vischeck/vischeckURL.php).

Use markup and style sheets, and do so properly. Using markup incorrectly hinders accessibility. This usually refers to using markup for presentation effects such as font size or layout tables.

FIGURE 5.28
Tool to Check Color Blindness Accessibility for Web Pages

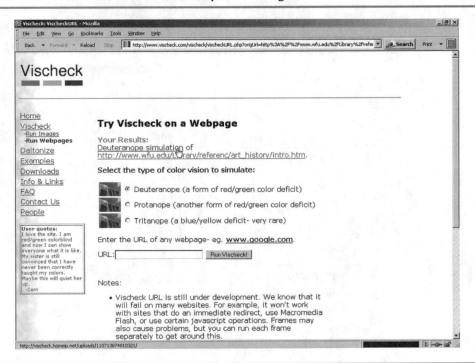

From Vischeck. Available: http://www.vischeck.com/vischeck/vischeckURL.php.

Clarify natural language usage. Use markup that facilitates pronunciation or interpretation of abbreviated or foreign text. Identifying this helps devices switch to the new language. For example, when using a word containing a diacritical mark, use the proper markup to display it rather than pasting the symbol into the document from a word processing document (that is, the proper markup to display ê is ê).

Create tables that transform gracefully. Tables should be used to mark up tabular information and should have their row and column headers labeled correctly. Using tables for layout makes it hard for users with assistive tools to navigate through the page. If you are going to use tables for layout, provide an alternate version.

Ensure that pages featuring new technologies transform gracefully. If using newer technologies that may not be supported by all browsers, alternative methods should be included so that the page still works.

Ensure user control of time-sensitive content changes. Some disabilities prevent users from reading moving or scrolling text. Make sure these can be paused or stopped.

Ensure direct accessibility of embedded user interfaces. Elements that are embedded into an HTML page should be directly accessible or compatible with assistive technologies.

Design for device-independence. Users should be able to interact with their preferred input device, whether it is by mouse, voice, or keyboard.

Use interim solutions. Some older assistive technologies and browsers do not interpret page elements correctly. Some elements that cause difficulty are pop-up windows, tables, forms, and adjacent links. Until these can be handled by newer technologies, consider avoiding their use or provide alternative versions.

Use W3C technologies and guidelines. Many non-W3C formats (such as Shockwave or PDF [Portable Document Format]) require viewing via a plug-in or stand-alone application. Some assistive technologies can't view or navigate through these.

Provide context and orientation information. Group different page elements, and provide contextual information. This guideline applies to frames in particular. Be certain to title each frame to help users navigate.

Provide clear navigation mechanisms. Navigation should be clear and consistent. Incorporate site maps and tables of contents. Make text links meaningful.

Ensure that documents are clear and simple. The key to this is consistent page layout, easy-to-understand language, and identifiable graphics with text alternatives.

In November 2004 the W3C published a working draft of Web Content Accessibility Guidelines 2.0 that is designed to build on the version 1.0. It has the same aim as the original document but attempts to apply the guidelines to a wider range of technologies and use a language that can be better understood by a more varied audience.[13] Because, at the time of this writing, it is only in draft form, the guidelines above should continue to serve until it is further developed (see http://www.w3.org/TR/WCAG20/).

The W3C also has compiled a page of links to tools that can be used to evaluate, repair, and transform pages to meet accessibility rules (see http://www.w3.org/WAI/ER/existingtools.html).

PAGE OPTIMIZATION

An important part of your students' experience with your tutorial is whether the pages load quickly. Users become impatient if they have to wait several seconds for a page to display. Slow-loading pages hinder the focus on the learning that is, after all, your main goal. Graphics can be one of the biggest hindrances to quick-loading pages. Solutions will be discussed in more detail in the next chapter. You should be aware, however, that there are other things that can slow down a page display. Even extra spacing can contribute to a bloated page. Ways to reduce this slowness include page optimization, the process of minimizing HTML file size to maximize page-display speed.

Visual-Based Web Editors

As discussed in chapter 4, visual-based (WYSIWYG) Web editors are more user friendly than code-based ones are. You don't need to know HTML to produce professional-looking Web pages. The down sides to this type of editor are that it does not always create code efficiently and often leaves unnecessary code behind during the editing process. WYSIWYG editors may be the biggest cause of code bloat.

Tables

You've read about some of the pros and cons of using tables in HTML. Unfortunately, tables slow down page display because browsers need to understand a table's structure before they can render tables on the screen. If you have used large or nested tables for layout, the page-download time can be seriously hindered. Optimally, make the switch to CSS2, and use its positioning power to get table-like layout at much greater speed. However, if you feel that tables work best for layout because your audience is running older browsers, try to use more and smaller tables instead of one larger one. Also, make sure you use the width attribute of the <table> and <td> tags properly. The widths defined in the <td> tag need to add up to equal what is specified in the <table> tag, or different browsers will interpret and display the code differently. A note of interest: WYSIWYG editors are notorious for bloating tables with inefficient code.

Optimization Tips

There's no reason you can't optimize manually if you are a code buff. Following are a few examples of some adjustments you can make by hand. These ideas and additional tips are available in Andrew King's book on Web optimization:[14]

Remove comments. Although they may be helpful to the author, they take time to download and are meaningless to the user of the page.

Simplify tables. (See above.)

Substitute style sheets for font tags. Designating style elements in one place in the head of the document or in a separate file can greatly reduce the size of the file.

Use attribute defaults where possible. (For example, the horizontal rule defaults to a width of 100 percent and align = center. If this is what you want to display, there's no need to specify it.)

Use named colors rather than hex, when shorter (for example, bgcolor = white rather than bgcolor = #ffffff).

Delete unnecessary characters—closing tags, spaces, returns, tabs, and quotes— within the tags in the code.

Optimization Tools

Some software programs are designed to automate the optimization process. Most work in a similar manner by removing excess spaces, tabs, quotes, unnecessary attributes, and so forth. Some provide you with a report of what changes were made and the percentage of file reduction.

An example of a Macintosh optimization program is VSE Web Site Turbo (http://vse-online.com/web-site-turbo/). A similar application for Windows is Web Page Analyzer (http://www.websiteoptimization.com), which also includes a free single page analyzer.

Notes

1. Donn C. Ritchie and Bob Hoffman, "Incorporating Instructional Design Principles with the World Wide Web," in *Web-Based Instruction*, ed. Badrul Huda Khan (Englewood Cliffs, NJ: Educational Technology Publications, 1997), 135–38.
2. Jakob Nielsen and John Morkes, "Concise, Scannable, and Objective: How to Write for the Web," *Useit.com*, http://www.useit.com/papers/webwriting/writing.html.
3. Ben Shneiderman and Catherine Plaisant, *Designing the User Interface: Strategies for Effective Human-Computer Interaction*, 4th ed. (Boston: Pearson/Addison Wesley, 2004), 74–75.
4. Jennifer Fleming, *Web Navigation : Designing the User Experience*, 1st ed. (Sebastopol, CA: O'Reilly, 1998).
5. Jakob Nielsen, *Designing Web Usability: A Guide to Simplicity* (Indianapolis, IN: New Riders, 2000), 85.
6. Shneiderman and Plaisant, 510–11.
7. Jakob Nielsen, "Guidelines for Visualizing Links," *Useit.com*, http://www.useit.com/alertbox/20040510.html.
8. Ibid.
9. Nielsen, *Designing Web Usability: A Guide to Simplicity*, 126.
10. Linda Loring, "Six Steps to Preparing Instruction for a Worldwide Audience," *Journal of Interactive Instruction Development* 14, no. 3 (2002).
11. Ibid.
12. Web Content Guidelines Working Group, "Web Content Accessibility Guidelines," *W3C*, http://www.w3.org/TR/WCAG10/.
13. Web Content Accessibility Guidelines Working Group, "Web Content Accessibility Guidelines 2.0," *W3C*, http://www.w3.org/TR/WCAG20/.
14. Andrew B. King, *Speed Up Your Site: Web Site Optimization* (Indianapolis, IN: New Riders, 2003).

6

Multimedia: Using Graphics, Sound, Animation, and Video

Multimedia is the integration of text, graphics, sound, and video or animation in a computer-based environment. Because the Web is a multimedia environment, it is easy to envision incorporating multimedia into an instructional tutorial to enhance the learning experience. This chapter examines the various media and issues surrounding their use.

MULTIMEDIA AND INSTRUCTION

When you contemplate how and when to incorporate multimedia into online instruction, there are an assortment of considerations to be made. This section examines the benefits and limitations of multimedia, explores some of the appropriate uses of multimedia for instruction, and discusses multimedia issues that can influence its effective use.

Benefits and Limitations of Multimedia

Why is multimedia good to use in an online learning experience? Students have different learning preferences, and for that reason alone, offering information in more than one medium is beneficial. Many researchers have found advantages and disadvantages to using multimedia as a part of instruction.

Advantages

Allows representation of knowledge in a variety of ways. Students can read text to learn abstract principles and see practical application through an animation, for example.[1]

Addresses different learning styles and preferences. Multimedia provides opportunities for teaching individuals and incorporating their preferred learning styles.

Some students learn best through an auditory channel (lecture), while others learn best through visual channels. Multimedia can provide both.

Can provide a more active learning environment. Allows teachers to bring the real world to the learner through the combined use of two or more media such as sound, images, text, animation, and video.

Better learning and retention. Multimedia engages students and provides multiple learning methods.

Motivation. Studies show that learners consistently show positive attitudes toward multimedia (particularly interactive multimedia, which will be discussed in chapter 7).

Disadvantages

Equipment requirements. The hardware and software required for multimedia development may be a burden on organizations that are limited in their abilities to install and maintain them.

Start-up costs. The initial costs for resources to support multimedia development can be prohibitive.

Complexity and lack of standardization. Much multimedia today is still proprietary. It is often difficult to configure various components so that they can work together.

Mayer's Principles of Multimedia Design

Richard E. Mayer studied the effects of multimedia and technology in learning and concluded that multimedia can be both beneficial and harmful. His conclusion: while a little multimedia can be a good thing, too much can be a bad thing. On the positive side his research found that when certain kinds of materials are presented via multimedia, retention increases by an average of 23 percent; when text and graphics are combined, it goes up an average of 42 percent; and if a text of a presentation is spoken rather than read by the student, retention goes up an average of 30 percent. One of the most important findings involves the "transfer" of information, or the ability of students to integrate new information into their existing knowledge base and use the knowledge to generate new ideas and solve problems. In his study, students who were tested on this ability to transfer information presented multimedia style showed an 89 percent improvement in performance over traditional book-based methods. But, paradoxically, he also found that multimedia can be detrimental to learning in different scenarios. From the research, he developed principles for effective use of multimedia:[2]

Multimedia principle. Students learn better from words and pictures than solely from words.

Spatial contiguity principle. Students learn better when on-screen text and graphics are physically integrated. For instance, if a graphic is explained by a block of text, retention is increased if the text is integrated in the graphic rather than being located beside or below it.

Temporal contiguity principle. Students learn better when corresponding words and pictures are presented simultaneously.

Coherence principle. Students learn better when extraneous material is excluded from multimedia presentations. Learning is hurt with irrelevant words and pictures and with interesting but irrelevant sounds and music. Learning is improved when unneeded words are eliminated.

Modality principle. Students learn better from animation with narration than from animation with printed text.

Redundancy principle. Students learn better from animation and narration than from animation, narration, and on-screen text.

Individual differences principle. The previous multimedia principles have a greater impact on students with low prior knowledge and high spatial abilities.

Appropriateness

Multimedia can offer an enhanced learning experience, but only if it is used properly. It should be used only when it can contribute something to aid student learning; for instance, as discussed in the previous section. Using it just because it is "cool" is not a suitable reason. Some viable reasons for including multimedia are identified in the following sections.

Navigation

The importance of navigation was discussed in the previous chapter. Using images to build a navigation tool bar is a popular design approach. Images can serve to highlight the navigation scheme for the tutorial. Regular Web users are accustomed to looking for navigation icons and images that will direct them through a site.

The global navigation in the tutorial shown in figure 6.1 from the Cleveland State University Library incorporates image buttons. As the cursor passes over a navigation image, a second image with a starburst effect appears.

Establish a Theme or Mood

Students may become more engaged if the appropriate tone is set for a particular learning. Images, audio, or animation are all possible means to create just the right setting. The tutorial shown in figure 6.2, from DiMenna-Nyselius Library, Fairfield University, uses an imposing graphic of the entry to Plagiarism Court. Plagiarism is a serious issue in education today and this splash screen to their tutorial sets a solemn yet engaging tone for the instruction.

Identification

Including a library logo or some other identifying graphic helps ensure that students know the origin of the instruction. If someone comes into your tutorial at a point other than the starting page, having identification helps to orient him or her to the current location. As shown in figure 6.3, an identifying UCSD Libraries logo appears at the top of each screen. There's no doubt about the origin of this instruction. Note that the image links back to the main UCSD Web site.

FIGURE 6.1
Images Used for Navigation

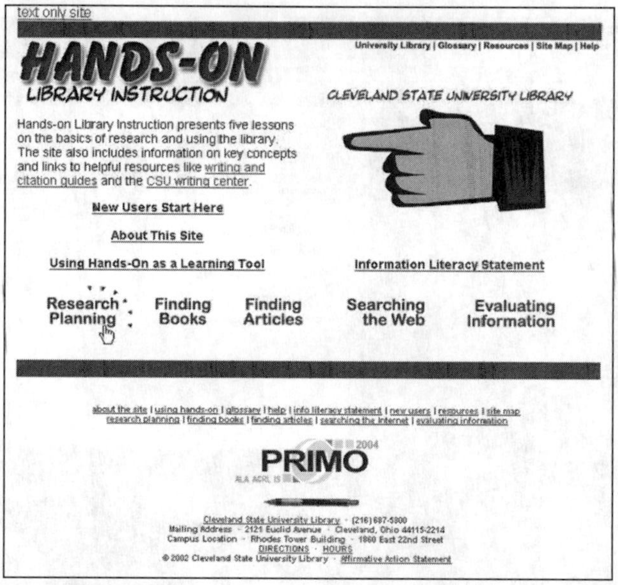

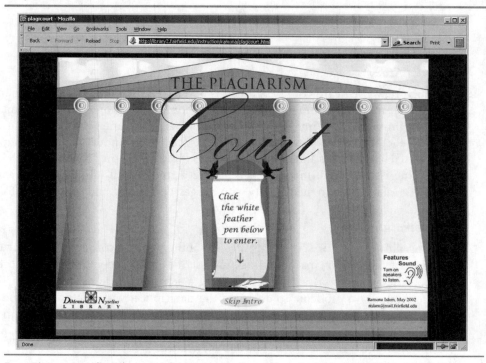

From Cleveland State University Library, Ohio. Available: http://www.ulib.csuohio.edu/help/hands-on.

FIGURE 6.2
Graphics Used to Set a Mood

From DiMenna-Nyselius Library, Fairfield University, Connecticut. Available: http://library2.fairfield.edu/instruction/ramona/plagicourt.html.

FIGURE 6.3
Logo Used for Identification

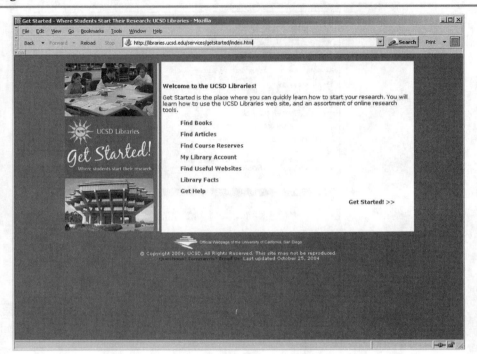

From UCSD Libraries, University of California, San Diego. Available: http://libraries.ucsd.edu/services/ getstarted/index.html.

Tell a Story

A picture, we've heard countless times, is worth a thousand words, and in many situations an image does in fact provide information much more effectively than words. One common use of images and illustrations is in conjunction with virtual library tours. Pictures of the different areas of the facility and floor maps help familiarize potential library users and give patrons a good way to become acquainted with how the building is organized. In figure 6.4, the German National Library of Medicine (ZB MED) orients users to their facility with images, floor plans, and a link to a QTVR tour.

Illustration

Using illustrations or screen captures is another way of conveying an instructional point effectively. For instance, you can describe what students should expect to see when they conduct a search, but showing a screen-capture image of what is being described allows students to associate the description with a representation of the screen they will see. The screen shown in figure 6.5 is instructing users how to output their results from an online catalog search. To better illustrate the options, a screen capture of the e-mail and save options is included.

FIGURE 6.4
Photos and Maps in Virtual Tour

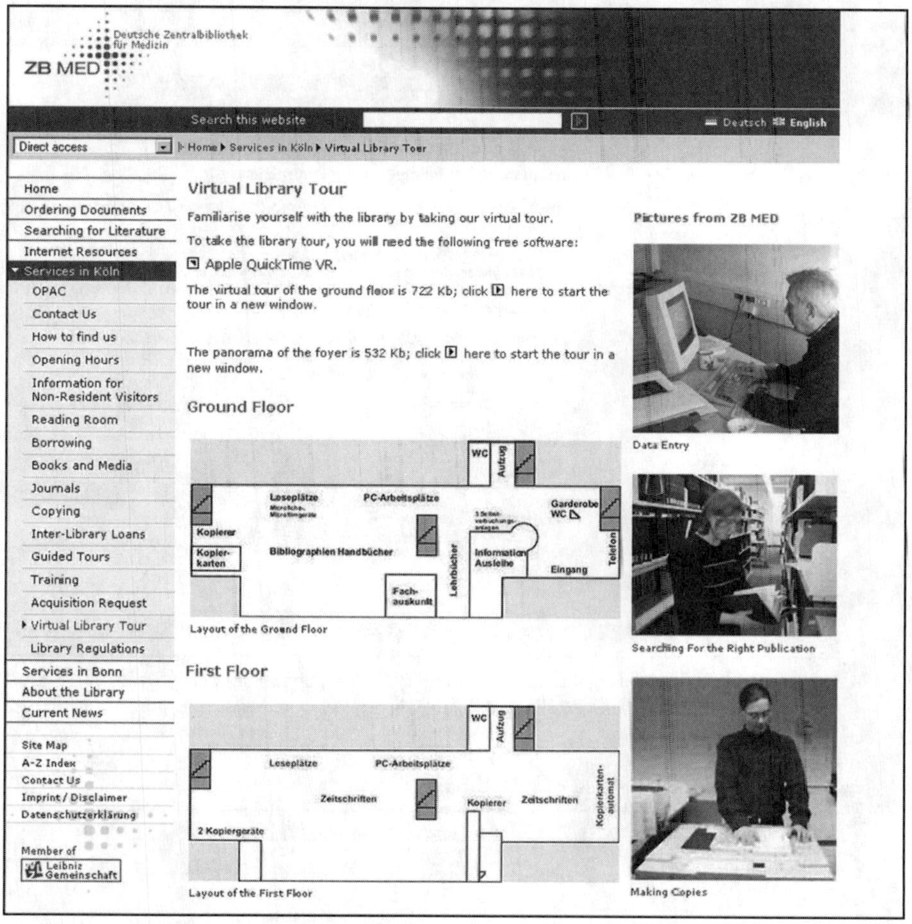

From German National Library of Medicine (ZB MED), Köln. Available: http://www.zbmed.de/koeln_rundgang.html?&lang=en.

Demonstration/Simulation

Often, the best way to get a concept across is through demonstration or simulation. One typical type of demonstration shows how to conduct searches using particular search software. In figure 6.6 students from University of Saskatchewan Library are guided through a demonstration of a search in InfoTrac. The tutorial is a series of screen captures transformed into a Flash presentation with accompanying highlights and explanation.

A more interactive approach is to set up a simulation where students are instructed to enter information and receive feedback as they successfully accomplish tasks. Figure 6.7 is a simulation of how to search WebSpirs using screen-capture images of the catalog and additional programming to deliver a level of reality to students.

FIGURE 6.5
Screen Capture to Illustrate Instructional Text

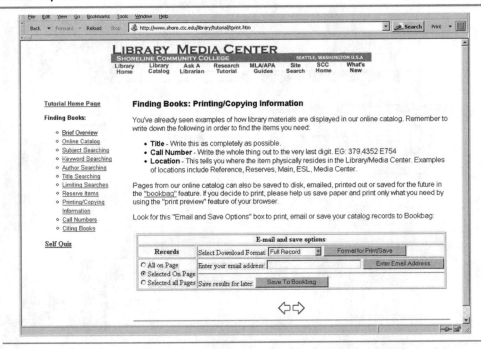

From Library Media Center, Shoreline Community College, Shoreline, Washington. © Library Media Center, Shoreline Community College. Available: http://www.shoreline.edu/library/tutorial/ttutorial.htm.

FIGURE 6.6
Demonstration of the Use of a Database

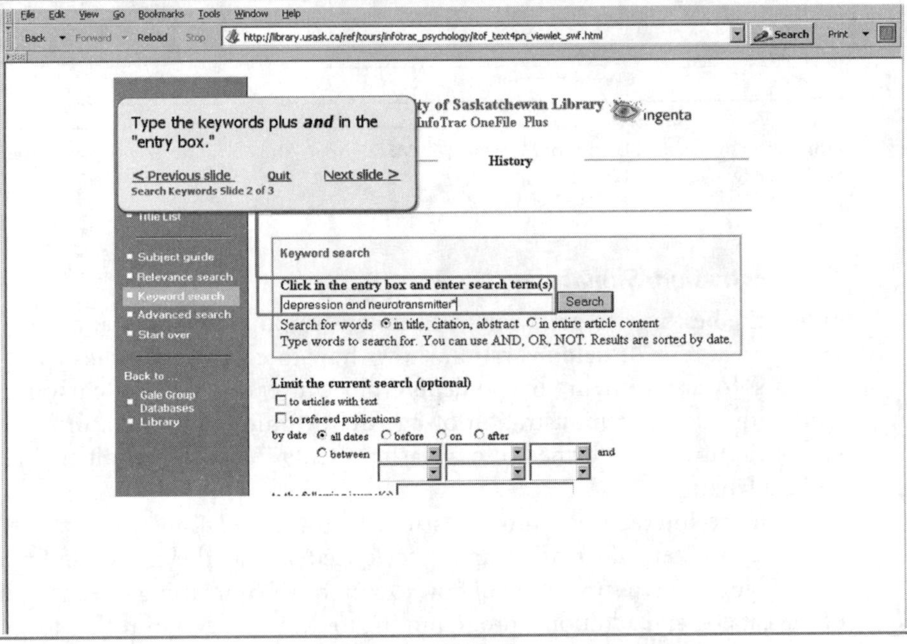

From University of Saskatchewan Library, Saskatoon, Saskatchewan. Available: http://library .usask.ca/ref/tours/infotrac_psychology/index.html.

FIGURE 6.7
Screen Capture Simulation of Database Search

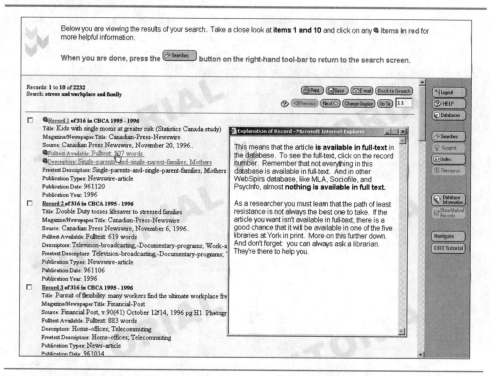

From York University Libraries, Toronto, Ontario. Available: http://info.library.yorku.ca/guides/webspirs/index.htm.

Visualization

Visualization is a way to help students grasp difficult concepts and ideas. By including graphics, charts, diagrams, animation, and even 3-D objects, designers can help students visualize to make content more understandable. One concept that students commonly have difficulty understanding is Boolean logic. Figure 6.8 shows how graphics can help students understand this idea. The image uses a Venn diagram to show the result set from the use of AND to connect two search terms.

Multimedia Considerations

As you are deciding on what types of multimedia to integrate into your tutorial, always keep your audience's best interests in mind. You will want to consider each of the following elements.

Bandwidth

Bandwidth is the amount of data that can be transmitted in a certain amount of time. Any type of multimedia requires additional bandwidth. Webmonkey's Adam Powell

FIGURE 6.8
Image Used for Visualization of Boolean Logic Concepts

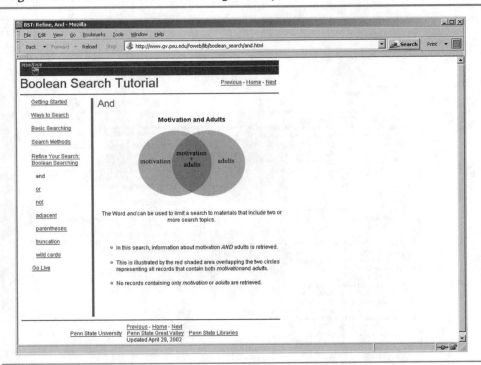

From Penn State Libraries, Penn State Great Valley, Malvern, Pennsylvania. Available:
http://www.gv.psu.edu/foweb/lib/boolean_search/start.html.

compares moving multimedia through the Internet to sucking a bowling ball through a garden hose.[3] Even when students have a good connection, non-streaming multimedia files have to be downloaded, and this takes time. Keep the size of multimedia files as compact as possible by using file compression. This will be discussed later in this chapter. If you are incorporating files of any size, communicate that to the user. It will help prevent the frustration of long download times.

Plug-ins

Plug-in applications are separate programs that are installed and run as part of your browser. Many of today's latest multimedia technologies require a plug-in so the media can be viewed or heard. Once installed, plug-ins permit multimedia to become integrated into the browser environment, but most people don't make the effort to download and install them until faced with the need to view a page that requires one. Be kind to your students. State at the beginning of the tutorial what plug-ins are required, and provide a link to their download sites.

Hardware and Software Requirements

It's worth mentioning again that your use of multimedia should not exceed your audience's capacity to access it. Before you invest a great deal of time and money in developing sophisticated multimedia elements, be certain your users have the hardware and software capabilities to play and view what you create. If you have a diverse user group, consider making a high-tech and a low-tech version of your instruction.

Accessibility

Incorporating multimedia into instruction presents a particular challenge in regard to accessibility to all potential users. By its nature, multimedia content can shut out users. Vision-impaired users can't see graphics or animations. They need a text alternative that can be spoken by a screen reader. Hearing-impaired users can't hear audio narration. They need a visual alternative to audible materials. Audio clips should have text alternatives and video clips should be captioned. The bottom line is that you should provide multiple representations of your multimedia content to address the needs of users with disabilities.

As accessibility issues have come to the forefront in the past years, developers have started to address building accessibility functionality into their multimedia development tools, along with providing instruction on their Web sites. The Macromedia site is a good example (http://www.macromedia.com/macromedia/accessibility/). Included are instructions for building accessibility into Flash and Dreamweaver, along with information about accessibility issues in general, tools, case studies, and examples of accessible sites.

Investigate to determine the most effective way to make your multimedia instruction accessible to all your potential users, keeping in mind that text is the most widely accessible content there is!

TYPES OF MULTIMEDIA

The basic divisions between types of multimedia with which most of us are familiar include graphics, sound, animation, and video. However, in the world of computer multimedia, the lines of distinction often blur. For instance, animations can include text, sound, and video. Videos can include text, animation, and still images. As you explore the various types of multimedia, be on the lookout for formats that overlap other categories and have more than one function. You will also see several references to interactivity capabilities, which are discussed in greater depth in chapter 7.

Graphics or Images

When the Web was first popularized, the combination of text and images constituted multimedia on the Web. Now, however, images are almost a given on any particular Web page. Nevertheless, creating graphics for the Web is different from creating them for print. The following subsections examine some of the basics of computer imaging and how to work with Web graphics.

Raster (Bitmap) versus Vector Images

Computer graphics come in two different flavors: raster (also called bitmap) and vector. It is helpful to have some understanding of what each type is and to understand their differences and the benefits and drawbacks of each type.

Raster images are made up of small squares called pixels that are arranged in a grid. Each pixel is a tiny unit of color that comes together with the other pixels to form the images you see on your screen. When you create a raster image, you set the number of pixels that will be in the grid, and this determines the resolution, measured in dots or pixels per inch (dpi and ppi). When you view raster images at the size they were created, you will not see the pixels. However, if you zoom in on an image with a photo-editing application, the individual pixels appear (see figure 6.9).

Raster images are resolution dependent. If you increase the size of a raster image, the pixels are simply enlarged and the edges appear jagged. Computer screens typically display at 72 or 96 dpi. That is why an image scanned in at 300 dpi looks so large on a computer monitor. If you are creating a raster image that will be displayed only on a computer monitor (and is not intended for printing), there is no reason to create it any larger than 72 dpi.

Because they are created on a grid, raster images are rectangular in shape. Some raster formats support transparency, which designates some of the pixels to be invisible to the eye, giving the illusion of a nonrectangular shape. Transparency permits one color to be specified as see through. This capability allows the rectangular raster image to appear to be other shapes because it permits a Web page's background color to show through the transparent pixels. Because they are resolution dependent, it is difficult to

FIGURE 6.9
Zoom-in View of Raster Image Pixels

resize raster images without degrading the quality. Making the graphic smaller forces your imaging program to throw away pixels. Resizing the image to a larger size forces the program to create new pixels, and it will have to guess what new pixels to create.

Resizing is different from scaling. Scaling takes place when you adjust the image size by dragging the corners of it in a page-layout program. This does not permanently change the image, but it does change how it displays. If you enlarge an image via scaling, the result will be pixelated much as the example in figure 6.9. It's best to create raster images at the size you plan to use them. Since scanners and digital cameras both produce bitmap images, you can control size creation from the image-editing software. For a discussion of potential imaging programs, refer to chapter 4.

Vector images are made up of mathematically described objects. The objects can be lines, curves, and shapes and have attributes such as color, fill, and outline. Vector graphics are resolution independent: they are scalable and can be manipulated without losing qualities, illustrated by the arrow in figure 6.10 that has had its size reduced and enlarged. A font is an example of a vector object.

Unlike bitmap images, vector images are not restricted to a rectangular shape, so they are much more flexible when combining with other objects. One major advantage of vector images is that their file size is small because the file really represents an equation the operating system uses to re-create the object. Another advantage is the ease with which a vector image can be edited and resized. The major disadvantage is that they are not suitable for photo-quality images. They are best suited for line drawings. Vector images are normally created using illustration software such as Adobe Illustrator.

As you will discover in the next section, most graphics on the Web today are raster images. However, nearly all illustration programs include the capability to convert a vector image to a raster image so that it can be viewed on the Web. Just be certain that the image is sized correctly before converting it. For a summary of raster and vector features and file formats, refer to figure 6.11.

FIGURE 6.10
Vector Images

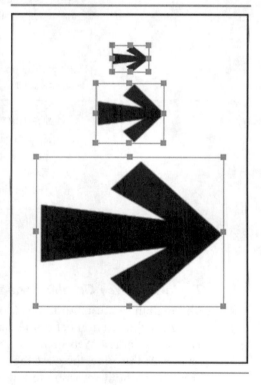

Metafiles

Metafile formats are those that contain both raster and vector data. They are vector overall but contain at least one object that is a bitmap.

FIGURE 6.11
Comparison of Raster and Vector Images

	RASTER (BITMAP) IMAGES	VECTOR IMAGES

Key points	Pixels in a grid
	Resolution dependent
	Resizing reduces quality
	Easily converted to other
	  bitmap formats
	Restricted to rectangle
	Minimal support for
	  transparency
		Mathematically described lines
		  and curves
		Resolution independent
		Scalable
		No background
		Cartoon-like
		Inappropriate for photorealistic
		  images

Common file formats	.bmp, Bitmap
	.gif, Graphics Interchange
	  Format
	.jpeg, jpg, Joint Photographic
	  Experts Group
	.png, Portable Network
	  Graphics
	.pict (Macintosh)
	.tiff, .tif, Tag Image Bitmap File
	.psd (Adobe Photoshop)
		.ai, Abobe Illustrator
		.cdr, CorelDRAW
		.cmx, Corel Exchange
		.cgm, Computer Graphic Metafile
		.dxf, Data Exchange Format
		  (Autocad)
		.svg (Scalable Vector Graphics)
		.wmf, Windows Metafile

SUPPORT FOR BOTH RASTER AND VECTOR
.eps (Encapsulated Postscript)
.pdf (Adobe Portable Document Format)
.fla (Flash)
.swf (Flash Movie)

Traditional Web Graphic Formats

Although there are a multitude of formats that can be used to create computer graphics, only a limited number of them are supported by browsers for display on the Web. The two standard Web image formats are GIF and JPEG, both of which are raster images. At this time, these are the only two image formats that can be displayed in all browsers without resorting to a plug-in. However, several newer formats have been developed for use on the Web. Their level of support and potential is discussed later in this chapter.

GIF (.gif)   The Graphics Interchange Format (GIF, pronounced "jif") was defined in the late 1980s by CompuServe. It incorporates a compression scheme that keeps file sizes at minimum with no loss of data (lossless compression) while preserving sharp detail. The compression used is LZW (which stands for its inventors Lempel, Zev, and Welch), a scheme that efficiently compresses large fields of homogeneous color. GIF files have a palette limited to 256 colors (8 bits). There are two GIF standards: the initial version, 87a, and 89a, which supports transparency. The GIF format also supports interlaced images; every eighth row in an image is displayed, then every fourth, then every second. This allows users to view emerging images as they are being downloaded to their computers, a particularly attractive technique if your audience includes those who use modems to access your tutorial.

GIFs are most useful for images that have a limited number of colors or large areas of solid colors, as with line art and cartoons. This format works nicely with logos and illustrations with type. Vector images convert well to GIF because of its lossless compression and ability to support transparency. You can also use the GIF format to create animated images, which will be discussed shortly.

JPEG (.jpeg, .jpg)   JPEG (pronounced "JAY-peg") is an acronym for Joint Photographic Experts Group, the committee that developed the standard in the late 1980s and early 1990s. The JPEG image format is designed to compress full-color or grayscale realistic images. The JPEG format supports 24-bit color, or more than 16 million colors. Because it provides significantly more image information than a GIF format (with its 256-color limit) does, JPEG is better suited for photographs and scanned artwork. It is, however, a lossy compression, meaning that some data is discarded during the compression process. This loss may or may not be discernible to the naked eye, depending on the quality of the original and the amount of compression. The ability to specify degree of compression with JPEG, giving you the control over the balance of size versus quality, is an advantage of this image format. JPEG has the capability to provide up to a 20:1 compression of full-color data without visible loss. This can make a big difference in download time without any significant loss of image data.

The JPEG format offers its counterpart of the interlaced GIF. Progressive JPEG allows the image to download in stages, so viewers get a low-resolution preview until the image downloads completely.

There is one caution worth mentioning about JPEG. Because it is a lossy compression, the information that is discarded is gone forever. Always maintain an uncompressed original of the image and work from it.

A new JPEG standard has been developed: JPEG 2000. Because it had been many years since the original JPEG standard was developed, the JPEG committee felt the evolution of computer technology warranted an effort to improve the standard. JPEG 2000 uses wavelet technology to enable an increase of 20 percent compression without any loss or distortion. Although still in the early stages of support for end users on the Web, it has potential for future use. Image size, as has been discussed here, is a major issue. "Images saved in JPEG 2000 format can be coded so that the data when transmitted and imaged gradually increases in resolution, starting with a thumbnail, or gradually increases in quality. A combination of these (and other) quality measures can also be achieved—and the user can stop the image transmission once they have enough detail to make their next choice, as the data is ordered in the file in the correct way to simplify its delivery by image servers."[4]

New Web Graphic Formats

Although GIFs and JPEGs dominate the Web, they are neither the only formats available nor necessarily the best in every circumstance. This section takes a look at some of the image formats that have been developed for several years but are now beginning to be viable for mainstream use on the Web.

PNG (.png)   PNG (pronounced "ping") is the Portable Network Graphics format, designed to be the successor to GIF. Interest in an alternative to GIF increased when the company that owns it announced that programs implementing GIF would require royalties. The PNG compression was developed expressly to be royalty free and contains a number of improvements over the GIF format. It was developed in 1995 and issued as a W3C recommendation in October 1996. You might wonder why, if it has been around so long, it is not more established, but it has taken some time for it to gain support in most browsers and authoring software. Most of the major browsers and imaging programs now support the format, so it is likely that you will see it used more frequently.

PNG supports three main image types: true color, grayscale, and palette-based. Because JPEG supports only true color and grayscale, and GIF supports only palette-based color, PNG offers a potential alternative to both of these formats in certain circumstances.

Like GIF, PNG is a lossless compression, but, unlike GIF, is not restricted to a 256-color palette. Because it supports up to 48-bit color, PNG can display complex color schemes with no loss of data. When rendered as to guidelines, PNG has a higher compression rate than GIF.

PNG also supports transparency, but here again improves on what GIF can offer. GIF supports transparency of one color and PNG allows for up to 254 levels of partial transparency.

Interlacing is also incorporated into PNG. Where GIF uses one-dimensional interlacing, PNG uses a two-dimensional scheme, which results in a more quickly displayed image. With only one-sixty-fourth of a PNG downloaded, a viewer gets a preview of the entire image, compared with only one-eighth of a GIF image.

Should you use PNG? If your authoring software supports PNG and your audience's browsers also do, then PNG may well be a worthwhile format. If you know that many of your users are viewing your tutorial through older browsers, you will probably want to postpone experimenting with the PNG compression. For more information on this promising Web format, visit the PNG home site (http://www.libpng.org/pub/png/).

SVG (.svg)   All the Web graphic formats discussed so far have been raster (bitmap). Because vector graphics have some benefits over raster images, developing a standard for supporting display of them over the Web has been a priority for some time. Currently, there are a number of proprietary vector graphic formats being used, but all require plug-ins, which prevents their being used as widely as raster graphics. Because no single format is widely supported for either viewing or design and there is little cross-platform support, W3C has taken on the development of a vector graphic standard. Called SVG (Scalable Vector Graphics), it is a language for describing two-dimensional graphics in XML, along with a set of APIs (application program interface) upon which to build graphics-based applications. The language issues instructions to describe how a figure should appear by assigning attributes to SVG elements. In other words, it is coded in plain text within an HTML document with no other files involved. SVG allows for three types of graphic objects: vector shapes (paths consisting of straight lines and curves), images (with color gradations), and text. SVG drawings can be dynamic and interactive. SVG is an open standard that has development support from many organizations, including major players such as Sun Microsystems, Adobe, Apple, and IBM. SVG has several advantages over the traditional Web graphic formats:

Scalability. Because it is a vector format, SVG can be scaled to any resolution without degradation of quality.

Smaller file size. Of course, this translates to faster download time.

Scripting and animation. SVG has the capability to render dynamic and interactive graphics.

Plain-text format. SVG language is written in plain text. This makes it possible to use a variety of tools to read and modify an SVG file. It also contributes to a smaller file size.

Ability to apply styles. SVG can be changed with CSS, unlike bitmapped images, which cannot be changed once they are created in anything but a graphics program. This means, for instance, that you can easily change text in objects to a different font or color.

Selectable and searchable text. The text content of an SVG graphic becomes searchable, can be indexed, and can be displayed in multiple languages. This has great benefit for disabled users.

Open standard. SVG is an open recommendation developed by a cross-industry consortium.

As of January 2003, SVG 1.1 became a W3C recommendation. A working draft for Version 1.2 was released in October 2004. For detailed information on SVG, visit the W3C's SVG site (http://www.w3.org/Graphics/SVG/).

For a comparison of the four Web graphics formats, refer to figure 6.12.

Icons

An icon is a small picture intended to represent a word or phrase. On the Web, icons are small graphic elements on a Web page that represent a topic or additional information on another page or, once clicked, a function for the user. Icons are quickly becoming a common tool on commercial sites; for instance, most people know what the shopping cart icon means. Appropriate icons on an educational site can be valuable also. A good icon contains a visual image that a user may recognize more quickly than written text. Figure 6.13 illustrates some of the well-known Web icons that have potential usefulness in a tutorial.

Clip Art

Clip art is off-the-shelf artwork originally designed for use in desktop publishing and prepared in a standardized format for nonspecific use and wide distribution. With the

FIGURE 6.12
Advantages, Disadvantages, and Uses of Web Graphic Formats

	ADVANTAGES	DISADVANTAGES	USE FOR
GIF	Can be indexed to a set color palette (helps with browser-safe color determination) Lossless compression scheme Supports transparency Superior when compressing a few distinct colors Supports interlacing Supports animations	Limited to a 256-color palette	Line art Logos Cartoons Type and fonts Black-and-white images Images with large areas of solid color
JPEG	Supports 24-bit true color Preserves broad range and subtle variations in brightness and hue Can specify degree of compression Supports progressive download	Has difficulty with sharp edges (which come out blurred) Lossy compression scheme Doesn't support transparency	Full-color or grayscale realistic images Images with lots of complex, gradient color variations
PNG	Supports 48-bit true color Cross-platform control of image brightness Two-dimensional interlacing Lossless compression, higher rate than GIF Variable transparency Supports true color, grayscale, and palette	Support for PNG is not universal in browsers and development software No multiple-image support for animations	Alternative to either GIF or JPEG if appropriate
SVG	Fully scalable for zooming and panning XML based W3C Recommendation Compact download size Editable and searchable text Multiple levels transparency Supports scripting and animation Ability to apply CSS Open standard Plain-text format (can use a variety of tools to create it)	May require use of a plug-in to view (Mozilla does support native display of SVG in its browser)	Implementing vector graphics that you desire scalability control over

FIGURE 6.13
Useful Web Icons for Tutorials

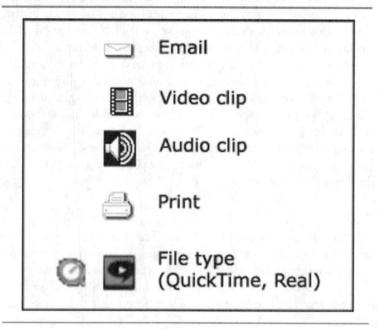

popularization of the Web, clip art libraries have become a common resource for artists and nonartists to incorporate art into their Web pages quickly and economically. Clip art includes visual elements such as bullets, lines, and arrows as well as subject-related illustrations on almost any topic under the sun.

Clip art is available commercially from many companies, but there are also plenty of clip art libraries on the Web. It is a simple matter to download clip art from the Web, but it is important to know that you can't assume that all clip art is freely available for download and use. Be aware that clip art may be copyrighted and that many clip art sites have terms and conditions for the use of their art. It is your responsibility to familiarize yourself with specified rules and to comply with them.

Finding clip art online is not difficult. You can use your favorite search engine or Web directory to find resources similar to these: Kid's Domain (http://www.kidsdo main.com/clip/) or Clip Art Warehouse (http://www.clipart.co.uk/index.shtml).

Image Maps

As mentioned in chapter 5, an image map is a graphic defined so that users can click on different areas to go to various destinations. These areas are called hot spots and are defined by x and y coordinates (the horizontal and vertical distance from the left-hand corner of the image). There are two types of image maps, server-side and client-side. The server-side map stores the map data on the server, which means a longer response time for the user, because the client browser must query the server for the map destination. With client-side maps, the map data is embedded in the HTML document and interpreted by the browser program on users' computers. Response time to the user is faster with a client-side image map, so it's best to use this type.

Image maps are often used as the main menu on a visually based introductory page. A designer with a little imagination, however, is likely to see opportunities to use them throughout an educational tutorial. Figure 6.14, for example, shows the construction of an image map to make a simulation of an online catalog search.

Image maps can be created in many Web editors, as illustrated in figure 6.14. Hot spots are selected by drawing one of three shapes (circle, rectangle, or polygon) and assigning a destination to that spot. The Properties window at the bottom of the screen shows the dialog boxes to create the hot spots. In the bottom design view screen in figure 6.14, the Guided Keyword Search, Course Reserves, and New Items tabs have been made into hot spots. The map coordinates are coded into the HTML document, as is shown in the upper code view window.

Rollover Images

A rollover (also known as a mouseover) is a JavaScript technique that allows a Web author to program a page element change when a user's cursor passes over something on the page. The page element is usually a graphic, and rollovers are often used in navigation tool bars. Rollovers invite a feeling of user interactivity because changes take place in response to the user's activity. To view a rollover, visit Stony Brook University

FIGURE 6.14
Creating an Image Map with Macromedia Dreamweaver

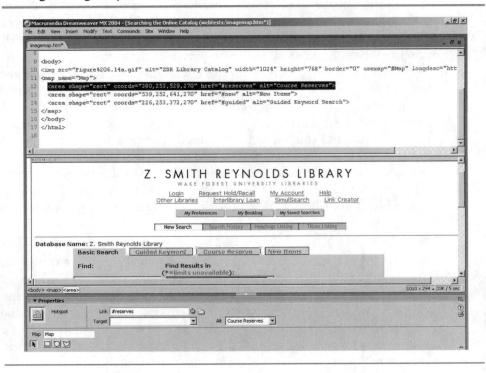

Libraries tutorial (see figure 6.15). The starred topic choices are images. When the user passes his mouse over one of them, an explanation of what the topic will cover appears. Figure 6.15 shows the screen with an inset that pictures both images used, along with the scripting included to make the action occur.

To make rollovers, create two graphics with the same dimensions. In figure 6.15, each of the images is 294 × 97 pixels. One will load when the page first displays. The second will swap places with the first when the cursor passes over the original image. Another common use is the remote rollover, which causes a previously invisible graphic element to appear when the user passes the cursor over a certain page element. In that case, you'll prepare a third image, which doesn't necessarily have to be the same size as the first two because it loads in a different part of the page. With a remote rollover, the third image will appear in a different location at the same time that the second image appears in place of the first. Don't hesitate to use rollovers just because you don't know how to write JavaScript. Many Web editors include behind-the-scenes scripting to create rollovers. It is also easy to find free rollover scripts on the Web. One such script is the Mouseover Machine, which has become available at many sites over the past few years. Figure 6.16 shows one site's implementation of it. This free utility creates a rollover script based on the information you enter into fields in a form at a participating site. Once the code is generated, you simply cut and paste it into your HTML document.

FIGURE 6.15
Rollover Images

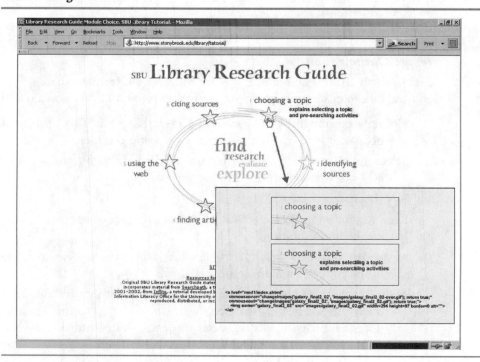

From Stony Brook University Libraries, New York. Available: http://www.stonybrook.edu/library/tutorial/.

FIGURE 6.16
JavaScript Magic: Mouseover Machine

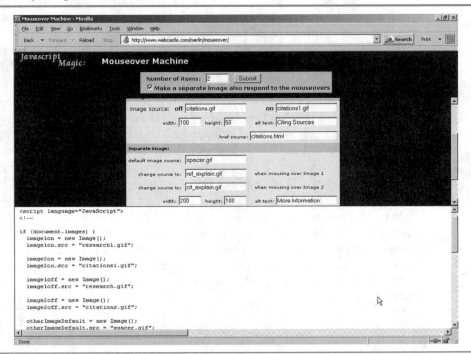

From WebCastle Productions, based on Charity Kahn's CoolTool. Available: http://www.webcastle
.com/merlin/mouseover/.

Image Optimization

Even though GIFs, JPEGs, and PNGs are compression formats, there are other steps
you can take to ensure that your images are optimized for faster download times.

- Use only meaningful graphics; remove everything else. This tip bears repeating
  because it is so easy to get carried away using graphics.
- Select the most appropriate format for the type of graphic you are using. Figure
  6.12 can help you decide which type is best.
- Size the images accurately.
- Keep resolution to 72 dpi. If you are not printing the image, there is no need for
  any higher resolution.
- Always use width and height attributes. This allows the browser to render the rest
  of the page while the graphic downloads.
- Make the width and height of the image the exact size that will display. Don't use
  the width and height attributes of the <image> tag to resize the image. If you
  do, either image quality will decrease or you waste bandwidth because the full
  image still needs to download.
- Crop images to discard extra space around the image's subject matter.

Reduce the number of colors (bit depth) in the image as much as possible in palette-based formats (GIF and PNG) to take out unnecessary color. If done carefully, the reduction will be invisible to the naked eye.

Optimize JPEG files. The less compression, the higher the image quality and the larger the file size are. Utilities such as JPEG Wizard (available at no cost from http://www.jpegwizard.com) will display your image at different compression degrees so that you can see which compression best reduces file size yet maintains image quality.

Reuse graphics sitewide. Because browsers cache files as they download, images that are repeated will appear quickly. If the browser recognizes a file name, it will look to the cache to retrieve it rather than to the originating server.

Store your images on the same server as your tutorial. This helps minimize the slight lag that an extra domain name server lookup entails.

Many graphics applications include the ability to optimize images for the Web. For instance, Adobe has incorporated ImageReady into Photoshop. This utility is used to prepare and optimize images for use on the Web. Figure 6.17 shows the original image displayed in the top left window. Three possible optimization choices are displayed alongside it to permit a visual inspection of all. Information about download time and file size are included to aid the decision-making process.

FIGURE 6.17
Optimizing Image for Display on the Web with ImageReady

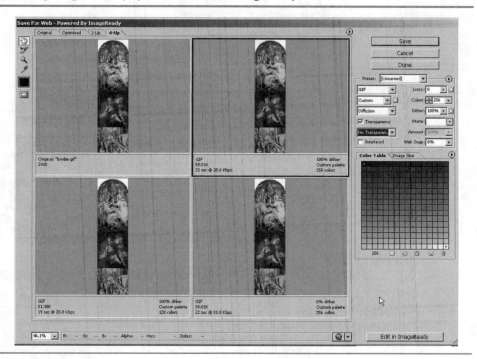

From Adobe Photoshop.

If you don't have access to an optimizing application, you can access utilities available on the Web, most of which involve a fee. One example is GIFBot (http://www .netmechanic.com/GIFBot/optimize-graphic.htm). You provide the URL to the image or a path to it for upload. The utility examines the file and displays several versions of it at different compressions. Information includes download time, file size, and size reduction percentage.

Image Slicing

Image slicing is a technique that combines image editing with HTML. It allows large images to be sliced into a number of pieces, which are then reassembled in an HTML table. Illustrated in figure 6.18 is an image as it displays in a browser (top) and the same image displayed in a Web editor with the border function turned on to demon-

FIGURE 6.18
Image Slicing

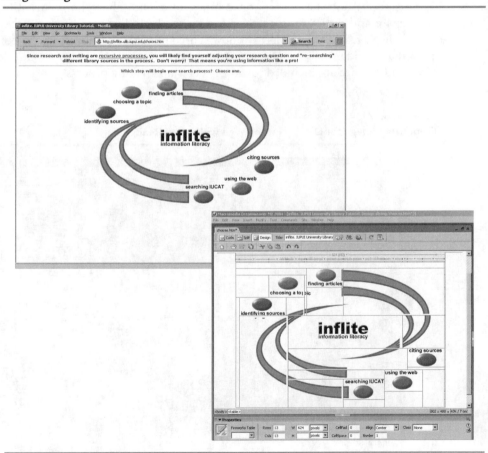

From Indiana University–Purdue University Indianapolis (IUPUI) University Library. Used by permission. INFLITE © by the Board of Trustees of Indiana University, which incorporates material from TILT, a tutorial developed by the Digital Information Literacy Office for the University of Texas System Digital Library, © 1998–2004. Available: http://inflite.ulib.iupui.edu/choices.htm.

strate that what appears to be a single image is really many smaller images reassembled into a table. Although the main benefit of image slicing would seem to be to facilitate faster download times, in reality no bandwidth is usually saved. The technique does, however, give the illusion of a quicker download, which sometimes can be just as important to the user. Slicing has some benefits worthy of consideration:

> Each sliced section can be individually optimized, which can result in a smaller overall size after all. For instance, if a graphic combines areas best suited to be GIFs and others that warrant being optimized as JPEGs, slicing allows you to define the sections so that each is treated separately.

> Blank areas of an image can be eliminated altogether to reveal background color and reduce download time.

> Slicing can be used to make graphic elements individual links. Although this can be accomplished with an image map, separate images for each link mean better compatibility when a page is viewed with the graphics off (using the ALT attribute) and makes updating links easier.

> Slicing makes rollover images for what appear to be single-image navigational elements possible.

> Large areas of identical image color can be sliced into a single smaller image that caches and displays much more quickly than if a single larger file.

> Slicing allows animation in a portion of a large image.

Labeling Images

The ALT attribute provides an alternative way to reveal the content of your images to those who cannot or choose not to view graphics. The ALT attribute looks like this in HTML code:

<img src="intromenu.gif" width="540" height="399" alt="Start Menu">

Users with visual disabilities or those who have turned off image loading in their browsers will either hear from a screen reader or see the text alternative. If this attribute is ignored or overlooked during the authoring process, the site will not be accessible to all visitors.

Audio

Although the Web is primarily a visual medium, as it has matured, the use of audio has become much more common. Proper use of audio can serve many purposes on an educational site—to set a mood, provide an alternate communication channel apart from the visual material, or give an audible clue for different actions within the interface, for example. As with other multimedia, the important thing to remember is to use audio for a specific purpose and not to overdo it.

File Formats

There are two main categories of sound on the Web today: self-contained (have to be downloaded to the local computer before they can be heard) and streaming audio. The following subsections explore the first category of audio file types. Streaming audio is examined within the presentation of streaming media later in the chapter.

AU (.au) The first audio file format used on the Internet, Audio File Format was intended for use on UNIX computers. It is also the standard sound format for the Java platform. This format supports a 2:1 compression ratio, which gives the format a relatively small file size of about 8 KB per second of audio. It is probably the closest to a nonproprietary audio standard available on the Internet and so can be found in quantity from sound libraries. Because the quality of AU files is not high, they work well for short clips and sound effects but would not be the first choice for a project that relies heavily on sound.

AIFF (.aiff, .aif) Apple developed the Audio Interchange File Format for the Macintosh platform. The AIFF format is uncompressed, so the files can be large. Its sound quality is better than the AU format.

WAV (.wav) Developed by Microsoft, the Waveform Audio File Format is the PC/Windows equivalent of Apple's AIFF. Because it is the native sound file format for the platform that has the overwhelming majority of presence on the Internet, it is common to see. However, it, too, is an uncompressed format, and just sixty seconds of WAV audio can take up more than 10 MB of disk space. WAV has a comparable sound quality to AIFF. Because it is uncompressed, WAV is the preferred format for saving archival versions of audio.

All three store recorded sound that originated as analog and was converted to digital. The next file type is quite different.

MIDI (.midi, .mid) The Musical Instrument Digital Interface is a protocol adopted by the electronic music industry for controlling music synthesizer devices (both keyboards and sound cards). It doesn't represent music sounds directly (as is the case with AU, AIFF, and WAV), but instead transfers information that tells the synthesizer what to play to produce a musical composition. MIDI might thus be compared with vector graphics in that both file types consist of instructions or commands. Like a vector file, the MIDI file sizes are smaller than their counterparts because the instructions consume much less data. One drawback to the MIDI format is that it plays only instrumentals, not voices.

MPEG Both an audio and a video compression format, MPEG is also the acronym for Motion Pictures Experts Group, and is explained in full in the video section of this chapter.

MP3 (.mp3) MPEG-1 Audio Layer-3 is the most popular audio format on the Web today. Although it is most famous for the illegalities involved with downloading files, MP3 is in fact just an efficient audio compression format. The compression ratio is 12:1, yet the sound quality is preserved. Although it has often been assumed to be an open (nonproprietary) standard, this isn't the case. Fraunhofer Institute was the main developer of the MP3 standard and joined forces with Thomson Multimedia to put together a patent portfolio and ask for royalties for developers to use it.[5]

Ogg Vorbis (.ogg) This led to the development of a completely open and free audio compression, Vorbis, from the Xiph.Org Foundation. The code for the latest release is available from the Vorbis Web site (http://www.vorbis.com). It is frequently used in conjunction with Ogg container, a fully open multimedia bitstream format designed for efficient streaming and storage. When used together, it is known as Ogg Vorbis. Ogg Vorbis has become popular with the open source communities, but MP3 technology is extremely entrenched in the public eye. However, an increasing number of audio players, including WinAmp for PCs (http://winamp.com) and WHAMB.com for Macs (http://www.whamb.com), support Ogg Vorbis in their products, so its use will surely increase over time as developers are required to pay royalties for MP3.

Windows Media Audio (.wma, .asf)   This Microsoft audio format is proprietary and compressed, designed initially as a competitor to MP3. It has now positioned itself as a competitor to the Advanced Audio Coding format used by Apple for iTunes. The initial reason for the development of WMA most likely was related to the patent issue with MP3, which had to be licensed to be included with the Windows operating system (OS). A WMA file is often encapsulated in an Advanced Systems Format (ASF) file. This format specifies how the metadata for the file is to be encoded. Advantages claimed over MP3 include being better suited to low bitrates (especially around 8–64 kbit/sec) and producing better quality at a given bitrate than MP3. To play WMA files, you can use the Windows Media Player or other players such as Winamp. It also has a digital rights component that protects against the unauthorized reproduction of copyrighted material.

File Download versus Inline

Linking to a sound file is the simplest way to include sound in a Web page. This method is the most appropriate when supplying certain types of files such as sound clips that accompany other material. Providing a link puts the control of the sound into the user's hands. When using a link, remember to include all the information about the file that is important to the audience: type of file format, file size, and estimated download time. A typical link might look like this:

<a href="boolean.wav">Hear about Boolean Logic</a>

When the user clicks on this link, either a player or a plug-in will be invoked, depending on the browser and its configuration.

Sounds may also be embedded, that is, be put in line so that they are a part of your page resulting in sound playing automatically in the background when the page loads. Since HTML version 4.01, the <object> tag embeds media in a Web page. The older <embed> and <bgsound> tags were never sanctioned and should not be used. You will find that there is only spotty support for embedded sounds from browser to browser, so be prepared to test in different browsers and across platforms to ensure that the sound works as you intend.

A third option for including sound files is JavaScript, whether having sound play when the screen loads or in response to different mouse actions.

If you decide to include background sound, do your audience a favor and give them the controls to turn the music on and off. What sounds great to one person may sound like fingernails across the blackboard to others.

Using Existing Sound Files

If you don't have the experience or expertise to create your own audio files, you'll probably want to access the many sound libraries that are available on the Web for clips. However, be careful when downloading others' sound files and always research the copyright requirements. Copyright issues in the music industry are complicated and rather a hot topic now. Several organizations deal with various aspects of music copyright, including the ASCAP (American Society of Composers, Authors and Publishers, http://www.ascap.com), BMI (Broadcast Music, Inc., http://www.bmi .com), RIAA (Recording Industry Association of America, http://www.riaa.com), and the HFA (Harry Fox Agency, Inc., http://www.nmpa.org/hfa.html).

Animation

Animation can be defined as the creation of the illusion of movement. This is accomplished through subtle changes in a sequence of stationary screen elements or images. Although motion across the screen is a primary type, animation also deals with any change in an object: change in brightness, color, size, shape, or into another object altogether (metamorphosis). It can include a variety of different media: text, vector and raster graphics, audio, and video. An animation is not just a viewable object; it can also incorporate elements of interactivity for user response.

When is animation appropriate to use? Good uses, as identified by Jakob Nielsen, include[6]

indicating transitions

illustrating change over time

showing multiple information objects in the same space

enriching graphical representations

visualizing three-dimensional structures

attracting attention

Basic Animation Concepts

In-depth instruction about animation is beyond the scope of this book. However, it is helpful to become acquainted with a few key ideas so that as you look at the various animation technologies, you can recognize similarities and differences in approach.

One common element of all animation is the capability to create sequential frames and then work with the timing and transition of those frames to ready them for playback. To best understand this procedure, it is worth becoming familiar with a few basic terms and concepts:

Cycling (looping). This involves creating cycles of motion that end the same way they start, allowing the reuse of the cycle as many times as needed. On the Web, cycling helps keep the file size of an animation smaller, thus conserving download time.

Keyframe. The animator designates specific objects at critical points on the animation timeline, and the computer program then fills in the motion between these frames.

Sprite. This is a graphic image that can move within a larger graphic. Software that supports sprites allows the designer to create individual animated images that can be combined into a larger animation.

Tweening. Short for in-betweening, this is the calculation (made by the application software) for determining the intermediate frames between two key frames to simulate motion.

Timeline. This is a scale measured either in seconds or frames that provides an editable, visual record of animation events.

The different types of animation will fall into one of two main categories: prerendered and real time. Prerendered (also called frame-by-frame) animations include those that are downloaded in their entirety to the users' computers before they can be played. These typically are rendered in raster (or bitmap) format, and are thus larger files. The real-time animations are often vector based, which means that the file being downloaded contains instructions only (meaning a much smaller file size) that the computer reads, interprets, and then renders all on the client side.

If you are new to the world of animation, refer to the resources at the end of this book for a list of links to animation information and tutorials. In the world of computer animation, you will find that technologies often overlap. It may not be necessary to try to pigeonhole the various technologies, but be aware of the major difference between animation and video. Remember that video takes a continuous motion and breaks it down into discrete frames, and animation starts in the opposite direction with independent frames that are then put together into a series to form the illusion of movement.

Types of Web Animation

The following subsections introduce you to some of the Web animation technologies available today. It is beneficial to have an overview of what each is designed to do because it is important to pick the right one for your purpose. Some of these animation technologies are easier to implement if you are a novice; others have a steep learning curve that requires an extensive investment of time.

Animated GIF (.gif)   In the GIF 89a standard, a GIF image can be animated by combining several images into a single file. Animations are easy to create and are supported by most Web browsers. Because this is a GIF format, it works bests with a limited number of colors and with illustration images instead of photographic ones. There are some drawbacks, namely that it tends to create large file sizes that don't compress well, and that it has no sound capabilities. But for small animations, animated GIF is serviceable.

To create animated GIFs, you will need a GIF 89a generating application. Some image-editing programs include this as part of the package, or you can download a freeware or shareware application from the Web. Begin by creating several images with identical dimensions. Make small changes in each image that will be the basis for the illusion of movement. Each of these images will become a frame in the animation. Use as few frames as possible to limit file size. Once you have opened all of your images in the GIF generating program, you will arrange them in order, set the timing for each frame, and run the optimization utility that is part of the program. This utility handles such tasks as generating a palette for the file based on all of the frames, applying special dithering to prevent flickering, and optimizing the frames so only areas that change from frame to frame are included—each of which greatly reduces the file size.

Figure 6.19 illustrates the construction of an animated GIF in JASC Animation Shop. The animation shows book pages flipping and is made up of eight individual images. The program includes functionality to optimize the animation and display it in your browser with file size and download time information (see inset).

FIGURE 6.19
Constructing an Animated GIF in JASC Animation Shop

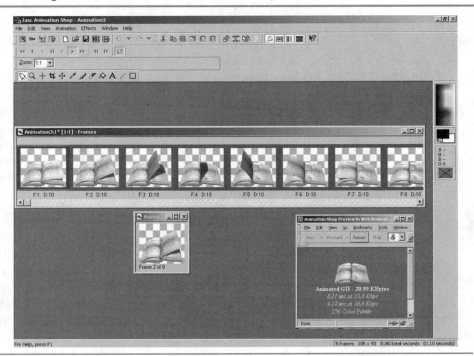

Copyright © 2003, Corel Corporation and Corel Corporation Limited. Reprinted by permission.

MNG (.mng) Multiple-Image Network Graphics (pronounced "ming") has been developed as the format to handle all of the multi-image capabilities that are not supported in PNG and is the PNG counterpart to an animated GIF. As of January 2001, the MNG specifications were upgraded and application support is starting to emerge. Its developers have included a number of features that show promise to improve on animated GIF capabilities:

object- or sprite-based approach to animation

nested loops for complex animations

integration of both PNG- and JPEG-based images

support for transparent JPEGs

unpatented compression either lossless (for PNG) or lossy (for JPEG)

Although the MNG format is not yet a practical choice for your animation because of its limited support for development and display, it is a format that you will want to keep tabs on for future consideration. For additional information, visit MNG's home page (http://www.libpng.org/pub/mng/).

Flash (.swf)   The Macromedia Flash file format has become the leading Web animation format. As of mid 2004, 98 percent of all Web browsers had the Flash player preinstalled.[7] It is created by using the authoring tool Macromedia Flash software, which now is available in two versions—Flash MX and Flash MX Professional. The program is a full-featured animation authoring system that has come a long way in the years since its inception in 1996. It can be used to create rich content via a WYSIWYG interface, uses a robust scripting language called ActionScript, and has a compact file format. The newest versions have support for CSS, accessibility, and Unicode. The professional version includes all of the features of Flash, plus it can be used to create forms, data-driven applications, and high-quality videos. Flash is vector based, which is one reason for its popularity. Vector-based animations are, of course, scalable and download quickly. In fact, Flash files can stream so that users don't have to wait for the entire file to download before viewing it. However, Flash is not limited to just vector graphics; it also allows the incorporation of bitmaps, MP3 and AVI audio, and interactivity. Flash animations can be exported as AVI, MOV, and animated GIF. Macromedia has opened the Flash file format so that third-party tools can be developed.

Flash is being used for a host of purposes on the Web, including education. The award-winning TILT (Texas Information Literacy Tutorial: http://tilt.lib.utsystem .edu) project from the University of Texas System Digital Library was one of the first good examples of the innovative animation possibilities of Flash for library instruction. In the six years since TILT was completed in 1999, many other institutions have turned to Flash to construct their Web-based instruction. Figure 6.20 shows a Flash tutorial about copyright called Primer from University of Maryland University College.

Director Shockwave (.swd, .dcr)   Shockwave is designed to be highly interactive; it supports audio, animation, and video. Shockwave files are created in Macromedia's Director authoring software. Director's (and therefore Shockwave's) strength lies in its ability to create advanced interactivity.

Which should you create—Flash or Shockwave files? Director preceded Flash and wasn't originally designed for the Web. Its main function was to create offline multimedia productions in stand-alone programs. It has a higher learning curve than does Flash and a higher price tag. However, if you are well versed in using Director, the latest versions are more Web-focused. If you are both creating for the Web and planning to publish to CD-ROM, you can do both with Director. If you are creating strictly for the Web, stick with Flash because it was designed as a Web authoring tool. Also, Flash is more universally available to users through their browsers. As mentioned earlier, 98 percent of browsers have the Flash player installed. Fewer than 60 percent have the Shockwave plug-in.

Authorware (.aam)   Macromedia Authorware is an authoring system (discussed in chapter 4) used mainly for producing instructional interactive e-learning. With Authorware you can create courseware that can connect to CMS/LMS systems and that complies with standards Shareable Courseware Object Reference Model (SCORM). Users work with a wizard to decide what information to get or send to the

FIGURE 6.20
Flash Tutorial on Copyright

From Center for Intellectual Property, University of Maryland University College, Adelphi, Maryland. Available: http://www-apps.umuc.edu/primer/enter.php.

LMS. Because it is an authoring system, there isn't a need to know programming to learn to use it, instead using dialog boxes to program. Authors can import Flash animations, synchronize media content, and incorporate MP3 audio. An Authorware plug-in is required to view .aam files. Several examples of Authorware tutorials are available online at Hennepin County Library's Interactive Tutorial site (http://www .hclib.org/pub/training/) (see figure 6.21).

dHTML Layer-Based Animation (.htm, .html)   Dynamic HTML is a marketing term used for a combination of the more recently developed HTML tags and options, including some topics that have been previously covered, such as cascading style sheets. One of the uses for dHTML is to provide animation capability. You won't be able to create the complex animation of Flash or Shockwave, but for simple animations, dHTML works well. Animations are created with layers that can overlay other page elements and move around the screen. You can place either plain text or a graphic in a layer. Multiple layers can be created, each with its own timeline and actors, behaviors, and property settings. Unless you are proficient at JavaScript, you will probably want to use a WYSIWYG Web editor to create your animations. Many Web editors incorporate this capability as illustrated by the screen shot of Macromedia Dreamweaver software shown in figure 6.22. The animation, in which two circles move across the screen to highlight two important pieces of information, is con-

FIGURE 6.21
Macromedia Authorware Tutorial

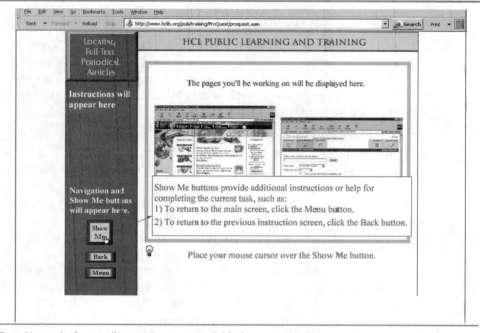

From Hennepin County Library, Minnesota. Available: http://www.hclib.org/pub/training/ProQuest/ proquest.com.

FIGURE 6.22
Macromedia Dreamweaver Used to Create Layer-Based Animation

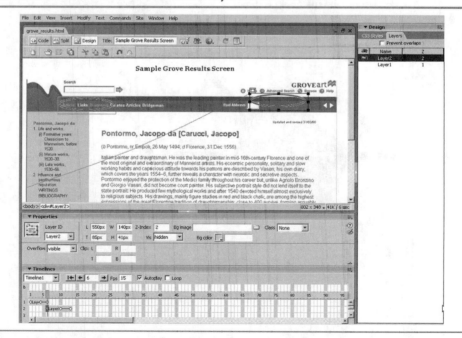

From Z. Smith Reynolds Library, Wake Forest University, Winston-Salem, North Carolina. Available: http://www.wfu.edu/Library/referenc/art_history/encyclopedia.htm.

structed by placing two images, each into its own layer, and timing their entry and travel across the screen using a time line and keyframes.

One major benefit of layer-based animation (besides the ease of authoring) is that a plug-in is not required for viewing because the animation script is part of the HTML page code. Support for layers does vary from browser to browser (layers are supported only in version 4 and above) and platform to platform, so it is important that you ascertain that your audience's browsers can interpret the code. An additional benefit of the ability to insert plain text into a dHTML animation is that the text will be able to be searched and indexed.

3-D Graphics   Three-dimensional graphics provide the perception of depth to two-dimensional images. When they are animated, they can be viewed from different angles and distances. Animation is what makes 3-D objects appear real to the user and makes them such effective visualization tools, but creating them requires both creativity and technical proficiency. Learning to produce 3-D objects and animations is not simple; even with 3-D authoring software, plan on a major commitment of time. Following is a simplistic summary of the steps involved in creating 3-D elements:

1. Most 3-D animations start with solid geometric objects that are called primitives (spheres, cubes, cylinders, and the like). When thinking about 3-D, it is helpful to understand about the three dimensions of space, the x (width), y (height), and z (depth) planes. The x and y axes are the 2-D coordinates, and the z axis adds the third dimension (see figure 6.23). Adding the z-axis to a 2-D object is called extrusion.

FIGURE 6.23
Axes of Three-Dimensional Graphics

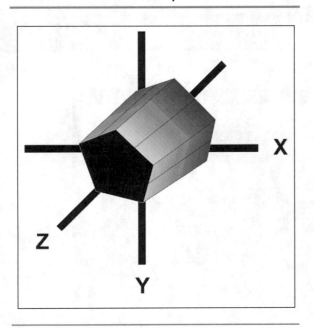

2. Combining, resizing, or re-forming the primitives can create other shapes, called modeling.

3. To make the shapes look realistic, you add color, textures, and light sources to the object. Other effects include reflection, transparency, and smoothness.

4. You create a 3-D space by positioning the objects, light, ground plane, and sometimes a background.

5. Animation is added via a timeline of movements and events.

6. The last step is to render the final scene, which is where you define the quality and type of the output.

X3D (.x3d, .x3dv, .xedb)   X3D is the new Web 3-D standard. It is the successor to VRML (Virtual Reality Modeling Language), which was developed as a screen-description language that describes the geometry and behavior of a 3-D scene or world. This language was originated with a goal of creating shared virtual worlds on the Internet. X3D extends the capabilities of VRML, supports multiple data encodings (XML, VRML classic and binary) and has improved graphics features. The X3D specification is designed to be more flexible than VRML to accommodate the evolution of the standard. It is an open source Web 3D Consortium project. To learn more, visit the project site (http://www.web3d.org), which offers an FAQ along with information about the specifications and available tools (viewers, authoring, and developer).

Video

Video is a multimedia format that requires careful planning to use appropriately over the Web. There are three traditional video file formats that are commonly seen online: AVI (Audio-Video Interleave), MPEG, and QuickTime (discussed in the following sections). All three of these are files that must be downloaded onto a user's computer before they can be viewed. Because of bandwidth constraints and the fact that video files can be quite large, it is best to incorporate video in short clips that are less than a minute long. Remember to always prepare your audience for the wait they will encounter in downloading by specifying the anticipated download time, the size of the file, and the playing time.

AVI (.avi)

AVI (Audio-Video Interleave) is Microsoft's proprietary video for Windows format. Because it has been a part of Windows, the majority of computer users can view it, which accounts for some of its rise in popularity. However, although you can find plenty of AVI files on the Web, its use is declining because of the characteristically large file sizes. AVI does have the advantage of being most likely playable on most PCs without the need to install a viewer or plug-in. A significant disadvantage is that it will not play on a Mac. Microsoft is no longer supporting video for Windows and is replacing AVI with an Active Streaming Format (ASF).

QuickTime (.mov, .qt)

QuickTime, developed by Apple, is both a file format and a software architecture for multimedia development, storage, and playback. It is a technology that is extensively used by developers, and it enjoys widespread support. QuickTime movies can incorporate a variety of media types, including audio, graphics, video, text, MPEG, vector media, VR, and 3-D. More than fifty file formats can be imported and more than twenty-five can be exported (see http://www.apple.com/quicktime/pro/specs.html). This flexibility in delivering multiple formats makes QuickTime versatile indeed. Although originally developed for the Macintosh, QuickTime now supports both platforms equally well. The QuickTime plug-in is supported in the major browsers but QuickTime movies cannot be played in Windows Media Player or Real Player.

An example of the use of QuickTime for delivering library instruction is available at DataLine BG (Bowling Green State University). Using a series of seven QuickTime movies, the University Libraries take an appealing look at "Research Stress Syndrome" (see figure 6.24). Take note that transcripts are included for each movie clip to address accessibility issues!

QuickTime is now involved in streaming technology (discussed later in this chapter). Not only that, another development that is sure to keep QuickTime in the forefront is that it was selected as the format that MPEG-4 is based on (see MPEG later in this chapter).

FIGURE 6.24
QuickTime Movies

From University Libraries, Bowling Green State University, Ohio. Available: http://www.bgsu.edu/colleges/library/infosrv/lue/dataline.html.

QTVR

QuickTime Virtual Reality is an enhanced version of Apple's QuickTime standard and adds the ability to tour through a virtual scene or examine 3-D objects by rotating them. A virtual scene in QTVR is a panoramic movie, a series of photographs taken in up to a 360° range and stitched together. The result is a cylinder-shaped image that surrounds the viewer, who can look in all directions, forward, backward, up, and down. Each one of the stitched photos is called a node, and when one or more nodes are connected, the viewer can move through the scene by clicking on designated hot spots. In figure 6.25, the virtual tour of Z. Smith Reynolds Library consists of more than 125 individual nodes stitched together, by floor level, so that visitors can stroll through all eight floors of the library. Accompanying this is a floor plan for each floor showing the path that can be taken and clickable hot links that will take a visitor to a specific area of the library.

The second type of QTVR format is an object movie, which allows users to simulate the action of picking up an object and turning it around to view it. As with the panorama, this is created with a series of still photographs that include shots of all sides, including top and bottom, of an object. The photos are stitched together and then can be rotated to view the object from any direction by using a mouse. QTVR production can be expensive because it requires specialized equipment, training, and photography skills. It can, however, give users a unique experience.

FIGURE 6.25
QTVR Tour of Z. Smith Reynolds Library, Wake Forest University

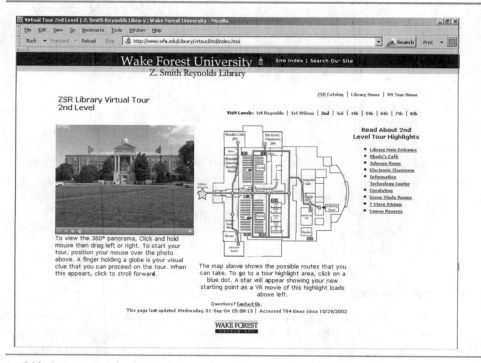

Available: http://www.wfu.edu/Library/vrtour/.

MPEG (.mpeg, .mpg, .mp3, .mp4)

MPEG (pronounced "EM-peg") is the acronym for the Moving Picture Experts Group, which develops standards for digital video and audio compression. There are various MPEG codecs. Commonly used for computer videos, MPEG-1 was created for use with CD-ROMs, video games, and other media that require high quality video and audio playback. It supports up to thirty frames per second, the same as a standard television, and a high compression ratio. This, combined with the fact of it having been designed as a digital video capture and playback technology, meant that it quickly became a popular method to deliver video content over the Web. MPEG-1 is also an audio compression standard; MP3 is part of the MPEG-1 family. MPEG-4 has been developed to become a compression standard for interactive multimedia on the Web, CD distribution, videophone, and broadcast television. MPEG-4 absorbs many of the features of MPEG-1 and 2 and adds others including support for 3-D rendering, object-oriented composite files, and Digital Right Management. Using MPEG-4, users can interact with a scene that can be composed from real sources such as video or from synthetic ones such as vector-based objects. Authors can empower users to modify scenes by deleting, adding, or repositioning objects. MPEG-4 supports scalable content. As mentioned earlier, QuickTime has been selected as the basis for starting development of the MPEG-4 standard (.mp4).

Flash Video (.flv)

This Flash video format is required if your video is to be included within a larger, more complex Flash environment. The encoding method is Sorenson Squeeze, which is included in the Macromedia Flash Video Kit. FLV files can be embedded in a Flash SWF file or delivered either in a progressive download or from a streaming server (see the following section). The delivery method will depend on factors such as file size and frame rate. Shorter and lower frame rates may do well embedded, but streaming is the optimal delivery for long, large video clips and broadcasting live events.

Screen-Capture Movie

Making a movie of the action that takes place over time on a computer screen is achieved with specialized software that acts like a video recorder. Most such programs also include an audio component so that the activity that takes place on the screen can be accompanied by narration. Many of the available screen recording applications support both AVI and streaming technology. Other names you may hear to describe this type of technology include screen recording, desktop activity recording, and screen-capture video. One popular screen capture application is Camtasia, available from TechSmith (http://www.techsmith.com) (see figure 4.9).

Streaming Media

Streaming media is fast becoming the multimedia delivery method of choice. With streaming audio, video, and other multimedia, users can play files without waiting for a download. Streaming technology works differently from the traditional Web transaction we are used to. A normal Web transaction occurs when a user clicks on a link of some sort. The request for a file, whether it is HTML, audio, graphic, or video, is sent to a Web server. The server takes the request and pushes out the file as quickly as possible and then disconnects. Back at the user's end, once the client (computer) receives the file that was sent, the computer is disconnected from the server, and the browser and plug-ins handle the display of the file. This works well for small files, like HTML and most graphics. However, with the larger files that are the norm for audio and video, the wait for the download is too long, and users get annoyed.

With streaming media, the data is fed to the user from the server as it is viewed. So rather than a quick connect and disconnect from the server, there is a continuous connection for the duration of the delivery of the media. On the receiving side of the data feed, the computer must be able to collect the data and send it to the player as a steady stream. If the data arrives more quickly than it is played back, it is stored in a buffer until it is needed.

Even though the data is delivered in a stream and plays as it arrives, there is still a need to compress the data as it streams. A lossy compression is used to reduce file size significantly, but entails degradation in image and sound. However, the main goal of developing streaming technology was to improve access, and it does accomplish that. We will continue to see a steady improvement in the quality as the technology matures.

The basic process for creating streaming video and audio is to capture the video and/or audio, digitize and edit it, encode the digitized file with the appropriate codec, and deliver the file through a Web site.

To include streaming media into a Web page, you can either provide a text or graphic link or embed the file into the HTML document so it is displayed as part of the Web page. Right now, streaming technology is primarily proprietary. The three major competitors in the streaming market are RealNetworks, QuickTime, and Windows Media.

RealMedia (.rm, .rmvb)

RealNetworks is one of today's leaders in the streaming technology race. Its streaming media is handled through RealSystem architecture. Two different kinds of streaming are available: true streaming that requires a server and serverless streaming that is known as progressive download. Using RealSystem with a server provides a much greater level of flexibility and scalability. For instance, one feature allows the creation of several versions of your audio and video tracks that are encoded for common user connections. Media production is done with one of two products—RealProducer Basic (a free tool) or RealProducer Plus. However, some third-party applications will also encode RealMedia content. RealNetworks streaming media requires a RealPlayer, which the author can embed in a Web page. In 2002, RealNetworks launched its Helix initiative with Helix Universal Server. Helix is RealNetworks' open source framework for delivering media. It uses RTP/RSTP (RealTime Protocol/RealTime Streaming Protocol) to stream files. A text file with an extension of *.ram* is created, and consists of a single line containing the URL (using rstp:// instead of http://) to the RealMedia file on the Helix Server. The result is that your Web page links to the ram file, which then links to the media file, which then streams from the server to the client. It is a universal platform with support for live and on-demand delivery of all major file formats, including RealMedia, Flash, Windows Media, QuickTime, MPEG-4, MP3, SMIL, and more.

Real has taken an important step by becoming an early supporter of SMIL, a language designed to synchronize multimedia (discussed in a following section).

QuickTime (.mov)

Apple has arrived on the streaming-media scene later than either RealNetworks or Microsoft and therefore has not developed its streaming technology as quickly. However, QuickTime does a lot of things well. It shouldn't be dismissed, if for no other reason than its potential in the number of file formats it supports. Also, as mentioned, QuickTime is deeply involved with the development of the MPEG-4 standard, which will incorporate streaming technology. Streaming QuickTime is viewed through QuickTime 6.5. Content can be created using QuickTime Pro. As with RealMedia, QuickTime streaming media can be delivered via a server or in pseudo-streaming form from a regular Web server. Apple's streaming server is QuickTime Streaming Server, which delivers both QuickTime (.mov) and MPEG-4 (.mp4) files in real time over the Internet via the Real-time Transport Protocol/Real-Time Streaming Protocol (RTP/RTSP). It runs on Mac OS. However, through the Darwin open source project, the Darwin Streaming Server is available for Linux, Windows, and Solaris, as well.

Windows Media (.asf, .wmv)

Microsoft's entry into the streaming media mix is called Advanced Systems Format (ASF), which stores audio, multibitrate video, metadata (such as the file's title and author), and index and script commands (such as URLs and closed captioning) in a single file. ASF does require a server component, specifically, Windows Media Services streaming server, to deliver the file. However, the tools to create, serve, and play ASF content are available at no charge from Microsoft's Web site. The player for ASF is Windows Media Player, and the production module is Windows Media Encoder. Windows Media supports the following file formats: WAV, WMA, WMV, ASF, AVI, MPG, MP3.

SMIL

Synchronized Multimedia Integration Language (.smil, pronounced "smile") is a markup language developed by a group coordinated by the W3C. SMIL is written as an XML (Extensible Markup Language) application and, as of May 2005, version 2.1 is a Candidate W3C Recommendation. With SMIL, authors can write interactive multimedia presentations and are able to define and use separate elements and synchronize them to work together on a page. In addition to the ability to time the playing of the elements, SMIL allows the description of the layout of the presentation on a screen. Another goal of version 2.0 is to allow reusing of the 2.0 syntax and semantics in other XML-based languages such as XHTML and SVG.

A SMIL presentation is a stand-alone document that looks similar to HTML, with the head of the document containing information about the layout of the presentation, and the body a collection of components placed in a certain order. These components can have different media types such as audio, video, image, or text, and can appear sequentially or run concurrently. Figure 6.26, an example of a SMIL document, is a tutorial developed by McKinney Engineering Library at UT Austin, viewed in RealPlayer. The authors provide a detailed online guide to the production of the tutorial (http://www.lib.utexas.edu/engin/usered/multimedia/index.htm).

FIGURE 6.26
Example of SMIL in Author Interactive Presentation

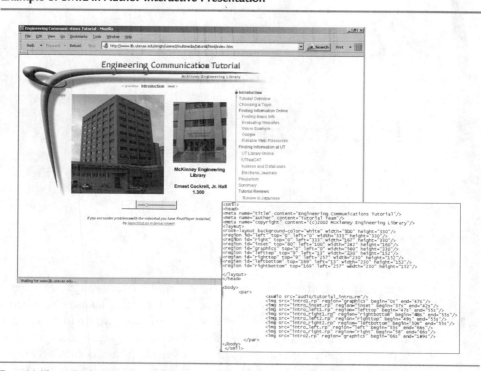

From McKinney Engineering Library, University of Texas at Austin. Available: http://www.lib.utexas.edu/engin/usered/multimedia/tutorial/html/index.htm.

Although the language has been developed so that it can be authored in a text editor, HTML editors are now adding support for the SMIL tags so that it is no more necessary to know every SMIL tag than it is to know every HTML tag. Vendors are also developing SMIL authoring tools. A SMIL player is required for viewing presentations, but again, players are available and both QuickTime and RealPlayer support SMIL. For detailed information on SMIL, including available development tools, visit the W3C site (http://www.w3.org/AudioVideo/).

Notes

1. Tony Bates and Gary Poole, *Effective Teaching with Technology in Higher Education: Foundations for Success* (Hoboken, NJ: Jossey-Bass, 2003), 60.
2. Richard E. Mayer, *Multimedia Learning* (New York: Cambridge University Press, 2001), 184.
3. Adam Powell, "Adam's Multimedia Tutorial," Webmonkey: the Web Developer's Resource, http://webmonkey.wired.com/webmonkey/multimedia/tutorials/tutorial3.html.
4. "JPEG 2000," JPEG, http://www.jpeg.org/jpeg2000/index.html.
5. Gabriel Bouvigne, "MP3' Tech," http://www.mp3-tech.org.
6. Jakob Nielsen, *Designing Web Usability: A Guide to Simplicity* (Indianapolis, IN: New Riders, 2000), 143–49.
7. "Flash Player Penetration Survey," Macromedia, http://www.macromedia.com/software/flash/survey.

7 Interactivity

Research tells us that students retain more and understand more when they are involved in active learning environments. Active learning takes place when a student is more than just a spectator and becomes a participant in the instructional process. With Web-based instruction, active learning is encouraged by incorporating interactivity. A simple definition of interactivity is "a dialog that occurs between a human being and a computer." It's easy to see that this can encompass a wide range of possibilities when you start to ponder what forms interactive Web-based instruction might take. It can mean that the student has some level of control over the sequence, pace, and content of the instruction. On a higher level, it can mean that the student can act on information and transform it into having some personal meaning. This chapter takes an in-depth look at interactivity as it applies to Web-based instruction, including

> categories of interaction
>
> interactivity methods
>
> interactivity languages and technologies
>
> interactivity development tools for nonprogrammers

CATEGORIES OF INTERACTION

A variety of technologies, both synchronous (same time, different place) and asynchronous (different time, different place), offer different kinds of interactivity on the Web. It is helpful to become familiar with the possibilities. The main categories of interaction can be divided into either individual interaction or social interaction.

Individual Interaction

Individual interaction takes place between a student and learning materials at a computer. It may also be expressed as student-resource interaction or student-content interaction. The level of interactivity depends heavily on how the instructional material is presented to the student on the computer screen. It encompasses such activities as the exchange of data, information, and knowledge from materials placed on the instructional site. Interaction can take place by various methods, which will be discussed in the next section. It can be a one-way delivery of content or a scripted exchange. Although often considered a lower (knowledge, comprehension), rather than a higher level of learning (analysis, synthesis, and evaluation), with the sophistication of programming possible today, this potential for interaction shouldn't be discounted.

Figure 7.1 shows an individual-content higher-level learning experience accomplished through scripted interactivity. This example illustrates an exercise designed to teach students to develop their critical thinking skills by learning to formulate effective search strategies. There is an opportunity to brainstorm for synonyms, alternate spellings, abbreviations, and acronyms (left column), which are compared with recommendations.

Social Interaction

The second category of interaction is social, which includes the various methods of communication that take place between various constituents, including learner-to-instructor, learner-to-learner, learner-to-guest lecturer, or learner-to-experts in the

FIGURE 7.1
Individual Interaction

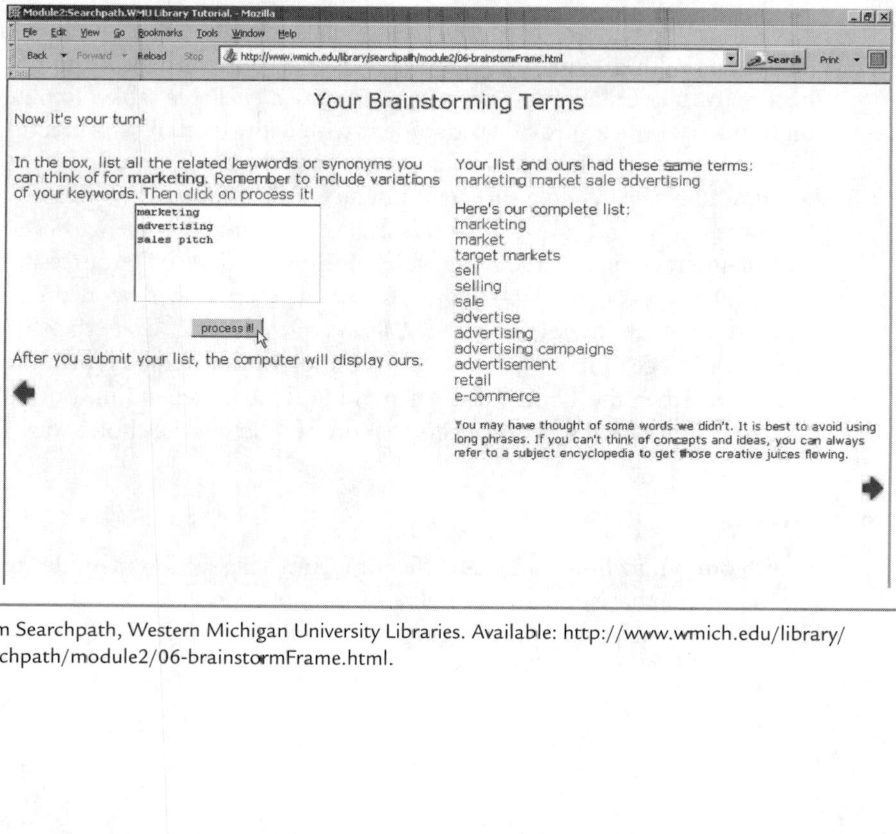

From Searchpath, Western Michigan University Libraries. Available: http://www.wmich.edu/library/searchpath/module2/06-brainstormFrame.html.

field. It can be an individual event or a group interaction. Because Web instruction is a remote learning experience, it is important to provide avenues for participants to become acquainted and comfortable with the instructors and other students, particularly with classes that extend into multiple sessions. Social interaction can be accomplished both synchronously and asynchronously through avenues including e-mail, chats, discussion forums, virtual experiences, and weblogs.

Learner-to-learner interactions can take many forms. There may be individual exchanges, but more often, students may be assigned to work collaboratively or participate in discussions to react to and evaluate other students' ideas and clarify thoughts and understanding.

Learner-to-instructor interactions are perhaps the most important interactions. They can provide encouragement, motivation, feedback, and responses to questions.

INTERACTIVITY METHODS

The decision about what level and types of interactivity to include in your instruction will be influenced by the scope and goals of your project and by the expertise of your development staff. However, there are simple, straightforward ways to incorporate interactivity into your teaching. The following subsections explore some common methods that are used to integrate interactivity: basic hyperlink interaction, communication, forms, skills practice, interactive animations, image rollovers, and dynamic database interaction. Refer to the chart in figure 1.1 for the synchronous and asynchronous types of interaction you might expect to see in online instruction.

Basic Hyperlink Interaction

At the most elementary level, point-and-click hypertext is a rudimentary form of interaction. With a hyperlink, the user makes a conscious choice to go in a certain direction or take an alternate path. In a tutorial, a clickable table of contents, navigation buttons, and text provide the student with a low level of self-direction. However, it is such a common function on any Web page that incorporating hyperlinks alone should not be considered a sufficient interactive solution.

There are ways, however, to use simple hyperlinks creatively to establish an element of interactivity. In their tutorial, "Libraries and Web Resources: Strategies for Success," University of Idaho Libraries use hyperlinks in several different ways to engage students to interact. Figure 7.2 shows one example where the student is asked to select the piece of information from a citation that would be typed into the catalog to learn whether the library owns a periodical title. Depending on which piece is selected, a responding screen appears to indicate whether the choice was the right one.

Communication

Online communications can take different forms. This section identifies types of communication that have potential usefulness in an online instruction environment: e-mail, discussion forums, chat, conferencing, and weblogs.

FIGURE 7.2

Hyperlinks to Create Interactivity in a Library Catalog Use Tutorial

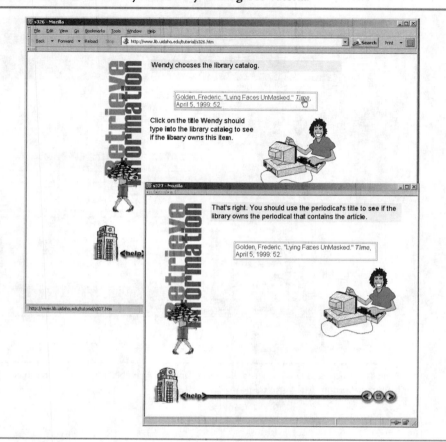

From University of Idaho Library, Moscow. Available: http://www.lib.uidaho.edu/tutorial/s326.htm.

E-mail

E-mail is one of the most straightforward methods of online communication. With a simple mailto: link, students can easily establish access to the instructor. E-mail is asynchronous, meaning that students can initiate communications with instructors at a time convenient to them (often after the midnight hour). If you are creating a multiple-session course, supplying e-mail links for all the class members can help promote student-to-student interaction.

Discussion Forum

Online discussion forums can be effective in facilitating information transfer, idea sharing, and collaboration. This method works well in a multisession course to stimulate class interaction. The instructor establishes a discussion topic, and participants respond to it and to each other's responses, creating what is called a discussion thread. Figure 7.3 pictures the main screen of a course's discussion forum in WebCT. Each

FIGURE 7.3
Discussion Forum as a Communication Method

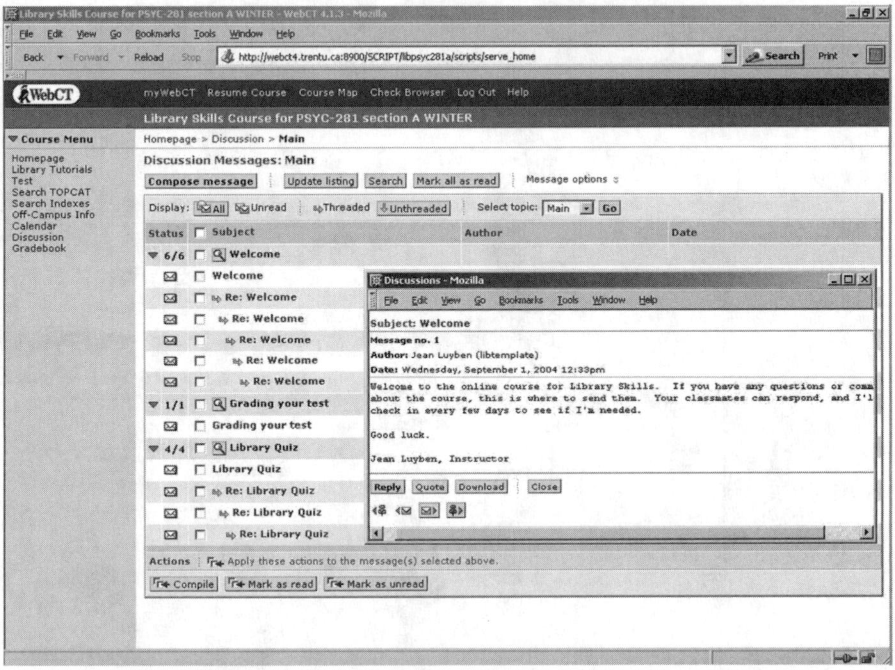

From Thomas J. Bata Library, Trent University, Ontario. Available: http://www.trentu.ca/webct
(username: primo; password: primo).

topic is shown on the screen. To participate students click on one of the hyperlinks to enter a thread. A built-in feature in many course management systems, a discussion board is an asynchronous form of communication.

Chat

A chat program is one where two or more people are connected online and converse by typing in text that is transmitted to the other person's computer screen. Real-time communication may be appropriate or necessary in a number of situations. Students in different geographical regions may be involved in a group project and need to meet to talk with each other. The instructor may determine that it is beneficial for the class members to meet with each other in a real-time situation, or want to establish office hours so that a student can talk with him or her. A chat program is a simple way to make these situations possible. During the past few years instant messaging (IM) has become almost ubiquitous among high school and college students. Savvy libraries are turning to IM as a tool to communicate with these students both for instruction reasons and research help. Chat is a synchronous mode of communication.

Conferencing

Conferencing takes real-time communication a step farther by incorporating audio and video capability. Some conferencing software applications also incorporate other features that facilitate online collaboration. For instance, Microsoft NetMeeting (http://www.microsoft.com/windows/netmeeting/) includes a white board, file transfer, and the ability to demonstrate or share control of a software application.

Weblogs (Blogs)

The popularity of weblogs is also widespread. They have evolved from being simple online journals to interactive communities. Many blogs are collaborative and support multiple user postings. Uses for weblogs in education are being identified and implemented. They can encourage independent thought, facilitate the free flow of ideas, foster discussion, and promote debate or reflection. They can be used in place of online discussion forums or e-mail lists.

A weblog is a Web-based tool (the front end is a Web page, the back end is database driven with an interface to update and edit content). Bloggers, as authors of weblogs are called, post discrete chunks of information called posts that are displayed in reverse chronological order and are date stamped.

They can be combined with an XML-based technology that is included in most blog software: RSS (Real Simple Syndication or Rich Site Summary). Weblog content is stored as XML. This code is called a feed, as in news feed. Instead of having to go to each weblog of interest, you can subscribe to the content of a blog and the RSS acts as an aggregator in collecting the information and feeding it to you on request. RSS is efficient for instructors who incorporate weblogs into their teaching. Instead of having to go to each student's blog to review new content, you can subscribe to their RSS feed and check their aggregator regularly.

The easiest way to start a weblog is to use one of many available free services. One of the best known is Blogger.com (http://www.blogger.com), but there are many to choose from and you will want to find one that offers the functionality needed to make an interactive blog. Refer to the resources section in this book for several pointers to weblog resources to help you get started.

Wiki

Wiki, developed in 1994/95 by Ward Cunningham, refers to both a Web site and the software used to create the site. Cunningham's goal was to create a simple Web site where programmers could exchange information without waiting for a webmaster to update the site. The term wiki comes from a Hawaiian word for fast, and a wikiwiki-web is a quick Web site. It is an example of what is being called social software, one that makes it easy for groups to work together in a virtual environment. Wikis emphasize a group's collective understanding rather than an individual point of view. The basic premise is that authorized users can add, edit, and delete content using nothing more than a Web browser and a form (see the next section about forms). Although this seems fraught with peril, most wiki engines have features that permit monitoring of changes and the ability to restore previous versions of a page if necessary.

Wikis come in a variety of types based on who can access them. Some are fully open to anyone. Others are *gated*, meaning that some pages may be restricted. There are members-only wikis and ones that are firewalled. An example of a well-known wiki is Wikipedia (http://en.wikipedia.org/wiki/Main_Page/), a free, open-content encyclopedia.

Typical wiki features include

page creation

page editing

text formatting

linking to an external Web page

a "sandbox" for new users to experiment in (learn to use the wiki)

a list of recent changes

a page history

site searching

There are more than one hundred different wiki software packages available today. The software is being developed in many different programming languages, the most popular being PHP, Perl, Python, and ASP (see the next section for more information).

Although not being used to any extent in library instruction as of this writing, look for its use in educational settings to increase as more libraries become familiar with the technology and its potential.

Forms

Forms are used to provide a variety of types of interactions. They can include text fields, buttons, check boxes, radio buttons, and drop-down lists. This variety of choices opens the way for multiple possibilities. Online forms can be programmed to process information that is made available to the instructor, or to give immediate feedback to the student. Forms don't necessarily have to be scripted to gather and transmit information; there are many examples of forms that are meant to be printed out by students for offline work to be subsequently turned in to the instructor in the old-fashioned way: hard copy. This section identifies some popular uses of forms for interaction: feedback, questionnaires and surveys, learning experiences, self-assessment, tests, and evaluation.

Feedback

Using a form to solicit feedback is a common use. A course-evaluation form is a feedback mechanism (see figure 7.4), but is normally designed to be more structured than a text field in which comments can be made. A feedback form can also provide an alternative way for students to communicate, perhaps anonymously, about any concerns. It is important to find out students' reactions to the experience, particularly if you are instructing distance-education students with whom you have no personal contact.

Questionnaires and Surveys

An online questionnaire can be a good tool to conduct a survey of your students. It can be valuable for gathering opinions and views from students. Surveys can be help-

FIGURE 7.4
Form Used for Feedback

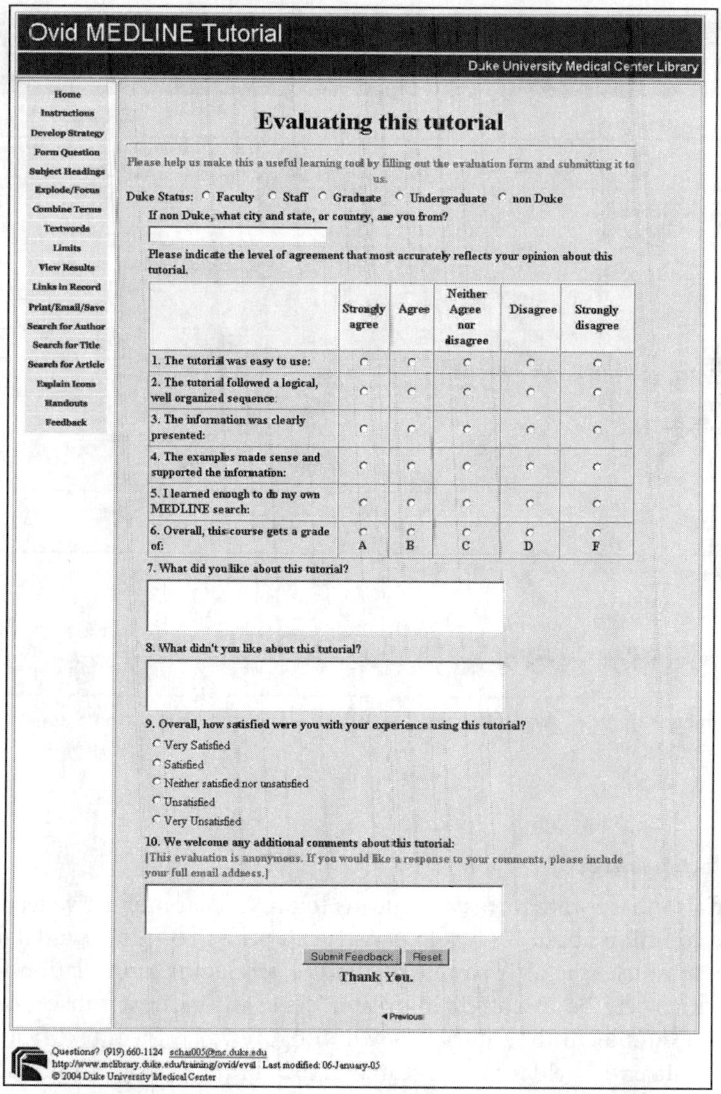

Ovid MEDLINE Tutorial

Duke University Medical Center Library

Home
Instructions
Develop Strategy
Form Question
Subject Headings
Explode/Focus
Combine Terms
Textwords
Limits
View Results
Links in Record
Print/Email/Save
Search for Author
Search for Title
Search for Article
Explain Icons
Handouts
Feedback

Evaluating this tutorial

Please help us make this a useful learning tool by filling out the evaluation form and submitting it to us.

Duke Status: Faculty Staff Graduate Undergraduate non Duke

If non Duke, what city and state, or country, are you from?

Please indicate the level of agreement that most accurately reflects your opinion about this tutorial.

	Strongly agree	Agree	Neither Agree nor disagree	Disagree	Strongly disagree
1. The tutorial was easy to use:					
2. The tutorial followed a logical, well organized sequence:					
3. The information was clearly presented:					
4. The examples made sense and supported the information:					
5. I learned enough to do my own MEDLINE search:					
6. Overall, this course gets a grade of:	A	B	C	D	F

7. What did you like about this tutorial?

8. What didn't you like about this tutorial?

9. Overall, how satisfied were you with your experience using this tutorial?
- Very Satisfied
- Satisfied
- Neither satisfied nor unsatisfied
- Unsatisfied
- Very Unsatisfied

10. We welcome any additional comments about this tutorial:
[This evaluation is anonymous. If you would like a response to your comments, please include your full email address.]

Submit Feedback | Reset

Thank You.

◄ Previous

Questions? (919) 660-1124 schar005@mc.duke.edu
http://www.mclibrary.duke.edu/training/ovid/eval Last modified: 06-January-05
© 2004 Duke University Medical Center

From Duke University Medical Center Library, Durham, North Carolina.
Available: http://www.mclibrary.duke.edu/training/ovid/eval/.

ful for assessing such things as student demographics including skill base, previous library experience, and level of subject interest and knowledge. The preassessment survey from the University of Massachusetts Amherst Libraries shown in figure 7.5 shows a questionnaire to aid instructors to determine the skill level of students prior to using the tutorial.

FIGURE 7.5
Forms for Pre-assessment Survey

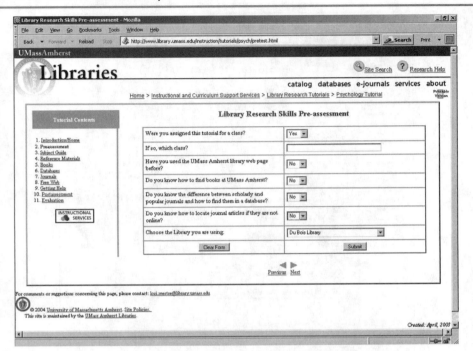

From UMass Amherst Libraries. Available: http://www.library.umass.edu/instruction/tutorials/
psych/pretest.html.

Learning Experiences

Many tutorials incorporate forms as a means to provide an interactive learning experience. One common application is to construct a page that mimics a database interface. This type of use is a fairly simple method of producing a simulation for exercise
purposes, which will be discussed in greater detail in the next subsection on skills
practice. For example, in the tutorial shown in figure 7.6, a form text field is used to
simulate the data entry field for a title search of the library catalog. If the student enters
the title incorrectly, a scripted response provides instructions to correct the error.

Self-Assessment

One of the most popular uses of forms is as a self-assessment tool. These forms are
scripted to accept input from students and return immediate feedback to them that
help them evaluate whether they have grasped the concepts being taught. With this
type of form, the results are communicated only to the person taking the assessment;
a score is not sent to the instructor. Often self-assessments are programmed to permit
the student to retake the assessment until all questions have been correctly answered.
For example, in TIP (Tutorial for Info Power) from University of Wyoming Libraries, form
elements are utilized to help students choose the best research questions (figure 7.7).

FIGURE 7.6
Exercise Using Forms in Library Catalog Tutorial

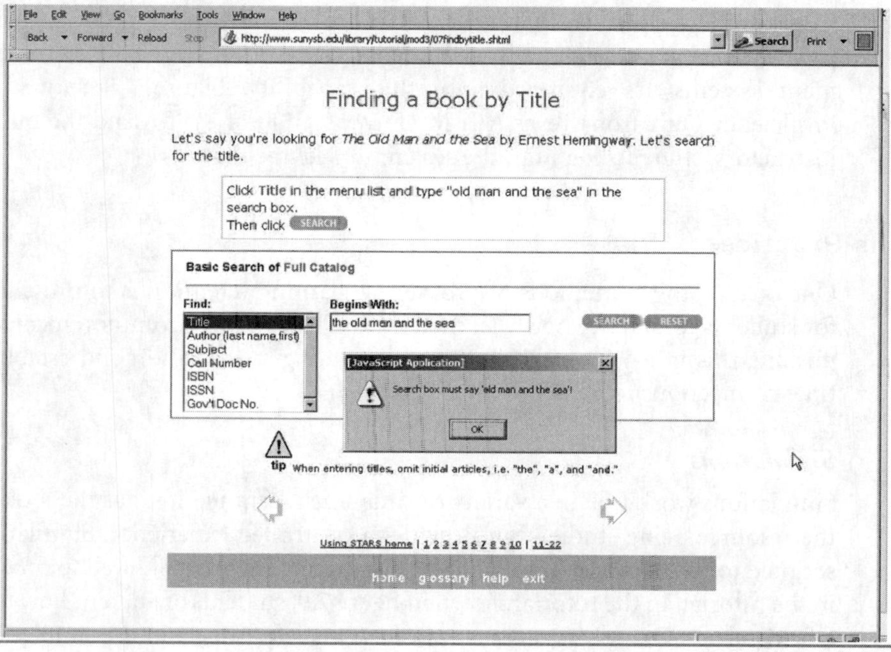

From Stony Brook University Libraries, New York. Available: http://www.sunysb.edu/library/tutorial/mod3/07findbytitle.shtml.

FIGURE 7.7
Self-Assessment Using Forms

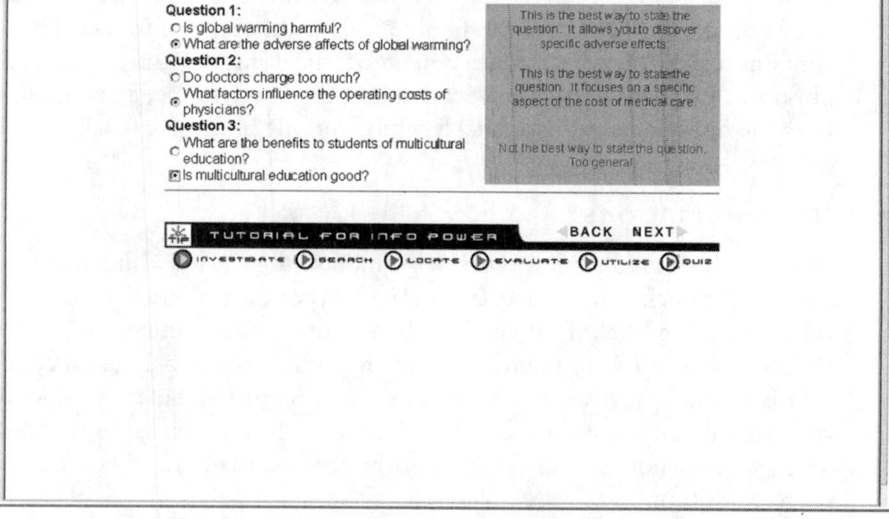

From University of Wyoming Libraries, Laramie. Available: http://tip.uwyo.edu/investigate/page2.htm.

Tests

Creating a test to assess student learning is another common use for a form. Often the form can be scripted so that test answers are submitted to a database, which can be programmed to grade it and track students' grades. Most of the major course management systems are equipped with this capability. Figure 7.8 shows a Citation Proficiency Quiz from Texas A & M University Libraries. To send the quiz results to instructors, students log in to the system to take the quiz.

Skills Practice

One of the proven methods of promoting learning retention is to provide a method for students to practice newly learned skills. The two most common means of accomplishing this in a Web tutorial are programming a simulation and establishing real-time connections to databases.

Simulations

Simulations work well in a variety of situations. A simulation has the look and feel of the resource being studied but provides a controlled experience. Simulations can be scripted to force users to make the right choice before being allowed to proceed further in the tutorial. In the tutorial shown in figure 7.9, students are taught how to use a specific database, Ovid. Instructions appear in the left frame and the simulation is in the right frame. If the student enters the incorrect data, a corrective message is displayed.

Live Access

When handled properly, incorporating the ability for students to practice real-time in a live database is an effective reinforcement. It is important to make sure, when planning a live interaction, that students don't become disoriented or lost, which is a possibility if you send them out of the instruction environment altogether. As mentioned in chapter 5, many designers use frames or pop-up windows to introduce external applications or resources so that students remain in the tutorial while accessing the live resources. In the example in figure 7.10, the tutorial uses frames. The upper frame contains the instructions for the student to follow when conducting a live search in the library's catalog. The catalog is loaded into the lower frame, allowing the student to keep the directions readily available while working in the live database.

Interactive Animations

Chapter 6 explored several types of animation that included interactive capabilities, Flash and Shockwave among them. These types of multimedia can add a sophisticated, engaging level of interactivity to a tutorial. They can be used to build simulations (see figure 7.9) or to create interactive activities that help teach concepts. Figure 7.11 is an example of an exercise from the Flyers tutorial that asks students to arrange the order of information types that should be consulted in a research project. They arrange their choices by clicking on the mouse and then dragging each selection to its correct position.

FIGURE 7.8
Testing Using Forms

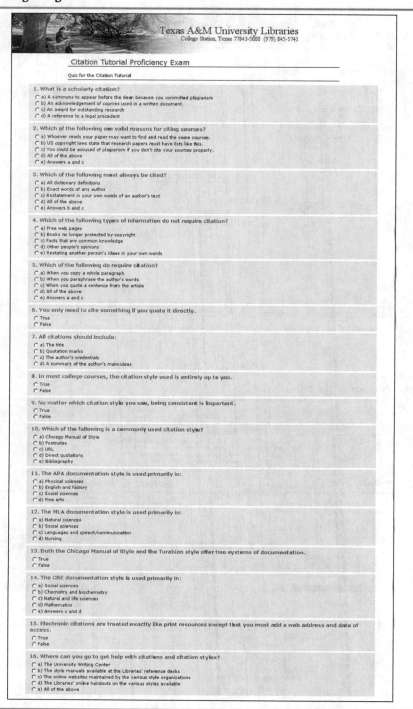

From Texas A&M University Libraries, College Station. Available: http://ednetold.tamu.edu/ast/qst/view/uncached/0,1238,0_91_6005690,00.html.

FIGURE 7.9
Skills Practice through Simulation of Database Searches

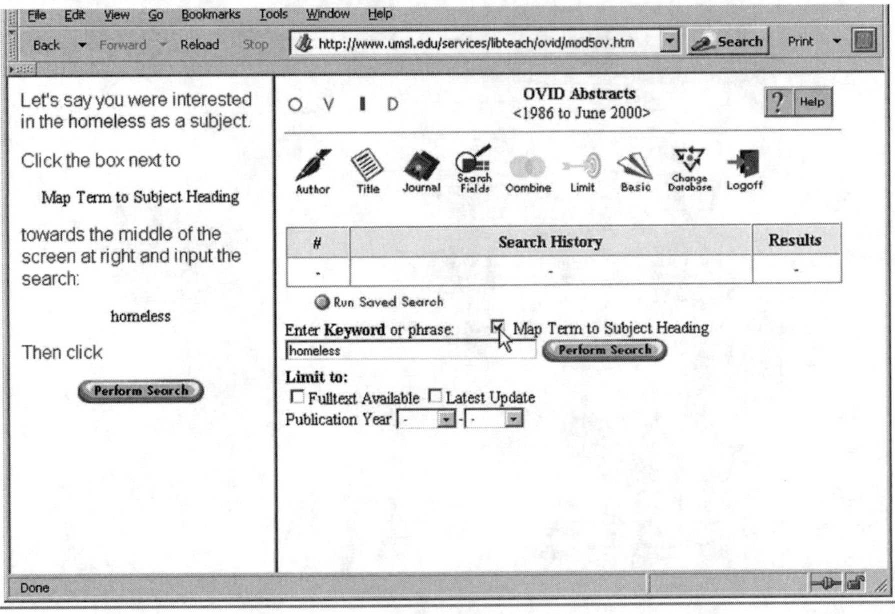

From University of Missouri, St. Louis. Available: http://www.umsl.edu/services/libteach/ovid/start.htm.

FIGURE 7.10
Skills Practice through Live Access

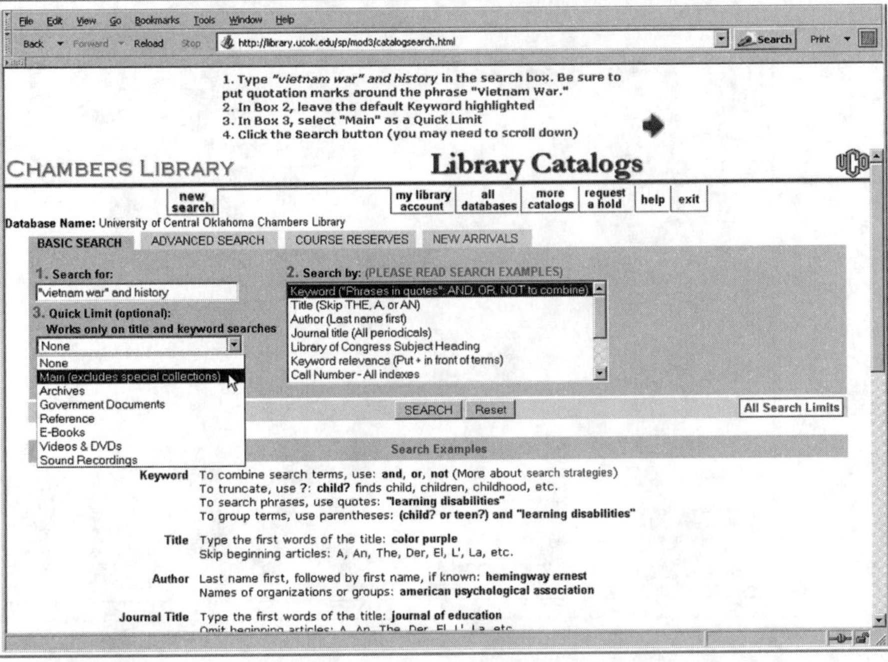

From Chambers Library, University of Central Oklahoma, Edmond. Available: http://library.ucok.edu/sp/mod3/catalogsearch.html.

FIGURE 7.11
Interactive Movement to Order the Research Process

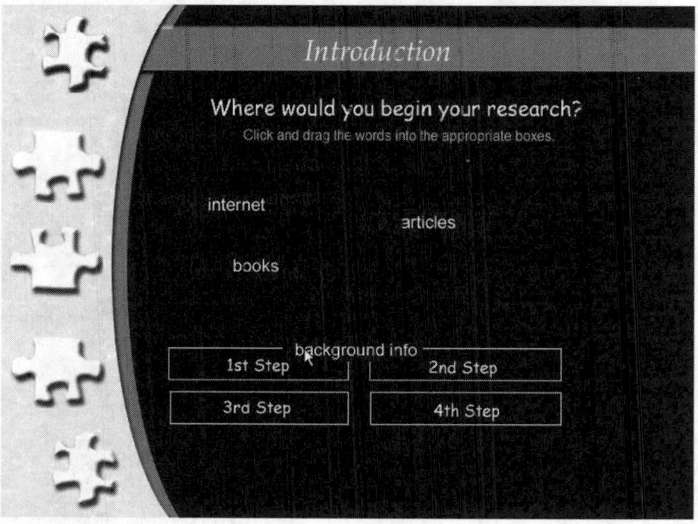

From Roesch Library, University of Dayton, Ohio. Available: http://library.udayton .edu/flyertutorial/.

Virtual Experiences

One type of sophisticated animated interaction, not seen extensively but intriguing to consider, is a 3-D virtual world to simulate a library experience. With a virtual environment, members of a community can intermingle, work cooperatively, and use resources. Library staff can interact, answer questions, and give instruction through bots, Web-links, and chats. Figure 7.12 illustrates one such world, Virtual Bibliographic Instruction (VBI) and Interactive Reference at Eastern University. The world comprises subject parks. Each park has its own reference center. Citizens and tourists (avatars) can stroll through each center and find book shelves and computer terminals that, when clicked, display Web-based resources and other information. Using VBI requires a separate 3-D browser (shown in figure 7.12). The top left window is the 3-D scene through which you can move and with which you can interact. The lower left panel is the chat panel where you can communicate with others. The panel on the right side displays the resources you have chosen.

Image Rollovers

Although rollovers are typically used to attract attention in a navigation system, they can offer a level of interactivity for active learning exercises as well. In figure 7.13, rollovers are used to explain the structure of a typical journal article citation. Students pass their mouse over each section of the citation, and the meaning is displayed.

FIGURE 7.12
Virtual Bibliographic Instruction and Interactive Reference: 3-D World

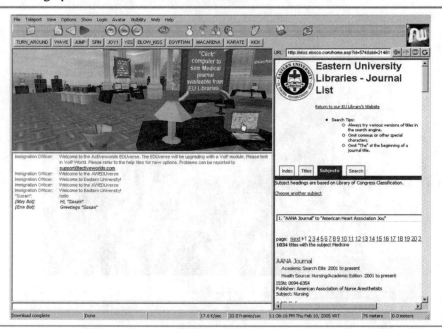

From Warner Memorial Library, Eastern University, St. Davids, Pennsylvania. Available: http://www
.eastern.edu/library/www/services/chat/vbintro.shtml.

FIGURE 7.13
Rollovers Used in Citation Identification Exercise

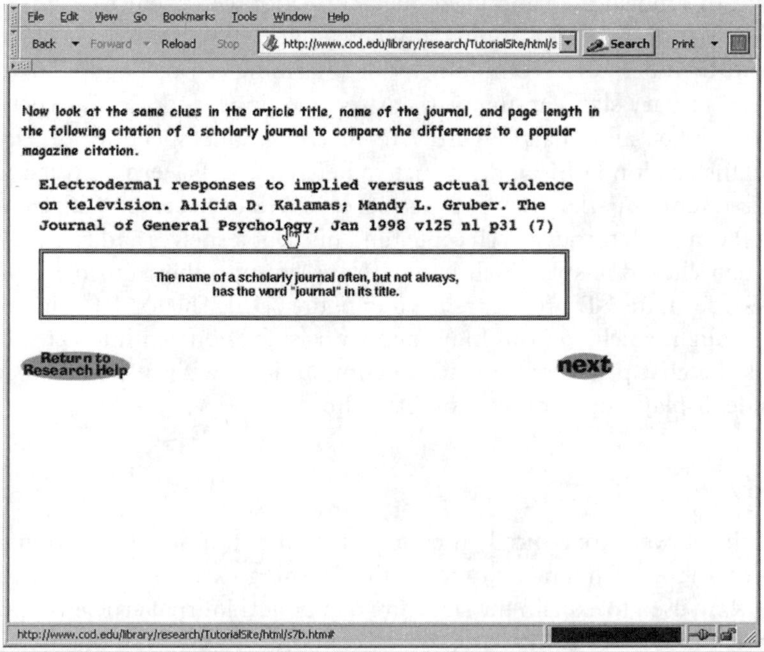

Now look at the same clues in the article title, name of the journal, and page length in the following citation of a scholarly journal to compare the differences to a popular magazine citation.

Electrodermal responses to implied versus actual violence on television. Alicia D. Kalamas; Mandy L. Gruber. The Journal of General Psychology, Jan 1998 v125 n1 p31 (7)

The name of a scholarly journal often, but not always, has the word "journal" in its title.

Return to Research Help   **next**

From College of DuPage Library, Glen Ellyn, Illinois.

Database Driven

Depending on the scope of your Web instruction project, you may find that you want to turn to a database solution. If you are planning on tracking test scores or progress of students, a database will facilitate the collection of data and data analysis and can make that data available to the students online. A database can be used to establish user accounts, build quiz pools, and authenticate access. Database-driven instructional Web sites allow knowledge to be captured into a reusable, dynamic form.[1]

If you are considering a database for these functions, there are many to choose from with a wide range of prices. As with other software choices, consider platform restrictions and complexity. If building a database from scratch and programming the interaction is beyond your team's technical capabilities, keep in mind that course management software programs use databases to accomplish interactive functions. For example, Blackboard uses Oracle as its back-end application.

LANGUAGES AND TECHNOLOGIES

Web-based interactivity is accomplished most often with Web programming languages. The most common types are known as script languages, and are often designed for interactive use, to connect diverse existing components to accomplish a new related task. A script consists of a sequence of instructions carried out (or interpreted) by another program rather than by the computer processor. Traditional programming languages (like C++) are compiled, meaning that the instructions or commands are transformed into machine language that is read by the processor. This results in a program that is executed much more quickly than one composed in a script language, but is far more complex to write. In contrast, a script language is designed to encourage rapid development because it is easier to learn and faster to code. Script languages are often called glue languages because they excel at gluing separate application components together—often necessary when bringing interactivity to a Web page.

Do you have to know one of these languages to integrate interactive elements into your tutorial? Of course not. (We will look at tools for nonprogrammers shortly.) However, it is useful to have an understanding of the different methods used to program dynamic, interactive Web sites. This section introduces the basic concepts of scripting (writing a program in a script language) and some of the common Web programming languages, including both interpreted and compiled ones. By no means is this intended to be a comprehensive discussion on writing programs, but it is a basic introduction to Web programming languages by a nonprogrammer to nonprogrammers. If you think you might want to learn to do your own Web programming, resources included at the end of this book will point you in the right direction.

Some considerations should be taken into account when selecting a Web programming language. There are several script languages criteria to examine before making your final choice:[2]

> *Ease of use.* Consider how easy it is to learn and to write. Is the syntax straightforward? This aspect can tie in closely with development.

Rapid development. By nature, script languages are faster to develop because they don't have to be compiled. But if quick development is a goal, then the time saved by writing a script may be more important than issues such as performance level.

Power and performance. Scripted tasks have to be executed either on the server (server-side) or on the client (client-side). Both ways have advantages and disadvantages, and the choice of which method to use will depend on the task being programmed and the power necessary to execute the program and how these requirements will affect performance. Again, you must consider the specifications of the computers your users will be using, the network connectivity, and the server capabilities. Compiled programs are usually quicker to execute, but if speed isn't the top priority, scripting advantages may outweigh this particular disadvantage.

Platform independence. As with HTML, you don't want to have to worry whether the application you create can function on a specific operating system. Your application should be platform independent. If that is not possible, choose a language that will work with your existing system.

Preserving intellectual property. Many script languages can easily be read by viewing the source of an HTML page. If code security is a concern, you may want to consider using a language that will offer some protection of your intellectual property.

Safety. Creating a safe environment for your users as well as your data and server is important. Some languages are safer than others, so this is something you should research.

Web Programming Languages

A few languages, such as Perl and JavaScript, have become familiar to Web designers. However, these are not the only Web programming languages out there. The following subsections, presented here in alphabetical order, briefly describe several languages that are used in Web programming. Refer to figure 7.14 for a comparison.

ActionScript

ActionScript is the scripting language for Macromedia Flash. The latest version (as of early 2005) is version 2.0. It is an object-oriented programming language (that is, programming that is organized around objects rather than actions) designed for Web site animation and to be similar to JavaScript. The code is frequently written in the Flash authoring environment and is saved along with the rest of the movie in a .fla file. However, it is possible to import ActionScript code from an external file stored on a server. In these cases, look for a .as file extension.

ActiveX

ActiveX has been Microsoft's answer to Sun Microsystems' Java technology. It is used to create a Component Object Model (COM) called an ActiveX Control, which is

FIGURE 7.14
Web Programming Languages Comparison Chart

LANGUAGE	PLATFORM SUPPORT	LOCATION	TYPE	FILE EXTENSION	NOTES
ActionScript	Cross-platform	Downloads from server to client	Interpreted	.as	Developed by Macromedia Specific to Flash
ActiveX	Cross-platform: Windows, Macintosh	Downloads from server to client	Compiled	.dll	Developed by Microsoft Being superseded by .NET platform
Java	Designed to be platform independent	Can be client-side or server-side	Compiled	.class (compiled) .jav, .java (source code)	Developed by Sun Micro-systems Applet programs run on clients; servlets run on server Unicode support
JavaScript	Platform independent	Can be client-side or server-side	Interpreted	.js	Developed by Netscape Not standardized to be handled uniformly in all browsers
Jscript	Multiplatform	Can be client-side or server-side	Interpreted	.js	Developed by Microsoft Microsoft's equivalent to JavaScript
Lingo	Cross-platform: Windows, Macintosh	Downloads from server to client	Compiled	.dcr, .swd	Developed by Macromedia Specific to Director
Perl	Cross-platform: Unix, Linux, Macintosh, Windows	Server-side	Interpreted, but can be compiled	.pl	Created by Larry Wall Used often to write CGI scripts Open source, freely available Latest version has Unicode support

(cont.)

FIGURE 7.14
Web Programming Languages Comparison Chart (*cont.*)

LANGUAGE	PLATFORM SUPPORT	LOCATION	TYPE	FILE EXTENSION	NOTES
PHP	Cross-platform	Server-side	Interpreted	.php, .php3, .phtml, .php4	Developed strictly to serve Web pages Open source, freely available No native Unicode support
Python	Multiplatform	Server-side	Interpreted but can be compiled	.py, .pyc (compiled)	Copyrighted but freely usable and distributable Unicode support
Ruby	Multiplatform	Server-side	Interpreted but can be compiled in JRuby implementation	.rb	Copyrighted but freely available Lacks Unicode support
Tcl	Multiplatform	Server-side	Interpreted	.tcl	Often used for CGI scripting Open source, available freely Full Unicode support
VBScript	Cross-platform	Can be client-side or server-side	Interpreted	.vbs	Developed by Microsoft Subset of Visual Basic Freely available Comparable to JavaScript

functionally similar to a Java applet. A control is a self-sufficient program that can run on an ActiveX network, though on a Windows or Macintosh platform only. ActiveX is being superseded by the Microsoft .NET initiative, designed for platform independence and rapid application development. .NET is a software development platform, not a programming language, but supports more than forty languages. A note of interest and caution concerning ActiveX: embedding it into the Internet Explorer browser created a way to exploit users' computers with viruses, trojans, and spyware infections.

Java

Java isn't considered a scripting language, but is included here because it is so closely associated with Web interactivity. Java is an object-oriented programming language, much closer to a full-featured language than the script languages. It was developed specifically as an Internet application by Sun Microsystems and with a goal to be platform independent. That has proved to be more difficult than desired and has not always been achieved. In addition, Sun and Microsoft went to court over Microsoft's desire to add platform-specific features. As a result, Microsoft decided to leave out Java system support in future versions of Windows. Sun and others have made Java systems available to those with Java-less versions of Windows.

Java can be used to create complete applications or to build small application modules called applets. In an HTML page, applets are handled much like an image. An <applet> tag tells the browser to transfer the compiled code to the browser and execute the code as long as the browser is Java enabled. An applet file is named with an extension of .class. Because a download to the browser is required, users' access speed capabilities should be a consideration when incorporating applets. Visit Sun's site for detailed information about Java (http://java.sun.com).

JavaScript

JavaScript is one of the best-known script languages for Web authors who want to create dynamic pages. It is commonly used to respond to user events such as mouse clicks, rollovers, page navigation, and validating form input and is a flexible way to integrate animation, sound, and other multimedia elements. Developed by Netscape, JavaScript is not a subset of Java, despite the similarity in the two names. JavaScript is an interpreted rather than a compiled language. Also, it is an open language that can be used by anyone with no need to purchase a license. A JavaScript script can be embedded right into an HTML page, meaning that it usually functions totally on the client side. However, JavaScript support is not standardized among browsers, each of which uses slightly different implementations. This means it may be necessary to write different scripts to work in different browsers. The two main ways to handle potential incompatibilities is through browser sniffing and object detection. With the proliferation of browser types and versions, sniffing has become more complex. Object detection works by testing for the existence of a property of an object and giving instructions for handling varied definitions of object.

To embed JavaScript, the code is inserted in a <script> tag in the <head> of HTML documents. If preferred, the code can also be a separate file that is called from the HTML page. These files end with the extension .js (for example, navigationscript .js). JavaScript is a safe language, meaning that it cannot access any system controls or hardware on a user's computer. Although JavaScript is best known as a client-side script, it is also available as a server-side language to accomplish such tasks as communicating with a relational database or conducting file manipulations on a server. It is handled a bit differently on a server. The script resides in an HTML document on the server, but the page is compiled into an executable file. Instead of the <script> tag, a <server> tag encloses the script. One benefit of a server-side JavaScript is that it can be read by any browser, not just those that are JavaScript enabled. Refer to the resources section at the end of this book for more information on JavaScript.

Jscript

Microsoft has developed Jscript specifically for use within Web pages. This is an interpreted, object-oriented language but not a cut-down version of a more powerful language. It adheres to the ECMAScript standard (http://www.ecma-interna tional.org), the Web's standard scripting language. Jscript is designed for use in browsers and other applications that use ActiveX controls and Java applets. It comes bundled with Microsoft Internet Explorer and with Microsoft Internet Information Server (MIIS), or it can be downloaded at no charge. It has multiplatform support. As with JavaScript, to embed the script in a document the code is inserted in a <script> tag in the <head> of HTML documents. For more information, see Microsoft's Scripting Technologies Web site (http://msdn.microsoft.com/scripting/).

Lingo

Lingo is the scripting language that drives Macromedia's Shockwave Director and is specific to Director. You will not encounter it anywhere else.

Perl

Perl (Practical Extraction and Report Language), created by Larry Wall, is popular in the world of Web development for being the primary language used to create dynamic content through CGI (Common Gateway Interface) programming. Perl is not synonymous with CGI, however, and can be used for a wide variety of purposes. It was designed to be a language to extract information from text files and generate that information into reports.

Perl works with HTML, XML, and other markup languages. Its database integration interface supports third-party databases including Oracle and MySQL. It derives from the C programming language and has its roots in the Unix environment. Yet because it is an interpreted language, it is portable across platforms, yet isn't strictly an interpreted language. Perl has been described as a compiled scripting language. This means a Perl program can be handled in different ways depending on its intended purpose. Without delving into complex details, the result is a language that is easier to learn and faster to code than traditional programming languages, but with more sophisticated capabilities than a strictly interpreted language. A program written in Perl will have an extension of .pl (for example, formmail.pl). For comprehensive information visit the Perl Web sites (http://www.perl.com or http://www.perl.org).

PHP

Originally written in 1994 by Rasmus Lerdorf and known as Personal Home Page and now called PHP Hypertext Processor, this interpreted language is similar to JavaScript and VBScript, runs on most major operating systems, and can interact with the major Web servers and relational database systems. Unlike JavaScript, however, PHP is a server-side HTML-embedded scripting language. This means that the PHP script is embedded in a Web page along with its HTML. Before the page is sent to the user who has requested it, the server interprets the code and executes the script. A Web page that contains a PHP script will typically be given a name with an extension .php, .php3, .php4, or .php5 (for example, webpage.php). Unlike most of the other languages, PHP was developed strictly to serve Web pages, that is, was not based on an existing language. PHP can be used to do the same sort of tasks that can be done with a CGI script, but, according to its developers, its strength lies in the large number of database applications it supports. The newest version of PHP has enhanced object-oriented functionality. A feature that has made it as popular as it is today (used by 18.5 million domains in January 2005) is the fact that it is a loose language, meaning that the rules aren't as strict with variables. What this means for a new programmer is an easier learning curve. It is open source and is freely available for download (http://www.php .net).

Python

Guido van Rossum, its creator, selected Python's name because he was a fan of Monty Python's Flying Circus. Python is similar to Perl because it, too, is an interpreted language that supports compilation. Known for its readability and portability to multiple operating systems, Python is deemed easy to learn because it is object oriented. In addition, it uses an uncluttered syntax that is designed to be highly readable, using English keywords rather than punctuation as is used in other languages. It runs on multiple platforms including Windows, Linux, Unix, Mac OS X, and Java. As with some of the other languages, it is available for download at no charge at a site full of comprehensive information (http://www.python.org).

Ruby

Ruby is another object-oriented programming language that was inspired by Perl and shares some features with Python. It was designed as an interpreted language but its JRuby implementation may be compiled. Ruby was created by Yukihiro (Matz) Matsumoto in 1995. The name Ruby was chosen to reflect its Perl heritage. It can be ported to many platforms including Unix, Mac OS X, Windows, and Linux. For more information on Ruby, visit the Web site (http://www.ruby-lang.org).

Tcl and Tk

Tcl stands for Tool Command Language (pronounced "tee cee ell" or "tickle"). It is an interpreted language, and like Perl, is used on the Web for CGI scripting, although not as extensively as Perl. It, too, is open source and is touted as being easy to learn and allowing rapid development. It is often compared with Perl, and both have their disciples. One advantage of Tcl comes with its Tk (Tool Kit), which is a tool for creating GUI (graphical user interface, pronounced "gooey") front-ends. John Ousterhout created Tcl. A good place to find thorough information is at the Tcl Developer Xchange (http://www.tcl.tk).

VBScript

Microsoft's VBScript (Visual Basic Scripting Edition) is a subset of the Visual Basic programming language. Like JavaScript, it is an interpreted script language. It is used in Active Server Pages (ASP) and in Windows Scripting Host as a general-purpose scripting language. As with JavaScript and Jscript, to embed a VBScript in a document you insert the code in a <script> tag in the <head> of an HTML document. Not surprisingly, it is a free language and enjoys cross-platform support. It is included with both Microsoft Internet Explorer and Microsoft Internet Information Server or can be downloaded from Microsoft's site. Visit Microsoft's Scripting Technologies Web site for further information (http://msdn.microsoft.com/library/default.asp?url=/library/en-us/script56/html/vbstutor.asp).

Web Server Technologies

This section presents a few important technologies often included when a discussion on scripting occurs but that can't really be classified as Web programming languages. These are instead technologies that permit a Web server to serve dynamic data.

CGI

The Common Gateway Interface (CGI) is actually a protocol for transferring information between a Web server and a program. Its purpose is to provide a means to process interaction between users and the server. A CGI script is stored and executed on the Web server in response to a request from a user. A typical example for a use for a CGI program is to process forms from an HTML page. The user fills in the form and clicks on the submit button. At that point, the CGI program takes control to process the submitted information. It might e-mail that data to a person, or it might write it to a spreadsheet. Although most people associate CGI with Perl, CGI is not language specific. CGI can be written in any language, including Perl, Python, and Tcl. The main shortcoming of CGI is that it tends to be slow because each request submitted by a user causes a new program to be launched. High traffic can overtax the server. Workarounds to this problem have been developed. For instance, Apache has embedded the interpreter into its Web server so that it can be executed without creating a new process each time. The big advantage of using CGI is that you are assured that all of your users will be able to use the program, unlike client-side technologies that can be turned off in the browser by users or may not be supported by a particular browser version. If you are interested in learning CGI or finding CGI scripts, check out the CGI Resource Index (http://www.cgi-resources.com).

ASP.NET

An Active Server Page (ASP) is a Web page that includes one or more embedded scripts that are executed on a Microsoft Web server before the page is sent to the user. The script responds to input from the user and then builds a Web page on the fly before sending it out. ASP works well to dynamically change, edit, or add content to a Web page; to respond to user queries; and to access databases and then return results. ASP is usually written in VBScript, although other languages can be used. Pages built with ASP have the extension .asp. The latest version of ASP is ASP.NET, which allows the replacement of in-HTML scripting with full-fledged support for .NET languages such as Visual Basic. Versions of ASP that predate .NET are now called classic. One benefit of the new version is that although ASP.NET is not compiled, it will automatically detect any changes made to a script, dynamically compile the files if needed, and store the compiled results to reuse for subsequent requests.

Because ASP is designed to run on a Microsoft Web server, required server software includes the latest Windows server OS and Internet Information Server (IIS). However, technologies are being developed that will permit ASP to run on non-Windows operating systems. One example is Sun Java System Active Server Pages (http://www.sun.com/software/chilisoft/index.xml), which markets the improved security of moving from IIS to Apache by using their product.

Because it is a server-side technology and ASP is delivered to the end users as plain HTML, there are no browser limitations for reading the output. A good starting point to learn more about ASP is at the Microsoft ASP.NET Developer portal (http://www .asp.net).

JSP

JavaServer Page is Sun Microsystems' technology similar to Microsoft's ASP. However, unlike ASP, JSP is designed to be platform and server independent. The language used to create JSP is Java. Small programs called servlets (the server-side version of an applet) are specified in a Web page and are run on the server, resulting in a modified HTML or XML page that is then sent to the requester. JSP technology is also known as the Servlet application program interface (API). JSP pages will end with an extension .jsp (for example, journalist.jsp). One benefit of servlet technology is that once a servlet is started, it stays in the server memory and can be executed multiple times to fulfill requests. Sun Microsystems' Java technology site is the place to find additional information (http://java.sun.com/products/jsp).

LAMP

With all the previous discussion of Web programming languages and technologies, with mention made of various databases, server operating systems, and Web server software, it doesn't take long to see that a combination of programs is required to deploy a dynamic Web site. LAMP is an acronym for a set of free software programs that are commonly used together to run dynamic sites: Linux (the operating system), Apache (the Web server), MySQL (the database management system) and Perl, PHP or Python (the scripting languages). They were not designed to work together, but due to their low cost and the fact that they are bundled with most Linux distributions, they have become a popular combination. When they are used in combination they are a solution stack of technologies to facilitate electronic enterprise. Comparable stacks include Microsoft's .NET architecture that has been mentioned here and Java/J2EEE (Java 2 Platform Enterprise Edition).

Markup Languages and Interactivity

By now, you understand that HTML and XML pages, by themselves, are static documents. Interactivity is added to them through the integration of scripts and other technologies. However, there are newer and more advanced markup languages that are associated with Web interactivity: dHTML, VRML, XML/XSLT, and XHTML. The following subsections discuss what they are and how they are considered interactive.

dHTML

Dynamic HTML, which is also discussed in chapter 6 in reference to animation, is not an actual specification. Rather, it is a collective term for a combination of new tags and options introduced in HTML 4.0 along with increased programming possibilities. A dynamic page is one that has the capability to change, even after it's been loaded into a browser. Some of the simple interactions that would be considered dHTML are rollovers and the ability to drag and drop objects from one place on a page to another. The three main technologies that are the primary components making up dHTML include client-side scripting, DOM, and CSS.

Client-Side Scripting

One of the best-known ways that Web authors create dynamic pages is through client-side scripting. It is the part of the equation that actually makes changes in a page. Scripts are embedded in the Web pages that are delivered to your client and your browser interprets the script to execute it.

DOM

DOM stands for Document Object Model, an application program interface (API) that allows HTML pages and XML documents to be created and modified as if they were program objects. The model encompasses the structure of a document as well as its behavior and the behavior of the objects that make up a page. All of the objects can be manipulated, and this is what makes interactivity possible. DOM is platform and language neutral; it allows programs and scripts to dynamically access and update page content, structure, and style of documents. This is accomplished by exposing DOM to scripting through browsers. While scripting makes the actual changes, DOM is the component that allows objects to be changeable. Because, originally, there were incompatibilities in the DOM implementation among browsers, the W3C came up with standard specification. The best place to find in-depth information about DOM is at W3C's Web site (http://w3c.org/DOM/).

CSS

Cascading style sheets (discussed in chapter 5) are a part of DOM, meaning that they are accessible to the scripting languages. Because CSS allows specific location placement of objects on a page (through specification of coordinates in the x, y, and z planes), a script can be used to move the object (or element), hide or show it, and otherwise change its properties (such as color and style).

X3D

X3D was previously known as VRML (Virtual Reality Modeling Language). As we learned in the section on animation in chapter 6, X3D is a screen-description language that describes the geometry and behavior of a 3-D world. This language is highly interactive as it allows users to determine how to move through a scene.

XML/XSL

XML (Extensible Markup Language) is similar to HTML in that both use tags to describe the contents of a page. However, in HTML, tags and attributes have specific meanings and control how elements will appear on a page. For instance, <p> stands for paragraph, and when it is used, a space is inserted in the line above it by default. With XML, tags are used to delimit pieces of data, and the meanings of tags are completely up to the application that reads it. If <p> is used in an XML file, it can stand for whatever data is being described (price, person, and so on). An XML tag describes the data that is contained within it. The meanings of tags can be decided on an individual level or can be determined by a group who may want to share information in a consistent way. Because the markup symbols are unlimited and self-defining, the language is said to be extensible. XML is actually a subset of SGML (Standard Generalized Markup Language). Because XML is designed to deal with data, it isn't meant to be a replacement for HTML because it isn't meant to be read. Instead, HTML and XML serve two different purposes and, thus, can complement each other. HTML handles presentation; XML handles content.

What is used to make the data from XML readable in an HTML document? The transformation is accomplished with the use of XSLT (Extensible Stylesheet Language Transformation), which we discussed in chapter 5. XSL is a family of languages, having three parts:

XSLT: an XML language for transforming XML documents from one syntax to another

XSL Formatting Objects (XSL-FO): an XML language for specifying the visual formatting of an XML document

XML Path Language (XPath): a non-XML language used by XSLT to access or refer to parts of an XML document

Where does interactivity come into play? Like HTML, XML is static. It is an effective means to structure data, but must be paired up with a programming or script language to extract data and to interface with different applications. Once again, W3C is the site to visit to find out all about XML (http://w3c.org/XML/) and XSL (http://w3c.org/Style/XSL/).

XHTML

XHTML (Extensible Hypertext Markup Language) is the W3C's recommendation to supersede HTML 4.01. It is a family of modules and document types that reformat and extend HTML in XML, which is designed to work in conjunction with XML user agents. As of this writing, XHTML 1.0 is the W3C's recommendation for the latest version of HTML (http://w3c.org/MarkUp/). Version 2.0 became a working draft in 2004. To convert existing HTML documents into XHTML, use HTML Tidy (http://tidy .sourceforge.net). If creating new pages, check your editor capabilities to default to making them XHTML compliant.

DEVELOPMENT TOOLS FOR NONPROGRAMMERS

The previous section showed that there are many choices for incorporating interactivity if you are a programmer or have one on your project team. However, what about all the rest of us who want to build an interactive tutorial but don't have the background, programming skills, or desire to do our own scripting? It is hoped that the previous section didn't scare you off, because now we are going to talk about the variety of existing tools available to nonprogrammers to facilitate building an interactive site. Keep in mind that this is a rapidly evolving industry, and between the time this is written and the time you are reading, many more tools will be available to help you. We will thus consider broad categories of interactivity development aids, but don't limit your consideration to the examples that are mentioned. Use your Internet searching skills to ferret out new and exciting utilities.

Open Publication License: yourTILT, yourSearchpath, TIP

By now, most practitioners who are investigating Web-based library instruction are acquainted with TILT (Texas Information Literacy Tutorial), which is available online (http://tilt.lib.utsystem.edu). It is an award-winning Web-based interactive educational site focusing on fundamental research skills for undergraduates, created in 1999 by the General Libraries Digital Information Literacy Office of UT, under the sponsorship of the University of Texas System Digital Library. In 2001, the TILT was made available to others under an Open Publication License (OPL). Called yourTILT, this version can be tailored to an individual institution's resources and particular user needs. A discussion list, TILTTALK exists to share questions and ideas about the use of yourTILT. To download the tutorial and join the list, visit the TILT Web site (http://tilt.lib.utsystem.edu/resources/index.html).

As part of the OPL, institutions who have customized TILT can also offer their versions to others. Searchpath (http://www.wmich.edu/library/searchpath/), from Western Michigan University, is one example of this model. They offer their customized tutorial as yourSearchpath, both in classic form and in a PHP version that can work in conjunction with a database to gather quiz scores and to e-mail instructors.

A third option for a potential adaptation of an existing interactive tutorial comes from TIP (Tutorial for Info Power) from the University of Wyoming Libraries. A grant project, developed in 2004, TIP has five modules and a quiz. It offers its tutorial to others through OPL also. Both the tutorial and the files are available at the TIP Web site (http://tip.uwyo.edu).

Web Editors

As Web editors evolve, many are including additional features that permit behind-the-scenes scripting functionality, cascading style sheets support, and sometimes, ready-to-use scripting actions. As mentioned in chapter 4, it's important to choose a Web editor that supports advanced features including CSS, layers, animations, JavaScript, applets, forms, and image maps. In addition, you want to investigate the major Web editors to see if they have extensions that can help you create more robust interactive components for your site. For instance, Macromedia Dreamweaver MX has an extension called CourseBuilder that has more than forty pre-scripted learning interactions, quiz and assessment templates, and the ability to track results to a learning management system or database.

Script Libraries

One of the greatest things about the Web is how willing people are to share what they have created. There are plenty of script libraries (sometimes called script archives) where you can find prewritten scripts that will perform just about any interactive function you need. It's easy to locate one; try going to your favorite search engine or directory and type in the kind of script library or interaction you would like to find, JavaScript script library or rollover script, for example. Depending on what type of script you are getting, the retrieval process may be a simple cut-and-paste or a file download for files like a CGI program that have to be copied to your server. For example, as shown in figure 7.15, a form is used to enter the information you need to create a popup window (top left). Then you click a button to generate the code, which

FIGURE 7.15
Scriptomizers Script Library

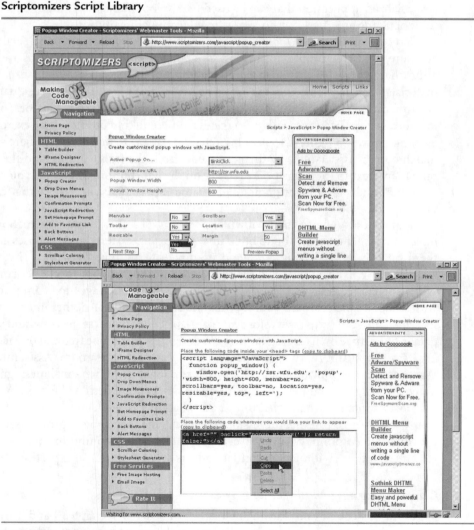

From Scriptomizers. Available: http://scriptomizers.com.

you then copy and paste into your page as directed (right bottom screen). Often a script is ready to use as written, but you may find that you will want to customize it to your situation. Good script libraries include instructions for modification and installation procedures.

Be sure to read and follow the rules that have been established at each library. Because most of these libraries collect scripts from many authors, there may be different use conditions for different scripts tied to the authors' wishes. Typical conditions include leaving author credit information inside the script or providing a link to the script library. You will find a list of several script libraries in the resources section at the end of this book.

Applications and Online Services

A specialized application that can be used to develop interactive components is a useful tool. Some are offered at no charge to educational institutions.

Hot Potatoes and Quandary, from University of Victoria and Half-Baked Software, are two examples of this type of application. These applications are offered at no charge to publicly funded nonprofit educational organizations that make their materials freely available over the Web. For others, there is a licensing fee. Quandary is an application for making Web-based action mazes. The Hot Potatoes program includes five applications; each one creates a different kind of interactive exercise. The example shown in figure 7.16 uses JMatch (top screen) to build a quiz where students match correct associations by dragging items from the right column and then dropping them next to the appropriate answer on the left (bottom screen). If you desire to track the results of student grades, hotpotatoes.net is a hosting service that can provide this for a fee.

Not all tools require you to download and install software to use them. Some sites offer services that permit you to build interactive quizzes, tests, and exercises and store them on site servers. Quia is a good example of this type of service (http://www .quia.com). For an annual subscription, it allows instructors to create games and quizzes, create classes and track quiz results, create class pages for communication with students, and maintain online schedules and a calendar. Another interesting service, FormSite.com (http://www.formsite.com), permits you to create forms and store the data in a database on its server. It offers two levels of service, one free and one fee-based.

NiceNet (http://www.nicenet.org) offers Internet Classroom Assistant, a free Web-based communication tool that provides conferencing, personal messaging, document sharing, scheduling, and link/resource sharing. It is designed for use by secondary, postsecondary, distance learning, and collaborative academic projects. NiceNet is an organization of Internet professionals who donate their time to provide services for the Internet community and have a goal of bringing communication tools and resources to those without substantial budgets or great technical expertise.

Course/Learning Management Systems

We examined course and learning management systems in chapter 4 and learned that they are designed to be a complete package to deliver all aspects of online education.

FIGURE 7.16
Hot Potatoes Quiz Creation Tool

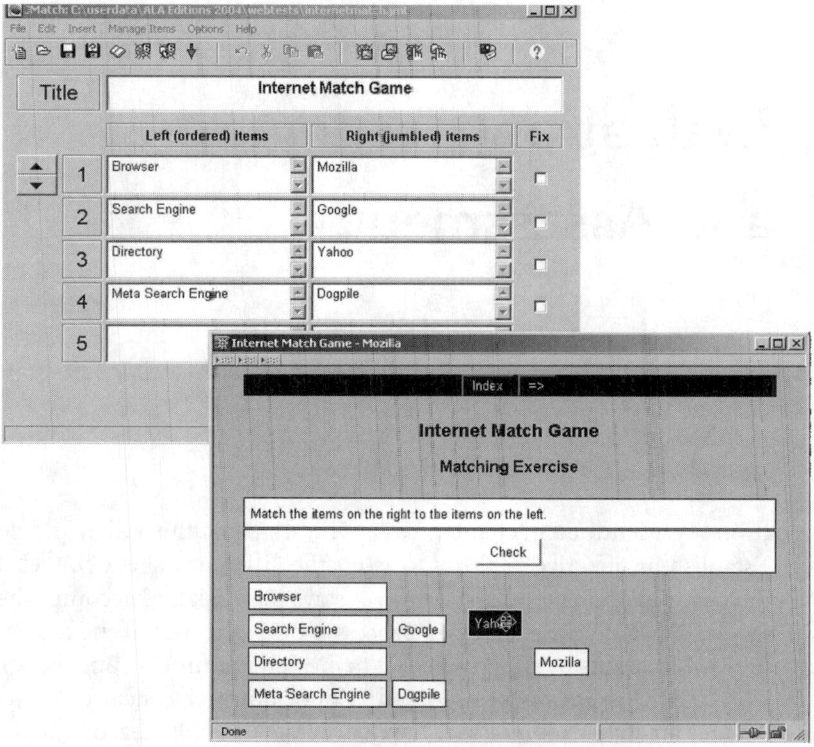

From Half-Baked Software and University of Victoria, Victoria, British Columbia.
Available: http://web.uvic.ca/hrd/hotpot/.

By definition, this includes interaction for communication, information transfer, file exchange, and online surveys and quizzes. If you have access to one, it can provide you with an environment that permits you to concentrate on instructional design and content building without having to be a technology guru.

Web Development Sites

Many sites are devoted to Web development issues. A great many of them also include tools to help Web authors build dynamic sites. WebDeveloper.com (http://www.web developer.com) is just one example of this type of site. The Web Design/HTML section of About.com (http://webdesign .about.com) is another.

Notes

1. Brenda Bannan-Ritland, "Web-Based Instruction," in *Education and Technology: An Encyclopedia*, ed. Ann Kovalchick and Kara Dawson (Santa Barbara, CA: ABC-CLIO, 2004), 643.
2. Steve Ford, David Wells, and Nancy Wells, "Web Programming Languages," 9 Jan. 1997, http://www.objs.com/survey/lang.htm.

8 Evaluation, Testing, and Assessment

Evaluation was identified in chapter 3 as a critical part of the design and development cycle. Establishing effective methods to assess the different stages of a Web-based project is the best way to make sure the project stays on track and accomplishes its established goals. However, the evaluation process is often the part of the design and development cycle that falls by the wayside. Whether due to time or budget constraints or to lack of knowledge on how to proceed, it's not unusual to hear of projects that are not evaluated in any fashion or that have chosen the wrong measurements altogether. In this chapter you will be introduced to an overview of evaluation and testing methods that have been determined to be useful for measuring the effectiveness of the interface design process as well as the effectiveness of the completed project. The goal is to provide you with some ideas about which method will best suit your project. It is beyond the scope of this book to cover research methodology and analysis, and there are many sources that address this in great depth.

WHY, WHAT, AND HOW MUCH EVALUATION?

You've assembled a knowledgeable team for your project who have good technical and design experience. You've done the analyses of your audience and have a good sense of how the project should be developed. Why, then, should you take on the extra time and expense of conducting tests and evaluations?

It's important to recognize that those most deeply involved in creating your Web-based instruction have become so immersed that it is impossible to maintain objectivity. The only way to find out if the design your team has developed functions as intended is to have it evaluated by people outside the project. What seems obvious to those closest to the project may not be understandable at all to outsiders. The goal of testing is to discover and correct usability flaws during the iterative design of the interface. External users can give you a fresh perspective.

Choices of evaluation methods can range from a costly multiphase test to a one-hour test with a few key users. Which method or methods you select will depend on several factors. Ben Shneiderman identified these determinants for the selection of an evaluation plan:[1]

Stage of design. Are you at the project's beginning, middle, or end?

Novelty of project. Is the project well defined, or is the project more exploratory in nature?

Number of expected users. Is the instruction for a class of twenty or for more than 1,000 students?

Criticality of the interface. How critical is the function of the interface you are designing? For example, an interface for a medical system will warrant a more comprehensive evaluation effort than an interface for a library tutorial.

Costs of product and finances allocated for testing. How much money has been invested in producing the tutorial, and what amount has been delegated for testing?

Time available. How much time is there to conduct an evaluation? If time is limited, a lengthy evaluation may not be the answer.

Experience of the design and evaluation team. Do your team members have any experience executing similar projects, or is this their first?

What should you try to discover through evaluation? Focusing on the wrong evaluation objective will result in a waste of time and money. Once again, Shneiderman has compiled a list of measurable human factors central to the evaluation of an interface:[2]

Time to learn. How long does it take a regular user to learn to use the interface?

Speed of performance. How fast can a regular user work through a set of tasks?

Rate of errors by users. How many and what kind of errors do users make?

Retention over time. How much of the knowledge obtained in the instruction do users retain after a length of time?

Subjective satisfaction. What do users think about the learning experience that took place?

CATEGORIES OF EVALUATION

The two main types of evaluation are formative and summative. Both are important components of the evaluation story.

Formative Evaluation

A formative evaluation takes place during the development or implementation of a project. The goal is to help the development team recognize problems in the design of the tutorial so that those problems can be corrected and improved before the project is completed. When the results of a formative evaluation are incorporated into the design, the process becomes iterative, because each modified interface is then a candidate for a new evaluation. A variety of methods can be used for a formative evaluation, some qualitative and some quantitative. Examples are surveys, focus groups, and observations. Time is an important factor in conducting a formative evaluation, however, because results must be analyzed and then be included in the modified interface quickly enough to stay on schedule.

Summative Evaluation

A summative evaluation occurs at the end of a project and is used to determine the impact of the project. It is used to measure whether the goals of the project have been met, including whether the final design and implementation were successful, as well as whether content was mastered. A summative evaluation is often the tool decision makers and other stakeholders use to judge the project's worth. In a multimedia project, this evaluation often serves as the basis for later revisions to the program. Some common summative evaluations are observation, student achievement, and interviews.

EVALUATION METHODS

Some of the established software evaluation methods may be more appropriate for either formative or summative evaluations, and others can be used for both processes. In addition, some methods involve users, and others rely on experts.

User Evaluation Methods

The intended audience for your project should be involved in the evaluation process. This section examines two common methods of evaluation that involve the user: prototyping and usability testing.

Prototyping

Prototypes are primitive interface designs that are assembled quickly and cheap to produce. A prototype allows user feedback at the beginning of the design process. Design issues can be discovered early before time and money have been invested in any actual production of the tutorial.

Prototyping may be at a low-, medium-, or high-fidelity level. Low-fidelity prototypes are those that are quickly constructed, such as paper sketches and storyboards that have no functionality but that demonstrate design concepts and layout. A low-fidelity prototype presentation for user feedback requires a facilitator who knows the intended functionality to demonstrate it. The users who will be part of the test should be representative of the targeted audience. In addition to having a facilitator present the test, development team members should act as observers and take notes on the participants' comments and reactions. If your budget allows, it may be useful to videotape the session for later reference.

Medium-fidelity prototypes simulate or animate some but not all of the features of the intended system. Some approaches to medium-fidelity prototypes are computer-based and slide/video simulation. High-fidelity prototypes are fully functional.

Both are more expensive than low-fidelity. Although most prototyping takes place in the early stages of the design process, medium- and high-fidelity prototypes make their appearances during the later stages because of the time required to produce them. Medium- and high-fidelity prototyping do not require a facilitator, but they do require an observer to record user actions. If you are interested in more detail about prototyping, read "Prototyping for Design and Development" (http://pages.cpsc.ucal gary.ca/~saul/681/1998/prototyping/survey.html).

Usability Testing

The purpose of usability testing is to assess your design and tutorial structure by having real users work through the program. This type of testing should be part of the formative evaluation so that any usability issues can be addressed and resolved.

Is it necessary to recruit a large number of users to get conclusive answers to your questions? According to Jakob Nielsen, good results can be obtained from testing no more than five users.[3] In research he conducted, he found that a single user provides almost one-third of all the data there is to know about a design's usability. With a second user, there is some overlap with what the first person found, and the second user therefore doesn't contribute as much new information as the first did. This trend continues as more users are added, but by the time the fifth user is tested, there is nothing much new to discover. Because of the iterative nature of the design process, you may choose to run a test at each stage of the redesign and involve five users for each test. The only time you really need to think about using more than five testers is when your audience straddles disparate user groups. Then you will want to include testers who are representative of each group. Be sure that the people you select to participate are typical rather than unusual users. Students who work in your library know more about how a library functions, so it is preferable to find students who are regular library users.

Testing should be held in a computer lab or wired classroom where there won't be interruptions. However, it doesn't have to be a sterile, noiseless location, and in fact should not be, because the more normal a setting you can come up with, the closer to reality the test will be.

If the testing method you are using requires interaction between the user and a facilitator, prepare a list of questions and key points you are interested in exploring so that the facilitator has a guide that will be the same for all participants. The guideline is just that, however, because issues that you never considered may crop up during a session, and these will need to be addressed with other participants.

The facilitator should have an assistant who acts as an observer and records the feedback. As with prototyping sessions, a video recording can be a valuable tool if it doesn't make participants self-conscious.

The final step in a usability test is to compile the findings and assimilate the results into potential solutions. Share these with your team, form a consensus about what actions are best, and proceed with the interface modifications. Different measurement methods can be used during a test. Some will provide you with quantitative data; others will give you qualitative insight into users' thinking.

Success rate. This is a straightforward way to test usability. You simply record the percentage of users who are able to accomplish the task they were assigned.

Thinking aloud. Users are asked to verbalize their thoughts as they work their way through the tutorial.

Task performance. With this measurement you simply time how long it takes users to perform assigned tasks.

Checklist-based testing. For budgetary reasons, you may decide that you prefer to do user testing without a facilitator or observer. A checklist-based test is cost effective and easily executed. Prepare a checklist of criteria that you want your testers to evaluate, and give them the list. Then leave the room, and let the testers work through the checklist as they interact with your program.

Subjective satisfaction. A big measurement of a design's success is how satisfied users are when they interact with it. A questionnaire can be useful in soliciting user satisfaction.

Usability Inspections

Users can provide important evaluation information. On the other hand, bringing in experts to review your interface design can be instrumental to design improvement during an iterative process. The term expert can refer to interface design authorities or to staff members who know the content and the tasks that are going to be included in the tutorial. As with user testing, usability inspections (also often called expert reviews) should involve more than one person because no single inspection will uncover every design flaw. Arrange for three to five experts to participate in the review process. Expert reviews can occur at any point in the design phase and are useful because they usually can be done quickly and cheaply. The reviews can be scheduled to take place at various stages of the design process when the development team is ready for feedback. Depending on the scope of the project, feedback from the experts can be a formal report or an informal discussion with the team. Several different methods of expert review you can choose follow.

Heuristic Evaluation

Developed by Jakob Nielsen, heuristic evaluation is one of the most popular types of usability inspection. Evaluators are given a short list of design-usability principles (heuristics), such as Shneiderman's eight golden rules (see chapter 5), or Instone's usability heuristics for the Web.[4] The experts inspect the interface on their own and determine its conformance with the list. They usually will go through the interface at least twice; the first time to become acquainted with the system and the second to focus on the specific principles. After all of the evaluators have completed their solitary inspections, they meet and aggregate their findings. Additional in-depth information about conducting heuristic evaluations is available at Nielsen's site (http://www .useit.com/papers/heuristic/).

Guidelines Review

If your organization has established specific guidelines to which your Web documents must conform, then you may want to perform a guidelines review. In this type of evaluation, the interface is checked for adherence to any organizational interface design requirements.

Pluralistic Walk-Through

In a pluralistic walk-through the users, developers, and usability experts meet in a group setting and work through task scenarios, evaluating how usable a system in fact is. A benefit of this type of evaluation is that the participants will be a diverse group, contributing different levels of skills and points of view. Normally, this type of session includes a facilitator who coordinates the discussion and participant input.

Consistency Inspection

The purpose of a consistency inspection is to ensure consistency across multiple products from the same development effort. In the case of library instruction tutorials, if you are developing two or more tutorials on various topics, having the same look and functionality across all of them will benefit the students who use them. Consistency can be checked in regard to such factors as color, screen layout, terminology, and navigation format.

Cognitive Walk-Through

A cognitive walk-through involves experts playing the role of users walking through the program interface to accomplish specific tasks. Often, users prefer to learn by exploring a new interface rather than by reading formal instructions. By putting themselves in the users' shoes, the inspectors can break down different tasks into specific steps and identify sequences that are likely to cause difficulty. To prepare for a cognitive walk-through, team members decide which tasks should be tested and then compile a list that breaks down each task into a sequence. Experts should have some knowledge of the targeted audience profile so they understand the goals. These goals should be defined and listed. During the evaluation phase, the information gathered in the preparatory stage is analyzed, and predictions are made about the degree of difficulty users are likely to encounter as they try to reach their goals.

Formal Usability Inspection

A formal usability inspection is the most structured type. Adapted from software inspection methodology, it formalizes the discovery and recording of usability problems. It is undertaken by a team of several people who, in addition to inspecting the design, each have a specific role: moderator, designer, recorder, and inspector. These roles are played during a formal meeting held after the design has been inspected. During the meeting, the moderator walks the team through each scenario or task, and the inspectors report each defect found at that particular stage. The recorder logs each reported defect. The final step is to assign the identified defects to be fixed to the appropriate development person. Because this method is detailed, it clearly takes longer to prepare and requires more people to carry out than some of the other methods do.

Inquiry Methods

In addition to user evaluations and usability inspections, asking users questions and soliciting their feedback can yield much valuable information. You can discover what they like or dislike, what their needs and expectations are, and how well they comprehend the program. Several avenues for collecting information from users are especially useful.

Questionnaires

A questionnaire is a written list of questions distributed to and completed and returned by one or more users. Although the term is often used interchangeably with the word survey, a questionnaire is in fact an instrument that can be used to conduct a survey. A survey, on the other hand, can also be conducted in person or over the telephone. Keep in mind when using a questionnaire that you are putting the burden on your users to return it to you. You are asking them to expend more effort on their part than with some other feedback methods. A possible compromise is to use an online questionnaire to survey users so that you reduce the cost of printing, mailing, and collecting paper forms.

Interviews

Interviews are direct person-to-person interaction with users. User opinions can be solicited and follow-up questions posed to clarify any issues that arise during the interview. Methods include structured sessions with specific predetermined agendas and unstructured informal exchanges. It is always a good idea to tape the interview so that the subject isn't distracted by the interviewer's note taking.

Focus Groups and Group Discussions

Focus groups and group discussions can be used to gather users' impressions both before design and after implementation. To run a focus group, you gather together six to eight people with a moderator who keeps the group on task. The moderator may demonstrate a prototype and then solicit response from the group. The main problem with focus groups as an information-gathering mechanism is that what is being collected are opinions about how participants think the program will or should work rather than data about how they would really interact if they were to sit in front of the screen and work through the program. Focus groups can be beneficial for exploring what users want from a program. What users want, however, may not be what they need.

Field Observation

Unlike observation in a usability test, field observation takes place in the users' environment. The purpose of this type of observation is to see users in action at their normal place of work or study. One component is to interview users about their work or study habits and how they would normally use the tutorial.

Online Feedback

As a part of the summative evaluation process, consider providing a vehicle for users to give you feedback from within the tutorial. This method can be beneficial because you receive impressions and opinions during or soon after users have worked through the tutorial.

ASSESSING CONTENT MASTERY

Up to this point, we have discussed how to evaluate the effectiveness of the Web instruction you are creating. Measuring the usability of the interface is an important part of ensuring the success of your project.

However, the most vital goal of an online instruction project is for learning to occur. Remember that Shneiderman identified "retention over time" as one of the factors central to the evaluation of an interface.

It is just as important to build in assessment methods into your instruction to determine if this is occurring. Many people use the terms evaluation and assessment interchangeably, but the words refer to two different activities. Evaluation is the process of judging the effectiveness and worth of the educational programs and products (such as Web-based tutorials). Assessment is the activity of measuring student learning.[5]

The tools to accomplish this are varied, and some methods are discussed in chapter 7. Some tools are traditional ones used to gauge retention, such as quizzes and tests. Assessment tools can be either formative or summative. They can be formal or informal. Optimally they will be integrated into the design of the instruction, be ongoing, and use diverse methods.[6]

Reeves discusses the need for alternative assessment approaches in an online environment and proposes three major directions that can provide more meaningful measurements:[7]

Cognitive. Students' higher order thinking abilities, attitudes, and communication skills are measured. One approach Reeves mentions is concept mapping, a strategy that permits students to represent the structure of their knowledge visually. Concept mapping software could be used with this method.

Performance. Learners demonstrate their capabilities by creating a product or engaging in an activity—applying their new abilities in a realistic context.

Portfolio. The students' work is accumulated and stored over time to be reviewed to show evolution of learning and the interim steps taken to get to the completion of a course of study.

As you plan evaluation procedures, build in assessment methods to measure if and to what extent students have mastered the content. Even if your institution or the class instructor doesn't require a grade, an assessment system can help determine how effective your online instruction has been. This can be a critical factor in decision making for future online instruction projects.

Notes

1. Ben Shneiderman and Catherine Plaisant, *Designing the User Interface: Strategies for Effective Human-Computer Interaction*, 4th ed. (Boston: Pearson/Addison Wesley, 2004), 140.
2. Ibid., 162.

3. Jakob Nielsen, "Why You Only Need to Test with 5 Users," *Alertbot useit.com*, http://www.useit.com/alertbox/20000319.html.

4. Keith Instone, "Site Usability Heuristics for the Web," *User-experience.org.* 1997, http://user-experience.org/uefiles/writings/heuristics.html.

5. Thomas C. Reeves, "Alternative Assessment Approaches for Online Learning Environments in Higher Education," *Journal of Educational Computing Research* 23, no. 1 (2000).

6. Trudi E. Jacobson, "Assessment of Learning," in *Developing Web-Based Instruction: Planning, Designing, Managing, and Evaluating for Results*, ed. Elizabeth Dupuis (New York: Neal-Schuman, 2003), 148.

7. Reeves, 107–8.

Glossary

3-D graphics   graphics that provide the perception of depth

accessibility   the capability of Web page content to be viewed or heard by everyone, especially people with impaired vision and other disabilities

animated GIF   the combination of several GIF images into a single file to create an animation

animation   the creation of the illusion of movement

application program interface (API)   a set of routines that an application uses to request and carry out lower-level services

application server   a program that handles transactions between a Web browser on a client computer and an institution's back-end (behind the scenes, usually on the server) applications or databases that reside on a server

assessment   the activity of measuring student learning

asynchronous   literally, "not at the same time"—a course in which the instruction is delivered at one time and the work can be done at another

audio   as used in this book, sound that has been digitized for storage and replay on a computer

bandwidth   the amount of data that can be transmitted in a certain amount of time

bibliographic instruction   *See* library instruction

binary files   digitized data that contains both text and nontextual information, in contrast to ASCII files, which contain only characters (plain text); include sound files, graphics files, and programming; frequently called binaries

bit (binary digit)   a single digit number in base-2, in other words, either a 1 or a 0; the smallest unit of computerized data

bitmap graphics   *See* raster graphics

bitrate   average number of bits that one second of video or audio data will transmit

blog   *See* weblog

Definitions adapted from a variety of sources, including Whatis.com (http://whatis.com), Wikipedia (http://en.wikipedia.org), Google (using the "define" function; http://www.google.com), and Webopedia (http://webopedia.com).

branching an instructional technique, usually programmed text, in which the learner's next step of instruction is determined by the response to a previous step

breadcrumb trail the part of the navigation that shows you where you are, similar to the fairy tale *Hansel and Gretel*; often found near the top of Web pages; defines both current location and primary pages above current page

browser *See* Web browser

byte the unit of data storage and transmission in computers; usually considered the code for a single character

cascading style sheets (CSS) a coding method that allows the separation of presentation from the content and structure of a document

CGI (Common Gateway Interface) a protocol for transferring information between a Web server and a program or processing the interaction between a user and the server

chat a program in which two or more people are connected online and type in text that is transmitted to the other's computer screen

chunk synonym for learning object

chunking the division of online material into small segments

clip art generic graphics that can be copied (clipped) and used again

codec (compressor/decompressor) any technology for compressing and decompressing data

compiled language programming in which the instructions or commands are transformed into machine language that is read by the processor

content management system (CMS) designed to streamline Web site content management by separating content from presentation

course management system (CMS) designed to facilitate the development, delivery, and management of online learning environments; known in the business world as a learning management system (LMS)

database a collection of organized information in which a computer can easily display and select different fields of data

deprecated an HTML element or attribute that has been outdated by newer constructs

design and development cycle the systematic process that incorporates planning, development, production, and evaluation of a software product from start to finish

digital the representation of information in the language used by computers, as a series of 0s and 1s, or binary digits

discussion forum an online platform to facilitate and manage online text discussions over a period of time among members of a group or class

distance learning a term for all learning that takes place at locations remote from the point of instruction

distributed learning a method of instructional delivery that includes a mix of Web-based instruction, media delivery, and face-to-face classroom time

dithering the process of juxtaposing pixels of two colors to create the illusion that a third color is present

Document Object Model (DOM) a programming interface that allows HTML pages and XML documents to be created and modified as if they were program objects; makes the elements of these documents available to a program as data structures, and supplies methods that may be invoked to perform common operations upon the document's structure and data; both platform- and language-neutral; a W3C standard

download/upload   transferring files between computers or other devices

dpi (dots per inch)   the number of dots that can be placed horizontally and vertically; also known as printer resolution

Dynamic HTML (dHTML)   marketing term applied to a mixture of standards including HTML, style sheets, the Document Object Model (DOM1), and scripting but not defined by W3C specification

element   the basic structural unit of an HTML document, indicated by start and stop tags, arranged hierarchically to define the overall document structure; can be empty; those with content also often called containers

evaluation   the process of judging the effectiveness and worth of educational programs and products

file format   a particular way to encode information for storage in a computer file

file sharing   refers to the sharing of computer data or space on a network

Flash   an animation authoring system by Macromedia

flowchart   a visual representation of the sequence of the content of a Web-instruction site

font   a complete set of characters in a particular style and size (for example, Times New Roman 12 point)

formative evaluation   an evaluation process that takes place during the development or implementation of a project

frames   a technique used in Web pages to divide the page into multiple windows, in which each window is called a frame and contains a separate page

freeware   software that is free to use indefinitely

GIF (Graphics Interchange Format)   a compression scheme that keeps graphics file size at a minimum with no loss of data

graphics   anything visually displayed on a computer that is not text

hard disk   a storage device that holds large amounts of data

HTML (Hypertext Markup Language)   coding used to create hypertext documents, primarily for use on the Web

highlighting   various methods used to make critical information prominent on a Web page to users

hybrid learning   *See* distributed learning

hyperlink   an image or portion of text on a Web page linked to another place on the same or a different page, either on the same or on another site

icon   a graphical representation of a concept, in Internet terms the small images on a Web interface that, when clicked, perform a function.

image map   an image containing one or more regions (hotspots) with assigned hyperlinks to other locations

image optimization   techniques used to reduce the file size of images to enable faster download time

image slicing   cutting a large image into several smaller segments for efficiency in online display

information literacy   the ability to locate, evaluate, and use information effectively

instant messaging (IM)   a combination of e-mail and chat room in which a user corresponds with others online by clicking on a name or names in a list and typing a message, which pops up in a window on the recipient's screen; others can join the conversation, much like a telephone conference call

instructional design   systematic process of translating general principles of learning and instruction into plans for instructional materials and learning

intellectual property   general term for intangible property rights that are a result of intellectual effort

interactivity   a dialog between a human being and a computer

Internet   a global network of networks connecting millions of computers

interpreted language   a script language that consists of a sequence of instructions carried out by another program rather than by the computer processor

iterative   a repetitive procedure that makes incremental corrections and changes in response to results of formative evaluation processes

JavaScript   a cross-platform scripting language used to integrate interactive actions on a Web page or site

JPEG (Joint Photographic Experts Group)   an image format to compress the size of realistic images such as photographs

learning management system (LMS)   *See* course management system

learning object   any digital resource that can be reused to support learning

learning style   an individual's preferred manner(s) in which to think, process information, and demonstrate learning

library instruction   instruction designed to teach library users how to use and locate library resources more efficiently

lossy compression   a method where compressing a file and then decompressing it retrieves a file that may well be different from the original, but close enough to be useful; used frequently on the Internet and especially in streaming media and telephony applications

markup language   a system (such as HTML or XML) for marking or tagging a document that indicates its logical structure (such as paragraphs) and gives instructions for its layout on the page for electronic transmission and display

media   the physical material on which information is recorded and stored

mock-up   a preliminary drawing or model providing a visual impression of a proposed Web site

modem (modulator-demodulator)   a device or program that enables a computer to transmit data over analog telephone lines

monitor   the part of a computer that contains the screen where messages to and from the central processing unit (CPU) are displayed

MPEG (Moving Picture Experts Group)   a standard for a digital video and audio compression

multimedia   the combination of text, still graphics, animation, audio, and video within a single technology such as a computer

navigation   the means by which a user can negotiate the content of a page or site

needs analysis   data collection and analysis to document the purpose and need for a given project

network interface card (NIC)   a board that provides network communication capabilities to and from a computer

object   a self-contained bundle of data and code

object-oriented programming   programming that features self-sufficient modules containing all the information need to manipulate a given data structure

open source   any software whose code is available for users to use and modify freely

optimization   the process used to minimize the size of Web page/site code or graphics to maximize speed of download to the user

pedagogy   the art of teaching

peripheral   any hardware device connected to a computer, such as monitor, keyboard, printer, scanner, mouse, and the like

Perl (Practical Extraction and Report Language)   the programming language most frequently used for writing CGI scripts

phishing   term coined by hackers who imitate legitimate companies in e-mails to entice people to share passwords or credit card numbers

PHP (PHP Hypertext Processor)   an interpreted scripting language similar to JavaScript

plug-in   programs installed separately but run as part of your browser to allow a user to view or hear specific multimedia

PNG (Portable Network Graphics)   an image compression designed to succeed GIF

protocol   any set of standardized rules for exchanging information among computers, with different protocols used for different kinds of communication

prototyping   a process in which versions of an interface are created to aid in designing the final product

QTVR (QuickTime Virtual Reality)   a program used to create a walk-through 360-degree panoramic virtual scene

QuickTime   by Apple, a file format and software for multimedia development, storage, and feedback

random access memory (RAM)   the area in the computer where data is stored during the short term for easy access

raster graphics   computer graphics in which the image is made up of tiny dots, called pixels, thus also called bitmapped graphics

resolution   the number of pixels per square inch on a computer-generated display

rich content   Web-based multimedia materials that are dynamic, interactive, or (preferably) both

rollover image   a JavaScript technique that allows one image to replace another on a Web page when a user's cursor passes over a page element

RSS (Rich Site Summary or Real Simple Syndication)   an XML format for distributing content on the Web

SCORM (Shareable Content Object Reference Model)   XML-based standard designed to ensure interoperability among systems and used to define and access information about learning objects so they can be easily shared between different systems

script language   one of several interpreted programming languages used to control the behavior of Web pages in response to user activities

search engine   a program that searches documents for specified keywords and returns a list of the documents or Web pages where the keywords were found

shareware   copyrighted software available for downloading and use on a free, limited trial basis

site map   a visual model of a Web site's content that allows the users to navigate through the site to find the information they are looking for

SMIL (Synchronized Multimedia Integration Language)   markup language that allows integrating a set of independent multimedia objects into a synchronized multimedia

software   a program, or set of instructions, that tells the computer what to do

spam   unwanted, unsolicited junk e-mail

spyware   a technology that surreptitiously collects information about a person without his or her knowledge

storyboard   a sketch of each screen of an instructional module to be designed and developed, including text, graphic information, design layout, color, sounds, and audience interaction

streaming media   audio or video sent in compressed form over the Internet and displayed by the viewer as it arrives rather than after it has finished downloading; plug-ins are required for playback and available for most browsers

summative evaluation   the evaluation that occurs at the end of a project and used to determine the impact of the project

SVG (Scaleable Vector Graphics)   a language for describing two-dimensional graphics in XML

synchronous   communication carried out with all parties present at the same time but not necessarily in the same physical location

syntax   the formal rules that determine how keywords or commands and their components must be combined in the source code of a computer program or in shell commands

tab   an image in a navigation system that mimics the tabs on file folders

typeface   a series of fonts

Unicode   character encoding standard developed to provide universal way of encoding characters of any language, regardless of the computer system, or platform, being used

URL (uniform resource locator)   unique address of a document or a resource on the Internet in the form protocol://server domain name/pathname

usability   the extent to which the intended user can meet his or her goals using a Web site or system

usability testing   testing a Web site to see how easy it is for humans to interact with

user agent   any software that interprets HTML documents, including graphical browsers, text-only browsers, nonvisual browsers (such as audio or Braille), and other systems and programs

user-centered design   a design approach in which the emphasis is on the user

user interface   the point of communication and interaction between computer and human

user interface design   the overall process of designing how a user will be able to interact with a system/site

vector graphics   digital images created and defined by a sequence of commands or mathematical statements that place lines and shapes in a two-dimensional or three-dimensional space

VRML (Virtual Reality Markup
Language)   a standard file format for
representing three-dimensional (3-D)
interactive vector graphics, designed particularly with the World Wide Web in
mind, and superseded by X3D

W3C (World Wide Web Consortium)
international industry consortium
founded in October 1994 to develop
common protocols that promote the evolution of the World Wide Web and
ensure its interoperability

Web-based instruction   teaching and
learning supported by the attributes and
resources of the Internet

Web browser   software installed on a computer that lets the user view material
designed for the Web

weblog (blog)   a shared on-line journal
where people can post entries on various
subjects depending on the subject focus
of the blog

WebQuest   inquiry-based activity that
involves students in using Web-based
resources and tools to transform their
learning into meaningful understandings
and real-world projects

white space   the open areas on a Web page
between design elements

Wi-Fi   short for wireless fidelity, used commonly when referring to the IEEE 802.11
wireless networking specification

wiki   a cooperative Web site, where anyone
can edit anything on any page

World Wide Web   the collection of all the
resources accessible on the Internet
mainly by HTTP

WYSIWYG (what you see is what you
get)   visually based Web site editing
software

X3D (Extensible 3-D Graphics)   a screen-
description language that describes the
geometry and behavior of a 3-D scene or
world, the successor to VRML

XML (Extensible Markup Language)
a text-markup language for interchange
of structured data, a subset of SGML

XSL (Extensible Stylesheet Language)
a language for creating a style sheet that
describes how data sent over the Web
using XML is to be presented to the user

XSLT (XSL Transformation)   a language
for transforming XML documents into
other XML documents

Resources

Accessibility

Hricko, Mary. *Design and Implementation of Web-Enabled Teaching Tools*. Hershey, PA: Information Science Pub., 2003.

Focuses on five issues in Web accessibility: legal implications, understanding Web accessibility guidelines, implementation in distance education, research in the application of accessibility, and a reference desk for additional information.

Web Content Accessibility Guidelines Working Group. "Web Content Accessibility Guidelines 2.0." Edited by Ben Caldwell, Wendy Chisholm, John Slatin, Gregg Vanderheiden, and Jason White. http://www.w3.org/TR/WCAG20/.

Working draft for version 2.0 that builds on WCAG 1.0. Aims to explain how to make Web content accessible to people with disabilities and to define target levels of accessibility. Attempts to apply guidelines to a wider range of technologies and to use wording that may be understood by a more varied audience than was the case in Version 1.0.

Web Content Guidelines Working Group. "Web Content Accessibility Guidelines." Edited by Wendy Chisholm, Gregg Vanderheiden, and Ian Jacobs. http://www.w3.org/TR/WCAG10/.

Guidelines explaining how to make Web content accessible to people with disabilities. Promotes accessibility.

Animation

Kirsanov, Dmitry. "The Art of Animation." *WebReference.com*. April 1999. http://www.webreference.com/dlab/9904/.

A thoughtful discussion on the basics of animation.

McMillan, Anna, and Emily Hobson. "Animation Tutorial." *Webmonkey: The Web Developer's Resource*. http://webmonkey.wired.com/webmonkey/multimedia/tutorials/tutorial1.html.

Includes profiles of the main animation technologies, before moving on to explain, in detail, how to use them. Design theories to use as guidelines for animations are examined. Adding audio to animations is included.

Roelofs, Greg. "MNG (Multiple-Image Network Graphics)." http://www.libpng.org/pub/mng/.

> Official site for MNG with its history, developer news, technical documentation, and list of supported applications.

Web 3D Consortium. "Web 3D Consortium: Open Standards for Real-Time 3D Communication." http://www.web3d.org/index.html.

> Dedicated to X3D, the replacement specification to VRML.

Assessment

Jacobson, Trudi E. "Assessment of Learning." In *Developing Web-Based Instruction: Planning, Designing, Managing, and Evaluating for Results*, edited by Elizabeth Dupuis, 147–64. New York: Neal-Schuman, 2003.

> An overview of assessment methods. Includes a discussion of assessment in online environments.

Merz, Lawrie H., and Beth L. Mark. *Assessment in College Library Instruction Programs*. Chicago: College Library Information Packet Committee College Libraries Section Association of College and Research Libraries, 2002.

> A survey of assessment instruments. Examples of assessment tools being used by college libraries are included.

Reeves, Thomas C. "Alternative Assessment Approaches for Online Learning Environments in Higher Education." *Journal of Educational Computing Research* 23, no. 1 (2000): 101–11.

> Describes need for alternative assessment approaches in online learning environments in higher education. Alternative options discussed include cognitive, performance, and portfolio assessment.

Audio

Bouvigne, Gabriel. "Mp3' Tech." http://www.mp3-tech.org.

> Focuses on the MP3 standard. Includes information about the MP3 standard and upcoming audio compression techniques, tests, MPEG source codes.

"Midi Manufacturers Association." http://www.midi.org.

> Official site of the organization that has overseen and coordinated the MIDI specification since its inception. Offers information on most aspects relating to the MIDI specification.

Tweakmeister, Rick. "Home Studio 101: How to Get Started with Midi and Digital Audio." *TweakHeads Lab: Electronic Music Cafe.* http://www.tweakheadz.com/how_to_get_started_ with_midi.html.

> An introduction to MIDI.

"Vorbis.Com." http://www.vorbis.com.

> Official Web site for information about Ogg Vorbis, a patent-free audio codec from Xip.org.

Best Practices

Carr-Chellman, Alison, and Philip Duchastel. "The Ideal Online Course." *Library Trends* 50, no. 1 (2001): 145.

> Addresses issues facing designers of Web-based university level courses based on experience in distance education. Components to be addressed when creating an online course; theoretical bases for ideal online course; issue of pacing students through the course; importance of face-to-face instruction.

Dewald, Nancy H. "Transporting Good Library Instruction Practices into the Web Environment: An Analysis of Online Tutorials." *The Journal of Academic Librarianship* 25, no. 1 (1999): 26–31.

> Criteria for good library instruction practices were applied to Web-based tutorials selected by the ALA Library Instruction Round Table. Face-to-face instruction and the online environment do not always lend themselves to exact parallels, yet in some respects the traditional criteria can guide librarians in developing good online instruction.

Hunt, Fiona, and Jane Birks. "Best Practices in Information Literacy." *Portal: Libraries and the Academy* 4, no. 1 (2004): 27–39.

> Discusses the application of the Association of College and Research Libraries' (ACRL) "Characteristics of Programs of Information Literacy that Illustrate Best Practices: A Guideline" to develop a successful postsecondary information literacy program.

Tancheva, Kornelia. "Online Tutorials for Library Instruction: An Ongoing Project under Constant Revision." Paper presented at the ACRL Eleventh National Conference, Charlotte, NC, 10–13 Apr. 2003. http://www.ala.org/ala/acrl/acrlevents/tancheva.PDF.

> A study of more than forty existing library tutorials and online library research aids and examines the experience of creating an interactive tutorial. Goals included to build on Nancy Dewald's study of twenty online tutorials. Additional goal was to determine to what extent an online library instruction tutorial addresses the principles of learning theories in distributed environments, as well as the accepted principles of effective library instruction. Compiled features for the ideal online tutorial. Includes a significant bibliography of case studies and research literature.

Cascading Style Sheets

Bos, Bert. "Cascading Style Sheets Home Page." *W3C.* http://www.w3.org/Style/CSS/.

> Offers in-depth information about CSS and links to resources.

Briggs, Owen, Steve Champeon, Eric Costello, and Matt Patterson. *Cascading Style Sheets: Separating Content from Presentation*, 2nd ed. Berkeley, CA: FriendsofED, 2004.

> Focuses guide to using cascading style sheets (CSS) for the visual design of Web pages. It provides coverage of all the essential CSS concepts, covers the syntax, how to structure a style sheet, and linking style sheets to (X)HTML documents.

Front Page–css discuss. http://css-discuss.incutio.com/?page=UsingFontSize.

The css-discuss Wiki is a companion to the CssDiscussList mailing list. It contains extensive discussions on cascading style sheet use.

Meyer, Eric A. *Cascading Style Sheets: The Definitive Guide*, 2nd ed. Sebastopol, CA: O'Reilly, 2004.

Second edition to definitive guide gives a thorough review of all aspects of CSS2.1 and a comprehensive guide to CSS implementation.

Raggett, Dave. "Adding a Touch of Style." *W3C.* http://www.w3.org/MarkUp/Guide/Style/.

An introductory guide to styling Web pages with CSS.

Schmitt, Christopher. *CSS Cookbook.* Sebastopol, CA: O'Reilly, 2004.

Quick solutions to common CSS problems. Intended for Web designers familiar with HTML and JavaScript, this book collects eighty-nine techniques for enhancing Web pages with cascading style sheets (CSS).

Scrivens, Paul. *CSS Vault: The Web's CSS Site.* http://cssvault.com.

Links to CSS sites, resources including reference materials, tutorials, articles.

Case Studies

Bacon, Pamela S. "Where the Kids Are." *School Library Journal* 50, no. 7 (2004): 28.

An article about a project to bring Web instruction to secondary students to help them master basic library skills.

Bender, Laura J., and Jeffrey M. Rosen. "Working toward Scalable Instruction: Creating the Rio Tutorial at the University of Arizona Library." *Research Strategies* 16, no. 4 (1998): 315–25.

Relates the process used to design and create RIO (Research Instruction Online), a Web-based tutorial designed to address identified competencies that comprise required information skills.

Blakeslee, Sarah, and Kristin Johnson. "Using Horizonlive to Deliver Library Instruction to Distance and Online Students." *Reference Services Review* 30, no. 4 (2002): 324.

Details a project from librarians at California State University, Chico, to collaborate with distance education professors to use HorizonLive and chat reference to provide traditional library instruction, albeit in an untraditional format, to distance students.

Cox, Suellen, and Elizabeth Housewright. "Teaching from the Web: Constructing a Library Learning Environment Where Connections Can Be Made." *Library Trends* 50, no. 1 (2001): 28.

Focuses on the evolving nature of the Introduction to Information Technology and Presentation course at California State University, Fullerton. Includes the background of the university; overview of the library instruction program at the university; and assessment techniques used to measure student learning and program effectiveness.

Dahl, Mark. "Content Management Strategy for a College Library Web Site." *Information Technology and Libraries* 23, no. 1 (2004): 23–29.

Presents the strategies used by Watzek Library at Lewis and Clark College to manage the content of its Web site. Informational pages are created with a template system based on the following tools: Macromedia Dreamweaver and Contribute, PHP, server-side includes, and cascading style sheets (CSS). They found that the system provides for collaborative content upkeep, flexible presentation options, structured data, and reuse of data.

Dennis, Stefanie, and Kelly Broughton. "Falcon: An Interactive Library Instruction Tutorial." *Reference Services Review* 28, no. 1 (2000): 31.

Bowling Green State University Jerome Library's Web tutorial, FALCON, models a standard library instructional session on the use of the library's Web-based catalog. The degree of interactivity and the design of a tutorial depend on the goals of its creators and the intended audience.

Diel, Eve M., and Theresa K. Flett. "The Role of Cooperation in Creating a Library Online Tutorial." *Reference Librarian*, no. 83/84 (2003): 175–82.

Reports the process of creating an online virtual library tour at St. Charles Community College.

Donaldson, Kelly A. "Library Research Success: Designing an Online Tutorial to Teach Information Literacy Skills to First-Year Students." *The Internet and Higher Education* 2, no. 4 (2000): 237–51.

Report on a collaborative effort undertaken between librarians and faculty at Toronto's Seneca College to develop and implement an online, interactive tutorial for first-year business students enrolled in the college's School of Business Management.

Duckett, Kim. "Online Instruction: Lessons Learned from Distance Education." Paper presented at the Loex 2004: Library Instruction: Restating the Need, Refocusing the Response, Ypsilanti, MI, 8 May 2004. http://www.emich.edu/public/loex/Proceedings04/duckett.doc.

Suggests that good online instructional content and tools are essential to library instruction for distance learners. Provides examples of online tools and services used to support a graduate-level distance education program and explore how planning instruction for distance learners benefits Web-based instruction for all library users.

Hansen, Carol. "The Internet Navigator: An Online Internet Course for Distance Learners." *Library Trends* 50, no. 1 (2001): 58.

Discusses the history and developments of the Internet Navigator, an online Internet course for distance learners in Utah.

Harasim, Linda. "Shift Happens: Online Education as a New Paradigm in Learning." *The Internet and Higher Education* 3, no. 1-2 (2000): 41–61.

Focuses on the Virtual-U, a Web-based environment especially customized to support advanced educational practices. The Virtual-U research team hosts the largest field trials in postsecondary education in the world with empirical results and insights generated from over 439 courses taught by 250 faculty to 15,000 students.

Izhaky, Smadar, and Beth Weil. "Using Streaming Video for Library Tutorials." Paper presented at the SLA Chemistry Division Forum Web Conference, Nashville, 7 June 2004. http://www.sla.org/division/dche/2004/izhaky.pdf.

Discusses several successful tutorial movies aimed at illustrating in real time the use and function of the electronic resources in their library.

Jacobs, Mark. "Speakeasy Studio and Cafe: Information Literacy, Web-Based Library Instruction, and Technology." *Information Technology and Libraries* 20, no. 2 (2001): 66.

Details the discussion tool Speakeasy Studio and Cafe.

Kaplowitz, Joan R., and David O. Yamamoto. "Web-Based Library Instruction for a Changing Medical School Curriculum." *Library Trends* 50, no. 1 (2001): 47.

Describes how librarians at the University of California Los Angeles Louise M. Darling Biomedical Library adapted to changes in the medical school's curriculum by using the Web as the primary mode of delivering instructions.

Kelley, Kimberly B., Gloria J. Orr, Janice Houck, and Claudine Schweber. "Library Instruction for the Next Millennium: Two Web-Based Courses to Teach Distant Students Information Literacy." *Journal of Library Administration* 32, no. 1/2 (2001): 281–94.

Analyzes the development of two online graduate courses by the library staff of the University of Maryland, University College (UMUC), including the process of designing, testing, and delivering of the graduate course; a comparison of the two course design processes, and students' perception of the value of the graduate course.

Ladner, Betty, Donald Beagle, James R Steele, and Linda Steele. "Rethinking Online Instruction: From Content Transmission to Cognitive Immersion." *Reference and User Services Quarterly* 43, no. 4: 329.

Details a study on the adaptation of bibliographic instruction from transmission of content to the creation of an interactive course to immerse students in a cognitive style of a discipline.

Lindsay, Elizabeth Balkesley. "The Best of Both Worlds: Teaching a Hybrid Course." *Academic Exchange Quarterly* 8, no. 4 (2004).

Discusses an example of capitalizing on the strengths of online courses to improve interaction and student performance within a traditional class setting.

Mach, Michelle, and Cathy Cranston. "You Can Take It with You: Portable Library Instruction." Paper presented at the World Conference on E-Learning in Corporate,

Government, Healthcare, and Higher Education (ELEARN), Phoenix, 2003. http://dl.aace.org/13741.

> Discusses the development of second generation tutorials, their initial evaluation, and implementation challenges. The tutorials cover both lifelong learning research skills and how to use current tools.

Manuel, Kate. "Teaching an Online Information Literacy Course." *Reference Services Review* 29, no. 3 (2001): 219–29.

> Discusses the development of a for-credit information literacy course for distance students at California State University and its challenges.

Matheson, Arden. "Blended Learning: A Model for Instruction." Paper presented at the SLA 2004 Annual Conference, 5–10 June 2004. http://www.sla.org/documents/blendedlearning.doc.

> Describes a local study to augment the traditional library instruction methods by incorporating options in the blended learning model and adopting a Web-based online tutorial as instruction enhancement for the marketing, human resources, and Management Essentials programs.

Minkel, Walter. "Talking Tutorials." *School Library Journal* 50, no. 5 (2004): 30.

> Describes a teacher's creation of an online tutorial to teach kids WordPad, a simple word-processing program, using an interactive mouse mascot named Mega Byte, which she adapted from some Microsoft clip art.

O'Hanlon, Nancy. "Development, Delivery, and Outcomes of a Distance Course for College Students." *Library Trends* 50, no. 1 (2001): 8.

> Provides an overview of the online information literacy course for college students at Ohio State University in Columbus, Ohio, for the academic year 1999/2000.

Parise, Pierina. "Herding Cats: Or, How Are Online Classes Changing the Education Paradigm?" *Library Computing* 19, no. 1/2 (2000): 93.

> Describes approaches needed in converting instruction to an online curriculum program, and reports reactions from both students and instructors. Calls attention to library support needs.

Perrone, Vye Gouver. "The Changing Role of Librarians and the Online Learning Environment." Paper presented at the Proceedings Distance Education: An Open Question? Adelaide (Australia), 2000. http://eprints.rclis.org/archive/00001687/01/perrone.pdf.

> Discusses the changing role of librarians in the online environment and the benefits for students after twelve months of course integrated information coaching by librarians at the University of Waikato.

Pival, Paul R., and Johanna Tunon. "Innovative Methods for Providing Instruction to Distance Students Using Technology." *Journal of Library Administration* 32, no. 1/2 (2001): 347–60.

Examines three methods tried at Nova Southeastern University in Fort Lauderdale, Florida, for providing quality bibliographic instruction to distance students: synchronous, asynchronous, and combination of both methods for delivering instruction.

Smyth, Joanne B. "Using a Web-Based Moo for Library Instruction in Distance Education." *Journal of Library Administration* 32, no. 1/2 (2001): 383.

Describes the development of a graphical interface service, Web-based Multi-User Dungeon, Object-Oriented (MOO), to create a forum for synchronous library instruction and to serve as an online meeting place for off-campus students.

Suarez, Doug. "Designing the Web Interface for Library Instruction Tutorials Using Dreamweaver, Fireworks, and CourseBuilder." *Information Technology and Libraries* 21, no. 3 (2002): 129–34.

Offers important tips that can be shared by all those developing Web tutorials similar to one created for classes in the Faculty of Applied Health Sciences, Brock University.

Tempelman-Kluit, Nadaleen, and Ethan Ehrenberg. "Library Instruction and Online Tutorials: Developing Best Practices for Streaming Desktop Video Capture." In *Connect: Information Technology at NYU*, 2003. http://www.nyu.edu/its/pubs/connect/spring03/ehrenberg_streaming.html.

Details the exploration of the possibility of using video desktop screen capture technologies as a way to generate an alternative to deliver instruction, in hopes of targeting more visual and audio learners.

Xiao, Daniel Yi. "Experiencing the Library in a Panorama Virtual Reality Environment." *Library Hi Tech* 18, no. 2 (2000): 177.

Investigates the potential of using panorama virtual reality to enhance Web-based library instruction; describes a project in Sterling C. Evans Library at Texas A & M University that emulates a physical tour and renders it into a virtual tour with 360-degree realistic views.

Clip Art

"Classroom Clipart." http://classroomclipart.com.

An example of one of the many clip art sites.

"Clip Art Warehouse." http://www.clipart.co.uk/index.shtml.

An example of one of the many sites offering Web clip art at no charge or for a small fee.

"Kid's Domain." http://www.kidsdomain.com/clip.

An example of one of the many sites that offer Web clip art at no charge, or for a small fee.

Color

Adam, Pegie Stark. "Color, Contrast and Dimension in News Design." *Poynter Online*. 2001. http://poynterextra.org/cp/index.html.

Online interactive version of the 1992 book, *Color, Contrast and Dimensions in News Design*. Explains color theory and shows how to use it in design through examples and exercises; six sections: the power of color, the physiology and theory of color, color, contrast and dimension, color on the Web, and eye-trac research; additional resources and bibliography included.

Ford, Janet Lynn. "Color Worqx." *Worqx.com*. http://www.worqx.com/color/index.htm.

A color theory tutorial and includes a bibliography with links to other resources on color.

Lehn, David, and Stern Hadley. "Death of the Web-Safe Color Palette?" *Webmonkey: The Web Developer's Resource*. http://webmonkey.wired.com/webmonkey/00/37/index2a .html?tw=design.

Examines the need to continue to use the 216 Web-safe color palette in light of development of increasing sophisticated hardware and the history of why the palette was needed. Discusses high and true color and test colors at different bits.

Content Management Systems

"Content Management." *CMS Watch*. http://www.cmswatch.com.

CMSWatch.com provides a source of information, trends, opinion, and analysis about Web content management and enterprise content management solutions.

Smith, Eleanor M., and May M. Chang. "Use of a Content Management System and Reusable Learning Objects to Develop an Integrated Suite of Instructional Materials for Scientific Information Literacy." Paper presented at the SLA Chemistry Division Forum Web Conference, Nashville, 19–25 July 2004. http://www.sla.org/division/dche/ 2004/smith.pdf.

A presentation on the use of a content management system in conjunction with reusable learning objects to manage and integrate a wide array of online instructional materials and systems.

Course Management Systems (CMS)

"Course Management Systems." *EduTools*. http://www.edutools.info/course/.

Designed to assist higher education in using a more rational decision-making process to review the many options for a course management system. Reviews each product by researching and describing more than forty product features.

Dabbagh, Nada. "Web-Based Course Management Systems." In *Education and Technology: An Encyclopedia*, edited by Ann Kovalchick and Kara Dawson, 622–30. Santa Barbara, CA: ABC-CLIO, 2004.

Provides an overview on the purpose of these systems and discusses some of the most significant products on the market. There is also a discussion of the pedagogical implication of course management systems.

Design and Development Cycle

Bichelmeyer, Barbara. "Rapid Prototyping." In *Education and Technology: An Encyclopedia*, edited by Ann Kovalchick and Kara Dawson, 483–89. Santa Barbara, CA: ABC-CLIO, 2004.

An overview of rapid prototyping in instructional design.

Burdman, Jessica R. *Collaborative Web Development: Strategies and Best Practices for Web Teams*. Reading, MA: Addison Wesley, 1999.

Guide to getting a handle on the issues and challenges involved with developing a Web site and includes strategies for effective coordination among team members and clients, a smooth development process, and a successful end result.

Dupuis, Elizabeth, ed. "Part I: Planning and Management." In *Developing Web-Based Instruction: Planning, Designing, Managing, and Evaluating for Results*, edited by Elizabeth Dupuis, 1–85. New York: Neal-Schuman, 2003.

Addresses the planning and management of a Web-based instruction project, including Scope, Timeline, and Budget; Teams and Partners; Audience and Stakeholders; Pedagogy and Andragogy; and Educational Technology.

Forte, Andrea. "Multimedia Tutorial Production Guide." http://www.lib.utexas.edu/engin/usered/funding/tutorialguide.pdf.

A guide to the production of multimedia library instruction using streaming media technology. Includes sections on planning the instruction, determining available technology/skills sets, script creation, visual media creation, audio media creation, synchronizing the tutorial with SMIL, publishing online, evaluation.

Ivers, Karen S., and Ann E. Barron. *Multimedia Projects in Education: Designing, Producing, and Assessing*. Englewood, CO: Libraries Unlimited, 1998.

Presents strategies for incorporating multimedia projects into the curriculum. The authors use the DDD-E model (Decide, Design, Develop and Evaluate) to show how to select and plan multimedia projects; use presentation and development tools; manage graphics, audio, and digital video; and evaluate student work.

University of Arizona Library. "Needs Assessment Tutorial." 2000. http://digital.library.arizona.edu/nadm/tutorial/index.htm.

Designed to help those with either no or basic knowledge of needs assessment practices and pitfalls.

Development Hardware

Anderson, Dave. *PCTechGuide: The PC Technology Guide*. http://www.pctechguide.com.

Covers the PC's major internal components and peripheral devices and, as its name implies, is more concerned with PC technologies than products. While its focus is current technology, the aim is to also convey a degree of historical perspective. Be aware that there is flashing advertising that can be irritating, but if one can get past that, there is good, solid technical information written so it can be understood by laymen.

Curtain, Dennis P. "A Short Course in Choosing a Digital Camera." *ShortCourses*. 2003. http://www.shortcourses.com.

Teaches how a digital camera works and what its features are used for. Includes links to sources and products.

Etchells, Dave, ed. *Imaging Resource*. http://www.imaging-resource.com.

Offers current, comprehensive, informative, and accurate digital camera information available. Includes digital camera, scanner, and printer reviews.

Houston, Patrick, ed. *CNET.com*. http://www.cnet.com.

Provides advice on technology products and services to inform users and expedite purchasing. Includes a directory of more than 200,000 computer, technology, and consumer electronics products as well as editorial content, downloads, trends, reviews, and price comparisons.

"Howstuffworks: Computer Stuff." *HowStuffWorks*. http://computer.howstuffworks.com.

Offers access to topics covering all aspects of computer and peripherals. Articles are clear and can be easily understood by laymen.

MacWorld: the Mac Product Experts. http://www.macworld.com.

Includes product information, news, forums, user help, and reviews relating to Macintosh hardware and software.

Miller, Michael J., ed. *PC Magazine: The Independent Guide to Technology*. 2005. http://www.pcmag.com.

Delivers comparative reviews of computing and Internet products.

"Monitor Technology Guide." http://www.necdisplay.com/support/css/monitortechguide/index.htm.

Covers all the technical aspects relating to computer monitors that are important to know when selecting them for purchase.

Distance Education

Johnson, Judith L. *Distance Education: The Complete Guide to Design, Delivery, and Improvement*. New York: Teachers College Press, 2003.

A comprehensive look at distance education from its beginning to the future.

Zvacek, Susan M. "Distance Education." In *Education and Technology: An Encyclopedia*. Edited by Ann Kovalchick and Kara Dawson. Santa Barbara, CA: ABC-CLIO, 2004.

Provides a concise overview on the topic, including history, theories, and implementations.

Distributed Learning (Hybrid, Blended)

Oblinger, Diana, Carole A. Barone, and Brian L. Hawkins. *Distributed Education and Its Challenges: An Overview*. Washington, DC: American Council on Education, 2001. http:www.ecs.org/html/Document.asp?chouseid=2707.

Designed to provide college and university presidents with an overview of distance education, e-learning, or distributed learning. Provides a general framework for understanding the key questions that distributed education poses to the higher education community.

Evaluation and Testing

Greenberg, Saul. "Prototyping for Design and Evaluation." 1998. http://pages.cpsc.ucalgary .ca/~saul/681/1998/prototyping/survey.html.

An overview of prototyping.

Hudson, Laura. "From Theory to (Virtual) Reality." *Library Journal* (Summer 2001 NetConnect): 12–15.

Discusses the steps involved in conducting usability testing.

Instone, Keith. "Site Usability Heuristics for the Web." *User-experience.org*. 1997. http://user-experience.org/uefiles/writings/heuristics.html.

Instone interprets Jakob Nielsen's usability heuristics as they relate to the Web.

Nielsen, Jakob. "Why You Only Need to Test with 5 Users." *Alertbox Useit.com*. http://www .useit.com/alertbox/20000319.html.

Nielsen's reasoning on why no more than five people are needed to conduct effective usability testing.

Norlin, Elaina, and C. M. Winters. *Usability Testing for Library Websites: A Hands-on Guide*. Chicago: American Library Association, 2002.

Provides the essentials to get a Web site usability project underway.

Starling, Andrew. "Usability Testing in Practice." *Web Developer's Virtual Library*. 15 Apr. 2002. http://wdvl.internet.com/Authoring/Design/UsabilityTesting/.

An overview of usability testing and tasks involved.

Grants and Fund Raising

Barber, Peggy, and Linda Crowe. *Getting Your Grant: A How-to-Do-It Manual for Librarians*, vol. 28, *How-to-Do-It Manuals for Libraries*. New York: Neal-Schuman, 1993.

Outlines the grant process for staffs of small and medium-sized public libraries, includes case studies for each step.

Becker, Bill. "Library Grant Money on the Web: A Resource Primer." *Searcher* 11, no. 10 (2003): 8–14.

Discusses the role of grant money in libraries and resources available to locate potential grants.

Camarena, Janet. "A Wealth of Information on Foundations and the Grant Seeking Process." *Computers in Libraries* 20, no. 5 (2000): 26–31.

> Highlights some of the top foundations and top grants in the library field, provides background information on the field of foundations, provides a guided tour of the grant-seeking process, and concludes with a list of fund-raising resources and components of key proposals.

Foundation Center. *Grant$ for Libraries and Information Services.* New York: Foundation Center.

> Annual publication that covers grants in the United States and abroad to public, academic, and special libraries, and to archives and information centers for construction, operations, acquisitions, computerization, and education.

Taft Group. *The Big Book of Library Grant Money.* Chicago: The Association.

> Biennial publication that profiles private and corporate foundations and direct corporate givers receptive to library grant proposals.

Hall-Ellis, Sylvia D., and Frank W. Hoffmann. *Grantsmanship for Small Libraries and School Library Media Centers.* Englewood, CO: Libraries Unlimited, 1999.

> Designed for educators and administrators in school and small public libraries, contains practical information needed to prepare and execute a successful grant proposal.

Hall-Ellis, Sylvia D., and Ann Jerabek. *Grants for School Libraries.* Westport, CT: Libraries Unlimited, 2003.

> Provides information to help school libraries and school library systems complete a grant application; includes listings of possible grants and recommendations for successful grant writing.

Graphics

Chastain, Sue. "About Graphics Software for Mac and PC." *About.com.* http://graphicssoft.about.com.

> Goal is to keep graphics software users abreast of the constant changes in the world of graphics software; includes resources for developing your graphics software skills.

Joint Photographic Experts Group. *JPEG.* http://www.jpeg.org.

> Official site of the Joint Photographic Experts Group, JPEG, and Joint Bi-level Image Experts Group, JBIG.

Roelofs, Greg. *Portable Network Graphics.* http://www.libpng.org/pub/png/.

> Official site; contains current information about the status of PNG support, the history of the format and its development, FAQs, news, specifications.

————. *PNG: The Definitive Guide.* 2nd ed. Sebastopol, CA: O'Reilly, 2003. http://www
.libpng.org/pub/png/book/.

Covers the main PNG-supporting applications, looks at PNG as a file format, and discusses programming with PNG.

World Wide Web Consortium. "Scalable Vector Graphics (SVG): XML Graphics for the Web."
http://w3c.org/Graphics/SVG/.

Official W3C Web site for SVG.

Image Optimization

Cook, Jason. "Site Optimization Tutorial: Lesson 1." *Webmonkey: The Web Developer's
Resource.* http://webmonkey.wired.com/webmonkey/98/26/index0a.html?tw=design.

Covers the issues involved with image compression: format basics, standard and advanced
compression techniques, progressive downloading, caching, and sizing.

"Gifbot." *NetMechanic.* http://www.netmechanic.com/GIFBot/optimize-graphic.htm.

Free service that will analyze your images and show different compressions that will save
download time.

Information Literacy

American Library Association. "Information Literacy Competency Standards for Higher
Education." ALA-American Library Association. http://www.ala.org/ala/acrl/
acrlstandards/informationliteracycompetency.htm.

Provides a framework for assessing the information literate individual. The standards outline the process by which faculty, librarians, and others can pinpoint specific indicators
that identify a student as information literate.

Brandt, D. Scott. "Information Technology Literacy: Task Knowledge and Mental Models."
Library Trends 50, no. 1 (2001): 73.

Describes and discusses the importance of information technology literacy as a precursor
to information literacy.

Institute for Information Literacy Executive Board. *ACRL Information Literacy Web Site.*
http://www.ala.org/ala/acrl/acrlissues/acrlinfolit/informationliteracy.htm.

Gateway to and gathering place for resources on information literacy focused on improving the teaching, learning, and research role of the higher education community.

Rader, Hannelore B. "Information Literacy 1973–2002: A Selected Literature Review." *Library
Trends* 51, no. 2 (2002): 242–59.

Review of the literature over thirty years. Draws conclusions on user instruction in different library types, includes notable Web sites, examples of model programs. The bibliography is annotated.

Webber, Sheila, Bill Johnston, and Stuart Boon. "Information Literacy Weblog: Sharing Relevant Items and Information Relating to Information Literacy Worldwide." http:// ciquest.shef.ac.uk/infolit/.

Focuses on facilitating the dissemination and sharing of relevant items and information relating to information literacy worldwide.

Instructional Design

Dewald, Nancy, Ann Scholz-Crane, Austin Booth, and Cynthia Levine. "Information Literacy at a Distance: Instructional Design Issues." *The Journal of Academic Librarianship* 26, no. 1 (2000): 33–44.

Discusses instructional design issues that must be considered to develop effective information literacy instruction for distance education students.

Ritchie, Donn C., and Bob Hoffman. "Incorporating Instructional Design Principles with the World Wide Web." In *Web-Based Instruction*, edited by Badrul Huda Khan, 135–38. Englewood Cliffs, N.J.: Educational Technology Publications, 1997.

Discusses how the seven common elements of instructional sequence can be incorporated in instruction designed for delivery on the Web. These include motivating the learner, specifying what is to be learned, prompting the learner to recall and apply previous knowledge, providing new information, offering guidance and feedback, testing comprehension, and supplying enrichment or remediation.

Interactivity

Kelsey, Kathleen D., and Alan D'souza. "Student Motivation for Learning at a Distance: Does Interaction Matter?" *Online Journal of Distance Learning Administration* 7, no. 2 (2004). http://www.westga.edu/~distance/ojdla/summer72/kelsey72.html.

Case study that evaluated a distance education program offered by a land-grant university agricultural college and the effect of interaction as a predicting factor for the success of such courses.

Reeves, Tom, and Patricia Reeves. "Effective Dimensions on Interactive Learning on the World Wide Web." In *Web-Based Instruction*, edited by Badrul Huda Khan, 59–66. Englewood Cliffs, NJ: Educational Technology Publications, 1997.

Presents a model that represents ten dimensions of interactive learning based upon research and theory in instructional technology, cognitive science, and adult education. These will help developers of Web-based instruction in considering the wide range of instructional attributes and the orientations that can be included in Web-based instructions.

Smith, Susan Sharpless. "Interactivity." In *Developing Web-Based Instruction: Planning, Designing, Managing, and Evaluating for Results*, edited by Elizabeth Dupuis, 191–208. New York: Neal-Schuman, 2003.

An overview of theories and models that promote interactivity, frameworks for interactive activities, and technologies for interactivity.

Interactivity Tools

"JavaScript Magic: Mouseover Machine." *WebCastle Productions.* http://www.webcastle
.com/merlin/mouseover/.

> An example of one of the interactivity tools available at no charge. Use the form to build
> the JavaScript code to make mouseover (rollover) images.

Invisible Web (Deep Web, Hidden Web)

Barker, Joe. "Invisible Web: What It Is, Why It Exists, How to Find It, and Its Inherent
Ambiguity." *Finding Information on the Internet: A Tutorial.* 7 Jan. 2004. http://www
.lib.berkeley.edu/TeachingLib/Guides/Internet/InvisibleWeb.html.

> A tutorial about the Invisible Web.

Lackey, Robert J. "Those Dark Hiding Places: The Invisible Web Revealed." http://library
.rider.edu/scholarly/rlackie/Invisible/Inv_Web.html.

> Provides links to directories, searchable sites, databases, and search engines useful for
> uncovering so-called hidden content.

Mardis, Marcia. "Uncovering the Hidden Web, Part II: Resources for Your Classroom." ERIC
Digest, 2001.

> Intended to help teachers find key resources—for themselves and their students—and
> develop techniques for keeping track of the hidden Web resources so that they can be
> accessed quickly and easily every time. Discussion includes clearinghouses, virtual
> libraries, full-text resources, learning objects, and managing hidden Web finds through
> good bookmarking and Web logging.

Sherman, Chris, and Gary Price. *The Invisible Web: Uncovering Information Sources Search
Engines Can't See.* Medford, NJ: CyberAge Books, 2001.

> Discusses many aspects of the Invisible Web, including search tools, specific disciplines of
> study, case studies, finding people, and the like. Includes bibliographic references and an
> index.

———. "The Invisible Web: Uncovering Sources Search Engines Can't See." *Library Trends*
52, no. 2 (2003): 282–98.

> Defines the Invisible Web and delves into the reasons search engines can't "see" its content.
> Discusses the four different "types" of invisibility, ranging from the "opaque" Web, which
> is relatively accessible to the searcher, to the truly invisible Web, which requires specialized
> finding aids to access effectively.

University Libraries, University at Albany, State University of New York. "The Deep Web."
Internet Tutorials. http://library.albany.edu/internet/deepweb.html.

> Provides an overview on the Deep Web, including terminology, sources of content, and tips
> for dealing with the Deep Web.

K–12

Bertland, Linda. "Resources for School Librarians." http://www.sldirectory.com/index.html.
Offers extensive links to resources covering all aspects of school media center activity.

Denton, Lisa. "Library Instruction in K–12 Schools." *Virginia Libraries* 45, no. 1 (1999).
Discusses the role of the school library media center.

Learning Objects

Center for International Education. "Learning Objects: What?" 13 Dec. 2002.
http://www.uwm.edu/Dept/CIE/AOP/LO_what.html.
Defines learning objects, links to learning objects collections, and includes a bibliography.

Smith, Eleanor M., and May M. Chang. "Use of a Content Management System and Reusable
Learning Objects to Develop an Integrated Suite of Instructional Materials for Scientific
Information Literacy." Paper presented at the SLA Chemistry Division Forum Web
Conference, Nashville, 19–25 July 2004. http://www.sla.org/division/dche/2004/
smith.pdf.
A presentation on the use of a content management system in conjunction with reusable
learning objects to manage and integrate a wide array of online instructional materials and
systems.

Smith, Rachel S. *Guidelines for Authors of Learning Objects.* 2004. http://www.nmc.org/
guidelines/.
Practitioner-focused monograph, produced with sponsorship from McGraw-Hill, provides straightforward suggestions and tips for authors of learning objects. Included topics
are the range and types of learning objects, pedagogical and design considerations, as well
as discussions of standards, metadata, interoperability, and reusability.

Tobey, Darren. "CLIP: Cooperative Library Instruction Project." *John Vaughan Library.*
http://library.nsuok.edu/tutorials/project/.
CLIP's purpose is to assist integration into the curriculum of comprehensive and systematic instruction in the use of information resources. Modules are in a standardized format
so that they can be shared and modified.

Wiley, David A., ed. *The Instructional Use of Learning Objects.* Bloomington, IN: Agency for
Instructional Technology Association for Educational Communications and Technology,
2002.
Designed to connect learning objects to instruction and learning. It is divided into five sections: learning objects explained, learning objects and constructivist thought, learning
objects and people, learning objects implementation war stories, and learning objects and
the future. An online version is available, licensed through Open Publication License
(http://www.reusability.org/read/).

Library Instruction

Heaton, Jordana. "The Instructional Role of the Librarian: A Selected Bibliography." 2001. http://www.slais.ubc.ca/people/students/student-projects/J_Heaton/l594/index.htm.

Contains a selection of major publications relating to library instruction, focusing on material published during the late 1980s through 2001. Citations compiled into a full bibliography, as well as being broken down into eight subject bibliographies.

Lorenzen, Michael. "The Librarian's Weapon of Mass Instruction." *Libraryinstruction.com*. http://www.libraryinstruction.com.

Offers library instruction lesson plans, articles about library instruction, a large library instruction bibliography, and links to library instruction resources. Also includes material relating to information literacy.

Library Instruction on the Web

Emerging Technologies in Instruction Committee of the Instruction Section. "Primo." *American Library Association*. http://www.ala.org/ala/acrlbucket/is/iscommittees/webpages/emergingtech/primo/index.htm.

PRIMO, formerly known as the Internet Education Project (IEP), is a means to promote and share peer-reviewed instructional materials created by librarians to teach people about discovering, accessing, and evaluating information in networked environments.

"Instruction Resources." *LOEX Clearinghouse for Library Instruction*. http://www.emich.edu/public/loex/resources.html.

Offers useful links to tutorials, teaching support, discussion forums, and more.

Markup Languages

Powell, Thomas A. *HTML and XHTML: The Complete Reference*, 4th ed. McGraw-Hill/Osborne, 2003.

Teaches Web markup with a focus on the standards in use today and the emerging standards of tomorrow. Presents layout and presentation techniques, including multimedia. Covers HTML, XHTML, XML, CSS1, and CSS2.

XML.com. *XML from the Inside Out*. http://www.xml.com.

The purpose of this site is to help one discover XML and learn how this Internet technology can solve real-world problems in information management and electronic commerce.

Multimedia

"Digital Formats for Library of Congress Collections." *Library of Congress Digital Preservation*. http://www.digitalpreservation.gov/formats/intro/intro.shtml.

Provides information about digital content formats. An initial offering is being compiled during 2004 and 2005, and the analyses and resources presented here will increase and be updated regularly. Digital formats will continue to evolve in the coming years and this or a successor site will also evolve to keep pace. Includes an extensive formats descriptions section, including an alphabetical listing of file formats.

Forte, Andrea. "Multimedia Tutorial Production Guide." http://www.lib.utexas.edu/engin/usered/funding/tutorialguide.pdf.

A guide to the production of multimedia library instruction using streaming media technology. Includes sections on planning the instruction, determining available technology/skills sets, script creation, visual media creation, audio media creation, synchronizing the tutorial with SMIL, publishing online, and evaluation.

"Macromedia Flash Learning Guides." *Macromedia Flash Developer Center*. http://www.macromedia.com/devnet/mx/flash/learning.html.

Guides to tutorials, samples, and documentation on learning and authoring Flash.

Mayer, Richard E. *The Cambridge Handbook of Multimedia Learning*. New York: Cambridge University Press, 2005.

Devoted to comprehensive coverage of research and theory in the field of multimedia learning. The focus of this handbook is on how people learn from words and pictures in computer-based environments. The book seeks to establish what works and to consider when and where it works.

———. *Multimedia Learning*. New York: Cambridge University Press, 2001.

A systematic summary of research studies done by the author and colleagues. The outcome is a set of seven principles for the design of multimedia messages and a cognitive theory of multimedia learning.

"Multimedia Authoring Web." http://www.mcli.dist.maricopa.edu/authoring/.

Offers a collection of pointers to Internet sites for those that develop or author multimedia.

Powell, Adam. "Adam's Multimedia Tutorial." *Webmonkey: The Web Developer's Resource*. http://webmonkey.wired.com/webmonkey/multimedia/tutorials/tutorial3.html.

Lessons that focus on RealAudio, RealVideo, and RealFlash technologies. A few years old, but solid information.

"QTVR Online Tutor." http://www.letmedoit.com/qtvr/qtvr_online/course_index.html.

A self-paced course in creating QTVR panoramas, objects, and scenes.

Roubini, Jonathan. "Audio and Video Formats." *PC Magazine* 22, no. 2 (2003): 108.

Discusses tests conducted by *PC Magazine* to answer the questions related to digital audio and video formats.

Multinational Design Issues

Collis, Betty. "Designing for Differences: Cultural Issues in the Design of WWW-Based Course-Support Sites." *British Journal of Educational Technology* 30, no. 3 (1999): 201–15.

Analyzes the cultural aspects of the Web-based course-support sites.

Loring, Linda. "Six Steps to Preparing Instruction for a Worldwide Audience." *Journal of Interactive Instruction Development* 14, no. 3 (2002): 24–29.

> Discusses six steps to follow to develop instruction for a multinational audience: address administrative issues, begin globally, consider cultural variables, design for worldwide use, express yourself clearly, and free training of rigid rules. Includes an annotated bibliography.

Navigation

Fleming, Jennifer. *Web Navigation: Designing the User Experience*. Sebastopol, CA: O'Reilly, 1998.

> Explores navigation design in depth, covering usability engineering, interface design, lessons from "real life," and more. Case studies of popular sites help show what works and what doesn't.

Online Learning Resources

Dringus, Laurie P. "Editor's Choice 2004: Selected Online Learning Resources." *The Internet and Higher Education* 7, no. 4 (2004): 343–64.

> The editor-in-chief of The Internet and Higher Education (INTHIG) compiles for the last issue of each year's volume resources that may be useful for researchers, teachers, administrators, or students who wish to locate information about the field of online learning and the uses of the Internet for instructional delivery. Resources are organized into several categories.

Page and Site Optimization

King, Andrew B. *Speed up Your Site: Web Site Optimization*. Indianapolis, IN: New Riders, 2003.

> Topics range from the psychology of user satisfaction on the Web; to CSS, JavaScript, HTML, and XHTML optimization tips; to graphics, audio, and video; and finally, search engine optimization and case studies of real Web sites.

Pedagogy

Dewald, Nancy H. "Web-Based Library Instruction: What Is Good Pedagogy?" *Information Technology and Libraries* 18, no. 1 (1999): 26.

> Reviews early pedagogical influences and some educators' ideas on Web instruction, then discusses how these theories are applied to Web-based library instruction, including selected exemplary sites.

Libraries, Association of College and Research. "Tips for Developing Effective Web-Based Library Instruction." *ALA Instruction Section*. http://www.ala.org/ala/acrlbucket/is/iscommittees/webpages/teachingmethods/tips.htm.

> Recommends that tutorials should follow the general principles for good Web page design. Offers tips on the pedagogy of Web tutorials.

Public Libraries

Stephens, Michael. "Here Come the Trainers!" *Public Libraries* 43, no. 4 (2004): 214–16.

> Public librarians have assumed the role of an Internet trainer to assist staffs and patrons seeking technology-training programs. This article offers several training tips designed to help library trainers.

Research Literature

ChanLin, Lih-Juan, and Barbara Chwen-Chwen Chang. "Web-Based Library Instruction for Promoting Information Skills." *Journal of Instructional Psychology* 30, no. 4 (2003): 265–75.

> Addresses the issues regarding the implementation of the Web-based library instruction from cognitive and instructional aspects. A Web-based library instruction was developed, implemented, and evaluated. Students' responses toward the Web-based instruction and the online interaction were analyzed.

Churkovich, Marion, and Christine Oughtred. "Can an Online Tutorial Pass the Test for Library Instruction? An Evaluation and Comparison of Library Skills Instruction Methods for First Year Students at Deakin University." *Australian Academic and Research Libraries* 33, no. 1 (2002): 25(14).

> The research compared and evaluated an online tutorial and face-to-face instruction. Findings were that students in face-to-face instruction gained higher posttest mean scores than did the students who used the tutorial. Face-to-face students were more confident following instruction than were the other group.

Drabenstott, Karen Markey. "Interactive Multimedia for Library-User Education." portal: *Libraries and the Academy* 3, no. 4 (2003): 601–13.

> Library educators at four academic libraries are using distance-education technologies to learn how to design and build Web-based interactive multimedia sites for library-user education. They will then test library users before and after using these multimedia sites to determine whether interactive multimedia is an effective approach to teaching library users about library research.

Fourie, Ina. "The Use of CAI for Distance Teaching in the Formulation of Search Strategies." *Library Trends* 50, no. 1 (2001): 110.

> Considers the use of computer-assisted instruction (CAI) as an effective method of teaching in Library and Information Science practices. Includes an overview of CAI and how it can be used in distance learning; design of a CAI tutorial for distance learning and analysis of learning content with regard to the formulation of search strategies.

Germain, Carol Anne, and Trudi E. Jacobson. "A Comparison of the Effectiveness of Presentation Formats for Instruction: Teaching First-Year Students." *College and Research Libraries* 61, no. 1 (2000): 65(8).

Compares the effectiveness of two library instructional methods used to teach a segment of students enrolled in the Project Renaissance first-year experience program at the University at Albany in New York.

Gregory, Vicki L. "Student Perceptions of the Effectiveness of Web-Based Distance Education." *New Library World* 104, no. 10 (2003): 426–31.

Study demonstrating that students perceive that the quality of their educational experience is significantly improved when there is included within or as an integral part of the course offering some meaningful level of real-time interaction.

Gutierrez, Carolyn, and Jianrong Wang. "A Comparison of an Electronic Vs. Print Workbook for Information Literacy Instruction." *The Journal of Academic Librarianship* 27, no. 3 (2001): 208–12.

Study comparing the attitudes and performance of two groups of freshman college students assigned print and electronic workbooks respectively. Findings included the fact that frequency of library usage was the significant factor in improvement of information literacy skills rather than instructional format.

Henke, Harold. "Evaluating Web-Based Instructional Design." *Chartula Press.* http://www.chartula.com/evalwbi.pdf.

Research project exploring design issues associated with the development of Web-based instruction (WBI). A Web-based instruction course with two sets of Web design guidelines was reviewed in an attempt to answer the question: What is good Web-based instruction design?

Holman, Lucy. "A Comparison of Computer-Assisted Instruction and Classroom Bibliographic Instruction." *Reference and User Services Quarterly* 40, no. 1 (2000): 53.

Report on a study that compares computer-assisted instruction (CAI) in the form of an online library tutorial to the more traditional classroom approach to bibliographic instruction. Designed to compare CAI and traditional classroom instruction as methods for teaching practical library skills. Focused on first-year students enrolled in English composition classes.

Magi, Trina J. "What's Best for Students? Comparing the Effectiveness of a Traditional Print Pathfinder and a Web-Based Research Tool." *Portal: Libraries and the Academy* 3, no. 4 (2003): 671–86.

For years, academic librarians have developed research guides and subject bibliographies to help students more quickly find information in various disciplines. Quantitative study compared a print pathfinder and a Web-based research tool in library instruction for two sections of a first-year business course. Intended to help the librarian decide whether it is in the best interest of students to replace the traditional printed pathfinder with an interactive Web tool.

Michel, Stephanie. "What Do They Really Think? Assessing Student and Faculty Perspectives of a Web-Based Tutorial To Library Research." *College and Research Libraries* 62, no. 4 (2001): 317(16).

Evaluates perceptions of the Highlander Guide, a Web-based tutorial for computer-assisted instruction in library research, by students and faculty in Radford University, Virginia. A correlation was found between students' perceptions of the guide and confidence in using the Web; a number of participants were in favor of using the tutorial to replace traditional library instruction.

Nichols, James, Barbara Shaffer, and Karen Shockey. "Changing the Face of Instruction: Is Online or In-class More Effective?" *College and Research Libraries* 64, no. 5 (2003): 378–88.

Study comparing student learning from use of an online tutorial with learning from a traditional lecture/demonstration for basic information literacy instruction in freshman English composition classes. Measures of both student learning and student satisfaction were comparable for online tutorial and in-class instruction.

Olson, Tatana M., and Robert A. Wisher. "The Effectiveness of Web-Based Instruction: An Inquiry." *IRRODL: International Review of Research in Open and Distance Learning.* 2002. http://www.irrodl.org/content/v3.2/olsen.html.

Conducted a meta-analysis of CBI as an appropriate benchmark to Web-based instruction. Forty-seven reports of evaluations of Web-based courses in higher education published between 1996 and 2002 were reviewed.

Orme, William A. "A Study of the Residual Impact of the Texas Information Literacy Tutorial on the Information-Seeking Ability of First Year College Students." *College and Research Libraries* 65, no. 3 (2004): 205(11).

"The study discussed in this paper investigated the residual impact of the Web-based tutorial Texas Information Literacy Tutorial (TILT) on first-year college students and their ability to perform tasks related to information research. Unique to this study is the investigation of ability beyond the semester in which instruction was provided. The study examined four groups of students, each of which received a different type of information skills instruction. Results and implications are discussed at the end of the article."

Russell, Thomas L. *The No Significant Difference Phenomenon: As Reported in 355 Research Reports, Summaries and Papers.* Raleigh: North Carolina State University, 1999.

Summarizes different research studies that support "no significant difference" between the effectiveness of classroom education and distance learning.

RSS Feeds

Carver, Blake T., and Steven M. Cohen. "Librarian RSS Feeds." *Lisfeeds.com.* http://www .lisfeeds.com.

A Web-based RSS headline aggregator. Scrapes headlines from sites and services that specialize in library-oriented news, and presents them in a convenient one-stop shop for library-oriented headlines.

Cohen, Steven M. "RSS for Non-Techie Librarians." *LLRX.com: Legal and Technology Articles and Resources for Librarians, Lawyers and Law Firms.* 2002. http://www.llrx.com/ features/rssforlibrarians.htm.

An overview of potential RSS use for providing library services. Also explains the basics of how RSS works.

McKiernan, Gerry. "Rich Site Services: Web Feeds for Extended Information and Library Services." *LLRX.com: Legal and Technology Articles and Resources for Librarians, Lawyers and Law Firms*. 2004. http://www.llrx.com/features/richsite.htm.

Discusses how RSS can be used to extend library services including instruction.

Montgomery, Molly. "RSS Tutorial." *Lone Star Librarian* 56, no. 2 (2003): 1–6. http://www
.sla.org/chapter/ctx/ls/lslv56n2.pdf.

Explains the basics of what RSS is and why you should want to use it.

Script Languages and Web Interaction Technologies

CGI Resource Index. http://cgi.resourceindex.com.

Contains more than 4,000 CGI resources.

Ford, Steve, David Wells, and Nancy Wells. "Web Programming Languages." 9 Jan. 1997. http://www.objs.com/survey/lang.htm.

Dated but solid discussion of script languages at the time and the characteristics of these languages.

Goodman, Danny, and Michael Morrison. *JavaScript Bible*, 5th ed. Indianapolis, IN: John Wiley, 2004.

Presents how to master JavaScript and DOM concepts, how to capture a target audience with Web sites featuring creative effects and instant interactivity, and how to optimize scripts for effective presentation on the newest browser versions.

Gousias, George, and Diomidis Spinellis. "A Comparison of Portable Dynamic Web Content Technologies for the Apache Server." Paper presented at the SANE 2002: 3rd International System Administration and Networking Conference Proceedings, Maastricht, The Netherlands, May 2002. http://www.dmst.aueb.gr/dds/pubs/conf/2002-SANE-DynCont/html/dyncont.pdf.

Focuses on Apache's extensibility, analyzing many techniques used to provide dynamic content. Available solutions are based either on extensions to the Web server itself or on the execution of user-space programs. Solutions include, among others, CGI scripts, PHP, mod_perl, mod_python, and Java Servlets. Basic design goals are presented for each technology, along with development facilities offered and technique drawbacks, with references to lessons learned during the complete deploy-and-test process.

"Java Server Pages Technology." *Sun Developer Network*. http://java.sun.com/products/jsp/.

The portal for Sun JSP technology. Includes technical articles, FAQs, documentation, white papers, and more.

Kanavin, Alexander. "An Overview of Scripting Languages." http://www.sensi.org/~ak/impit/studies/report.pdf.

Attempts to define what scripting languages are and then describes the most popular ones and their particular features.

MicrosoftASP.Net. http://www.asp.net.

A portal site for the ASP.NET development community. Includes tutorials, downloads, resources, and forums relating to ASP.

"MicrosoftASP.Net Developer Center." *MSDB*. http://msdn.microsoft.com/asp.net/.

Official Microsoft site for information about ASP.NET.

The Perl Directory. http://www.perl.org.

Designed to be the central directory to all things Perl. Contains Perl programming resources including documentation, history, articles. Perl can be downloaded from this site.

PHP: Hypertext Preprocessor. http://www.php.net.

Offers tutorials, events pertaining to the PHP community, documentation, and a wide assortment of other PHP information.

Python. http://www.python.org.

Official Python Web site. Includes articles, information for the Python community, documentation, and more.

Ruby: Programmer's Best Friend. http://ruby-lang.org.

Official site. Offers in-depth information about Ruby.

Tcl Developer Xchange. http://www.tcl.tk.

Primary resource for information about Tcl.

Script Libraries

Dynamic Drive: DHTML Scripts for the Real World. http://www.dynamicdrive.com.

A JavaScript code library. Scripts can be freely used but not redistributed or sold. A copyright statement is required.

JavaScript Source. http://javascript.internet.com.

Offers free JavaScript, tutorials, example code, reference, resources, and help.

Scriptomizers. http://www.scriptomizers.com.

Offers different types of code generation tools to help create popup windows, customize style sheets, or build tables, all without having to know any programming languages.

Scriptsearch.com. http://www.scriptsearch.com.

A resource for JavaScript, Perl, PHP, Python, Java, and Flash source files and information.

Site Analyzers

Dr. Watson. http://watson.addy.com.

A free service to analyze a Web page or entire site on the Internet. Analysis includes link validity, download speed, search engine compatibility, and link popularity.

Special Libraries

Haverkamp, Laura J., and Kelly Coffey. "Instruction Issues in Special Libraries." *Special Libraries Management Handbook: The Basics.* http://www.libsci.sc.edu/bob/class/clis724/SpecialLibrariesHandbook/instruction.htm.

Handbook written by students in CLIS 724 (Special Libraries and Information Centers) at the University of South Carolina College of Library and Information Science over the period 1999–2004. The assignment was to produce a chapter in a class-produced practical handbook on the management of special libraries and information centers. These chapters are written from the perspective of the beginning special librarian and are intended to provide basic "how-to" instructions on dealing with the issue or problem addressed.

Streaming Media

Schumacher-Rasmussen, Eric, ed. *StreamingMedia.com.* http://www.streamingmedia.com.

Contains industry news, information, articles, directories, and services. The site features thousands of original articles, hundreds of hours of audio/video content, breaking news, research reports, industry directory, and case studies that showcase the latest real-world streaming media implementations.

"What Is MPEG-4?" *MPEG Industry Forum.* http://www.m4if.org/mpeg4/.

A overview of MPEG-4 from the groups whose goal is to further the adoption of MPEG standards.

Technology in Education

Bates, Tony, and Gary Poole. *Effective Teaching with Technology in Higher Education: Foundations for Success.* Hoboken, NJ: Jossey-Bass, 2003.

Offers four chapters on theoretical foundations before moving to the more practical aspects: how technology is being used for teaching in higher education and in particular how teaching is being organized around the use of technology. Authors examine how to use technology to enhance classroom teaching but also discuss alternative ways to organize teaching, such as a reduction but not elimination of classroom teaching combined with online learning and teaching fully at a distance.

Kovalchick, Ann, and Kara Dawson. *Education and Technology: An Encyclopedia.* 2 vols. Santa Barbara, CA: ABC-CLIO, 2004.

Introduces educational technology and its relevance to those unfamiliar with the field. Entries are assigned to one of seven categories: foundations, implementations, issues, leaders, professional associations, projects (best practices), or research and theory.

Tutorial Examples

Farquhar, Betsy. "What's It Worth?: A WebQuest about Website Evaluation." http://www
.albany.edu/~ef8043/webquest.htm.

> Activity requiring students to work in groups to view a variety of available resources on
> Web site evaluation, and then generate, test, revise, and evaluate their own list of Web site
> evaluation criteria. Each group produces an end product, a usable resource for the class or
> library, in any one of a variety of formats.

Holmes, John, Anne Graham, Zach Hooker, Madolyn Nichols, Devang Patel, Doddy Samiaji,
and Jill Yetman. "Research 101." *University of Washington Information Literacy Learning.*
http://www.lib.washington.edu/uwill/research101/basic00.htm.

> Interactive online tutorial for students wanting an introduction to research skills. Covers
> the basics, including how to select a topic and develop research questions, as well as how
> to select, search for, find, and evaluate information sources.

Kentucky Virtual Library Kids and Teachers Workshop. "All the Information in the Known
Universe." http://www.kyvl.org/html/kids/f_portal.html.

> Research tutorial for K–5 children. Designed to be interactive. Guides students through six
> steps in the research process.

Swartz, Pauline, Ben Benjamin, Ellen Watanabe, David Yamamoto, Sharon Farb, Chisato
Uyeki, and Stephanie Brasley. "Bruin Success with Less Stress." *UCLA Library.* http://
www.library.ucla.edu/bruinsuccess/.

> Designed as an introduction to academic integrity and intellectual property, Bruin Success
> with Less Stress educates students about their role in the academic community to help
> them make informed choices.

Webb, Kathleen. "Flyers Tutorial." *University of Dayton Roesch Library.* http://library
.udayton.edu/flyertutorial/.

> Developed by librarians at the University of Dayton to assist students doing research in the
> English composition courses. Students complete the tutorial prior to coming into the library,
> so that librarians can spend the instruction session answering questions and allowing the
> students to actually get started with their research. Can be used to review research skills.

Typography

Shannon, Ross. "Web Typography." *HTML Source.* http://www.yourhtmlsource.com/text/
webtypography.html.

> Introduces typography, starting with font classifications and then going into the practical-
> ities of online text.

"Typography." *Web Page Design for Designers.* http://www.wpdfd.com/wpdtypo.htm.

> Addresses the problems with type on a Web page and offers tips on ways to make text show
> the way you prefer on a Web page.

Usability

Instone, Keith. *User-experience.org*. http://user-experience.org.

> Instone is a user experience expert. This is his Web site and has links to his articles and presentations.

Krug, Steve. *Don't Make Me Think! A Common Sense Approach to Web Usability*. Circle.Com Library: Que, 2000.

> "This book is for the people in the trenches, the designers, the programmers, the webmasters, the project managers, the marketing people, and the folks who sign the checks. Its easily absorbed principles will help you arrive at both the right questions to ask the experts you hire, and practical answers so you can make difficult technical, aesthetic, and structural decisions."

Nielsen, Jakob. *Useit.com: Jakob Nielsen on Usability and Web Design*. 2005. http://useit.com.

> Jakob Nielsen's Web site that contains years of content by Nielsen on his usability views relating to Web sites.

———. *Designing Web Usability: A Guide to Simplicity*. Indianapolis, IN: New Riders, 2000.

> Definitive guide to usability from Jakob Nielsen, the world's leading authority.

User Interface Design

Lynch, Patrick, and Sarah Horton. *Web Style Guide*, 2nd ed. March 2004. http://www.webstyleguide.com/index.html.

> Fundamentals and advice to help designers think and design for users. Teaches basic design principles as well as tricks of the trade, ranging from interaction design to typography. Attempts to give a broad framework that will help you understand the big picture of Web design.

Nielsen, Jakob. "Guidelines for Visualizing Links." *Useit.com*. 10 May 2004. http://www.useit.com/alertbox/20040510.html.

> Recommendations on handling hyperlinks in Web interfaces. Textual links should be colored and underlined to achieve the best perceived affordance of clickability, though there are a few exceptions to these guidelines.

Nielsen, Jakob, and John Morkes. "Concise, Scannable, and Objective: How to Write for the Web." *Useit.com*. http://www.useit.com/papers/webwriting/writing.html.

> Discusses research findings on how users read on the Web. They found that users do not actually read: instead, they scan the text. Recommendations include concise writing, using scannable text and writing in an objective manner.

Powell, Thomas A. *Web Design: The Complete Reference*, 2nd ed. Berkeley, CA: Osborne/McGraw-Hill, 2002.

> Combines design theory and detailed information on implementation. Addresses topics like design methodologies, usability, navigation theory and practice, linking, text handling,

building interactivity, server-side scripting, Web technologies, multimedia, site management, and the future of Web design.

Shneiderman, Ben, and Catherine Plaisant. *Designing the User Interface: Strategies for Effective Human-Computer Interaction.* 4th ed. Boston: Pearson/Addison Wesley, 2004.

Provides a comprehensive, authoritative introduction to the dynamic field of human-computer interaction (HCI). Includes practical principles and guidelines needed to develop high quality interface designs—ones that users can understand, predict, and control. Covers theoretical foundations, and design processes such as expert reviews and usability testing. Recent innovations in collaborative interfaces, online help, and information visualization receive special attention. A major change in this edition is the integration of the World Wide Web and mobile devices throughout the book.

User-Centered Design

Garrett, Jesse James. *The Elements of User Experience: User-Centered Design for the Web.* Indianapolis, IN: New Riders, 2003.

Introduces the big picture of Web user experience development, focusing on ideas rather than tools or techniques.

Sachs, Tammy, and Gary McClain. "Back to the User: Creating User-Focused Web Sites." *Web Developer's Virtual Library.* Indianapolis, IN: New Riders Publishing, 2002.

Integrates design, navigation, and content considerations with branding and marketing guidelines through engaging users in development early on.

Video

"Flash Video Learner's Guide." *Macromedia Developer's Center.* http://www.macromedia.com/devnet/mx/flash/articles/video_primer.html.

Provides an introduction to Flash Video, including information on how to create and publish.

The MPEG Home Page. http://www.chiariglione.org/mpeg/.

Official site of the Moving Picture Experts Group (MPEG), a working group of ISO/IEC in charge of the development of standards for coded representation of digital audio and video.

Voice over IP

Tyson, Jeff, and Robert Valdes. "How VoIP Works." *Howstuffworks.* http://computer.howstuffworks.com/ip-telephony.htm.

A straightforward introduction to VoIP technology.

Web Development

Kyrnin, Jennifer. "Web Design/Html." *About.com*. http://webdesign.about.com.

Includes tutorials, resources, and articles pertinent to developing Web sites.

Web Developers Virtual Library. http://www.wdvl.com.

Offers Web development tutorials and resources, including JavaScript, HTML, PHP, ASP, favicon, Perl, Flash.

Webdeveloper.com. http://www.webdeveloper.com.

Portal to information about developing Web sites, script programming, and forums on many Web development topics.

Webmonkey: The Web Developer's Resource. http://webmonkey.wired.com/webmonkey/index.html.

Offers articles and tutorials that address most aspects and technologies involved in building Web sites. It includes sections for different skill levels, or provides access to subject matter by tasks and technologies categories.

Web-Based Instruction

Driscoll, Margaret. *Web-Based Training: Creating E-Learning Experiences*, 2nd ed. Hoboken, NJ: Jossey-Bass/Pfeiffer, 2002.

Includes chapters on the strategic advantages of Web-based training, best practices, principles of adult education, and instructional design. Covers needs analysis, designing interactions, implementing and evaluating programs.

Dupuis, Elizabeth A., ed. *Developing Web-Based Instruction: Planning, Designing, Managing, and Evaluating for Results*. Vol. 7, New Library Series. New York: Neal-Schuman, 2003.

Fourteen chapter authors examine the entire process of creating Web-based library instruction. Emphasis is on instructional design and educational technologies chosen in terms of instructional goals. Divided into three main categories: planning and management, evaluation and assessment, and design and development.

Germain, Carol Anne, and Gregory Bobish. "Virtual Teaching: Library Instruction via the Web." *Reference Librarian* 77 (2002): 71–88.

Examines key aspects of virtual teaching and learning using the Web: development of Web-based instruction tools; library instruction Web resources; emphasis on Web page design and layout; technical and copyright issues; and usability and evaluation of Web pages.

Hook, Peter A. "Creating an Online Tutorial and Pathfinder." *Law Library Journal* 94, no. 2 (2002): 243–65.

Explores the educational potential of Web-based tutorials and pathfinders. Discusses how the multimedia environment can effectively reach a broad range of learner types. Explains how the disciplines of information architecture and information visualization can contribute to designing a successful tutorial and pathfinder.

Khan, Badrul Huda, ed. *Web-Based Instruction*. Englewood Cliffs, NJ: Educational Technology Publications, 1997.

Addresses design, development, delivery, management, and evaluation aspects of Web-based instruction. Includes an introduction to the subject, a discussion of critical issues, and case studies.

Pyle, Ransford C., and Charles D. Dziuban. "Technology: Servant or Master of the Online Teacher?" *Library Trends* 50, no. 1 (2001): 130.

Proposes different formats for utilizing the Web in online and classroom instruction. Discusses the danger associated with instructional technology; includes a description of models of Web use in teaching and opportunities offered by online teaching.

Weblogs

Berger, Pam. "Are You Blogging Yet?" *Information Searcher* 14, no. 2 (2003): 1–4.

Introduces features and benefits of adding a blog to a school library's site and touches upon the value of blogs to curriculum building and student collaboration and learning.

Booth, Stephanie. "Hosted Blog Platform Test Write-Up." *Climb to the Stars*. 12 Sept. 2004. http://climbtothestars.org/archives/2004/12/11/hosted-blog-platform-test-write-up/.

A review of thirteen free hosted weblogs.

Coggins, Sheila Ann Manuel. "Education Blogs." http://weblogs.about.com/od/educationblogs/.

Weblogs for and by teachers, educators, and learners. Offers ideas, resources, and tips that may be used in schools, universities, colleges, workshops, and the rest of the academic world.

Estep, Erik Sean, and Julia Gelfand. "Weblogs." *Library Hi Tech News* 20, no. 5 (2003): 11–12.

Discussion on using blogs in information literacy. Offers exercise where students are required to analyze a number of political blogs, an exercise that is intended to encourage critical thinking and evaluation.

Etches-Johnson, Amanda. *Ablogwithoutalibrary.net*. http://www.blogwithoutalibrary.net.

Blog about what libraries are doing with blogs. Includes a bibliography of articles written on using blogs in libraries.

Harder, Geoffrey, and Randy Reichardt. "Throw Another Blog on the Wire: Libraries and the Weblogging Phenomena." *Feliciter* 49, no. 2 (2003): 85–88.

Introduces blogging in general and blogging in libraries. Discusses components of a successful weblog, variation in writing blogs, and sources of information on blogs. Offers suggestion for potential blog use in public and academic libraries.

"Library Weblogs." *LibDex: The Library Index.* http://www.libdex.com/weblogs.html.

   Portal to an assortment of weblogs from and relating to libraries.

Nackerud, Shane. "Blogging and the U of M Libraries." *University of Minnesota Libraries Staff.* http://staff.lib.umn.edu/ug/uicd-blogmore.phtml.

   Explains why the University Libraries at University of Minnesota decided to host weblogs for their faculty and students.

Richardson, Will. "Blogging and RSS—the "What's It?" and "How to" of Powerful New Web Tools for Educators." *Multimedia and Internet@Schools* 11, no. 1 (2004): 10–13. http://www.infotoday.com/mmschools/jan04/richardson/shtml.

   Discussion of blogs in an education context that includes the possibilities of collaborative blogging as a teaching/learning experience.

———. Weblogg-ed. 2005. http://www.weblogg-ed.com.

   Dedicated to discussions and reflections on the use of weblogs, wikis, RSS, and other Internet-related technologies in the K–12 classroom.

University Libraries, University of Minnesota. *Uthink: Blogs at the University Libraries.* http://blog.lib.umn.edu.

   University Libraries developed a project to offer weblogs to the university community and manage them.

WebQuests

Dodge, Bernie. "Some Thoughts about WebQuests." *WebQuest Page.* 1997. http://edweb.sdsu.edu/courses/edtec596/about_webquests.html.

   An introduction to the subject of WebQuests by the person who developed the concept.

———. *WebQuest Page at San Diego State University.* 2004. http://webquest.sdsu.edu.

   Offers extensive support and examples for faculty and instructors who are using WebQuests to help students learn.

Lamb, Annette. "Locate and Evaluate WebQuests." *Teacher Tap: Professional Development Resources for Educators.* July 2004. http://eduscapes.com/tap/topic4.htm.

   Explains WebQuests and links to additional resources and various WebQuests.

Wikis

Chawner, Brenda, and Paul H. Lewis. "Wikiwikiwebs: New Ways of Interacting in a Web Environment." Paper presented at the LITA National Forum, St. Louis, MO, 7–10 Oct. 2004. http://www.ala.org/ala/lita/litaevents/2004Forum/CS_WikiWikiWebs.pdf.

   Describes the history and development of wikiwikiwebs, lists typical wiki features, and outlines factors to consider when choosing a wiki engine.

Hayes, Chris. "Enter the World of Wiki." *LLRX.com: Legal and Technology Articles and Resources for Librarians, Lawyers and Law Firms.* http://www.llrx.com/features/wiki.htm.

Overview of what a wiki is and its purpose as a collaborative discussion site.

Leuf, Bo, and Ward Cunningham. *The Wiki Way: Quick Collaboration on the Web.* Boston: Addison-Wesley, 2001.

Introduces open source collaborative server technology that enables users to access, browse, and edit hypertext pages, and can be used to coordinate collaborative documents, databases, and projects. Describes how to set up, customize, and run a Wiki server, with examples that demonstrate how to apply and adapt Wiki to the demands of various situations.

McKiernan, Gerry. "Sandbox (Sm): Wikibibliography." Cyberstacks (sm). http://www.public.iastate.edu/~CYBERSTACKS/WikiBib.htm.

A bibliography that links to articles about wikis.

Wireless

Drew, Bill. "Wireless Libraries." http://wirelesslibraries.blogspot.com.

This blog's goal is to advance the use of wireless technology in libraries.

Index

Susan Sharpless Smith, the Technology Team Leader for the Z. Smith Reynolds Library at Wake Forest University in Winston-Salem, North Carolina, has been deeply involved in developing and implementing ResearchExpress, a new service for managing, searching, and linking digital collections. Now adept at XML/XSL, she developed her interest in Web-based library instruction while studying for her MA in Educational Technology Leadership at George Washington University. She is active in state and national organizations and enjoys presenting on a variety of technology-related subjects. She earned her MLIS from the University of North Carolina–Greensboro.